CONTEMPORARY JAZZ UK

Twenty one lives in jazz

CONTEMPORARY JAZZ UK

Twenty one lives in jazz

Chris Horne

$P_i J$

Published in Great Britain in 2004 by
Perspectives in jazz
48 Lynette Avenue
London SW4 9HD

A catalogue record for this book is available from the British Library.

ISBN 0 9547982-0-1

Cover design by Roland Williams.
Photography and body text set by Chris Horne.
Printed and bound in Great Britain by
Biddles of King's Lynn, Norfolk.

Contents

Acknowledgements

First and foremost, may I thank all the musicians who gave their hospitality, their time and advice to enable this informal picture of UK jazz life to be assembled. The help and encouragement of a number of musicians in particular is appreciated namely, Alan Barnes, John Donaldson and Geoff Gascoyne.

I am really appreciative of the friendship and support of Dave Gelly. As a player as well as a writer on jazz, he also readily provided a Foreword that gets to the nub of many of the reasons for this book. Also many thanks to Celia Wood and Brian Blain of Jazz Services, Paul Pace of Ray's Jazz and Charles Alexander and Jon Newey of Jazzwise Magazine.

I would also like to thank Roland Williams, my designer and covert jazz fan for his excellent cover, his designs, website and for almost effortlessly keeping the ship on course.

To the many friends and relatives who have ventured ideas - Jim, Ray, Allan, Peter and Margaret for the council of ideas staged round an agreeably liquid lunch, Trevor, David and Philip, who have contributed their useful thoughts - my thanks to them too.

Recognition is due to The Bull's Head in Barnes, both as a legendary home for mainstream jazz of quality and a venue where I have listened with delight for more than two decades. It is also where many of the photographs were shot, a freedom not granted everywhere.

A word of thanks to Mary Greig in York, who has compiled the London Jazz Listings, unpaid, for over three decades.

Finally I would like to thank my wife Ann who has offered constant encouragement and ideas and is as excited about this project as I am. A meticulous editor, she has donated many hours. She has my heartfelt thanks, while any final errors must remain my own.

Foreword

Complaining is a British folk-custom, and British jazz lovers and British jazz musicians are as zealous as anyone when it comes to expressing dissatisfaction with their lot. But if you stand aside for a moment and look at the British jazz scene objectively, it is actually a success story. Few musicians become either rich or famous, but many of them pursue busy, creative and reasonably sustaining careers. This wasn't the case half a century ago, when there was only a handful of full-time, professional players in the whole country.

That being the case, it is remarkable how little Britain's jazz lovers know about the artists whose recordings they buy and whose live gigs they attend. How did they start off playing - and how did they settle on which instrument to start on? How did they learn? Did they set out to become professional jazz musicians, or did it just happen? How hard was it to get noticed in the first place? Do they have to practice every day, and if so, how they manage it if they're on tour? How disciplined do you have to be?

The best people to ask are those who are currently among the leaders in their field, the ones who have been through most of the ups and downs and are still at the top of their game. Their names are the ones you see on the CD covers and in the review columns. They're the ones who come round to your local jazz venue or appear at your favourite festival. But you have to ask the right questions. Sometimes press interviews do this, but quite often they don't. And, anyway, you might miss that issue of the paper or magazine.

That's what I find so valuable about Chris Horne's book. He asks the right questions, and gets straight, sometimes quite surprising, answers. His informal photographs go a long way towards completing a set of fully rounded portraits. This really is a picture of Contemporary Jazz UK at the beginning of the 21st century.

Dave Gelly

Introduction

I like to think that jazz is for people who don't enjoy hearing exactly the same music twice. They prefer more active listening, taking in fresh interpretations, innovative or beautiful new tunes presented with confidence and flair by performers who possess their own unique jazz voices.

That's fine but how do the players learn this special craft? Certainly many jazz musicians start with some classical training but what follows? The real battle for the aspiring jazz musician is internal, the absorption of a broad spectrum of skills - harmonic, rhythmic, styles and idioms - and this is developed over many years, in fact throughout a lifetime's learning process. Not a lot of non-musicians know much of what is involved.

This leads to the two main reasons prompting my production of this book. Firstly the increasing level of expertise and professionalism amongst contemporary jazz talent playing in Britain has so far not been acknowledged by many books that explain and present the current players to a wider public. Certainly none from the players' perspective.

For the keen jazz lover there are fine jazz magazines to broaden and deepen knowledge – amongst them Jazzwise, Jazz UK, Jazz Review - and some useful reference works such as *Who's Who of British Jazz, The Penguin Guide to Jazz on CD* and *Jazz – The Rough Guide*. But even *The Rough Guide*, good like *Who's Who* for covering British talent, has a world-wide and historical perspective. Indeed only around one in eight entries is British and approximately half the artists covered were born before 1940. So while covering the jazz tradition is important, it can seem pretty daunting for a player today to make his or her own mark in the shadow of those early legends.

Fortunately the players in this book are carving out life long careers and have much impressive music and many notable recordings to their names. They include a selection of our leading jazz playing and composing talent who, I believe, will be attracting much attention for decades to come.

The second reason for the book was that I had started down the long road to acquiring modest jazz skills and had some questions for leading experienced players. So besides asking them about early developments, the teenage years of rapid musical absorption, the bands they have played in, I wanted to extract some insider knowledge, to learn a little about improvisation and how they worked to develop it. This book therefore contains some quite basic 'how to' questions but rather interesting answers from individuals who have been there, understood and conquered the challenges.

The players in this book have paid their dues on the way up and are very roughly in their *prime* – though this is probably a rather hazy, moveable concept in jazz - and mainly keep up an active programme often based around gigging, composing, teaching and recording. I thank them for the generosity with their time and even more for the insight and the candour with which they talked about their musical lives. Jazz is an intricate art form and some of the questions must have seemd pretty naive at times - but their straight-forwardness and frankness were unshakeable!

I regret that only a selection of the leading jazz musicians in Britain could be covered for reasons of space and time – I fully recognise that many other wonderful talents exist. But taken together, the players in the book do shed light on many of the major segments within today's British jazz world.

It's been said that, before the mid-1920s, all the best players couldn't read music. After that time, jazz musicians mainly couldn't survive if they couldn't read music. As a result of this increased complexity, there is a growing range of jazz education at college level. For many of the players here there was a classical music degree or major jazz course - the Leeds College of Music, the Guildhall School of Music, Trinity College of Music or Berklee in Boston. Tim Garland and Julian Joseph studied composition, Julian on the grounds that his hero Herbie Hancock had gone down that route.

But there will always be a minority largely self-taught, such as Iain Ballamy, Jamie Cullum, Geoff Gascoyne – if you allow that jazz summer schools are used by nearly all.

Back in the Sixties the self-taught Jim Mullen started jazz with the guitar but, realising its complexity, took up the bass as a way to get on the bandstand and learn how all the harmonies and other elements were assembled.

This learning period is followed for all by a gradual process of gaining experience in gigging and surviving financially while feeling their way towards what would be for them the most meaningful, rewarding, improvisational music. Even the legendary pianist, McCoy Tyner, admits to taking a couple of factory jobs during lean periods, but strongly denies he drove a New York cab. Though he thought about it!

Players are more ready for commercial gigging after they have gained playing and listening experience through sitting in with existing bands. The 606 Club in Chelsea and the Jazz Cafe in Camden, are favoured London haunts where a lot of quality late night jamming gets done. The help extended by older established players to those who need experience is a remarkable ongoing feature of the jazz culture. London's Weekend Arts Centre at the time Julian Joseph was passing through was taught by the redoubtable Ian Carr, trumpeter and leader of band Nucleus [Best Band, Montreux Jazz Festival, 1970]. The saxophonist, Tim Whitehead has been active in conducting workshops that moved Denys Baptiste's and many other players' skills up a gear. The Dune organisation, besides its established artists, maintains Tomorrow's Warriors for emerging players and a schools' teaching programme that continually presents jazz to new audiences and nurtures latent talent. There are many more spread over the country.

What more *individual* revelations have come out of the interviews? Maybe a nice starter is how all these experienced players insist they are still learning. Guy Barker, who as a teenager was discussing playing technique with Clark Terry and Dizzie Gillespie, still likes to say his occupation is 'eternal music student'. John Donaldson develops one aspect of this - how the ear learns additional new ways of hearing, so that revisiting jazz records reveals new aspects of the music you could never hear before.

Ben Castle, in great demand, is a delightfully natural musical craftsman with a beautiful tone. He explains how, as his experience grew, he needed to break free from his early idol, US tenor player Michael Brecker. He describes some of the rigours of jazz training, playing a Miles Davis tune that is styled like an improvisation, Donna Lee, in all the keys and how sax players work to develop better tone. His friend and fellow tenor sax player from their Guildhall School of Music days, Denys Baptiste, explains how even the shape of your skull influences your sound and so no one can *fully* imitate Coltrane's sound. He sees his future focussing more on composition following the good reception given to *Let Freedom Ring*, his major piece commemorating Martin Luther King. Both he and Ben are certain to figure strongly on the British jazz scene in future decades.

Nigel Hitchcock was the youngest alto player – at eleven – to join the National Youth Jazz Orchestra and he now combines session work with dazzling jazz performances in a number of leading groups such as the Stan Tracey Quintet. He has a very quick musical brain and loves to analyse the relationships of music with mathematics.

For Tim Garland, a wonderful player and composer who has toured with Chick Corea in America, a key message is how jazz is best experienced *live* to understand the excitement of this music. After the interview I listened again to his Suite, 'Enter the Fire'. Tim had made a point about soloing while leaving space for other soloists to contribute and on *Spiritual*, I could hear he practices what he preaches with great results.

Iain Ballamy on tenor has grown strongly since he and Django Bates were leading figures in the innovative Eighties big band *Loose Tubes*. He describes his own very personal history of education in the big band and experiences after

Loose Tubes such as immersion in Indian music, playing in electronic as well as acoustic set-ups and what it feels like to play free jazz. A major, very individual talent led by a sound gut feel in matters musical.

Ingrid Laubrock arrived from Germany some fifteen years ago and began her jazz career by picking up an alto and busking. Much application and sweat, Guildhall training and masterclasses later, she is a seriously accomplished modern stylist with notably fresh and wide-ranging composing strengths. She is in parallel continuing her love for Brazilian music and hers is a name to watch.

One of the main past masters most pianists owe a debt to is McCoy Tyner. Steve Melling has absorbed elements of his style and mainly plays with Alan Skidmore [tenor] and Peter King [alto] who are significantly Coltrane and bop influenced. Steve has been working with them over many years to hone the group sound, maturing it into an exciting contemporary version of that idiom. Demonstrating his versatility, Steve can, in contrast, also be heard as a light, sparkling stylist working behind Trudy Kerr's vocals in her quartet.

Similarly John Donaldson is a pianist of wide musical influences and styles and a 'touch' player of beautifully presented solos. John's candid belief is that stylistic flexibility, a chameleon-like quality, is now an essential survival skill for pianists. After ten years' playing on America's West Coast, John now works primarily with Alan Barnes and Don Weller, two very popular bandleaders. He is additionally an experienced, sensitive supporter of vocalists.

Another pianist whose work demands careful attention is Nikki Iles, who is influenced by Bill Evans and Paul Bley. As a long term teacher and composer in the evolving English/European school of jazz stylists, which probably moves jazz closer to classical music, her speciality lies in her highly developed choice of harmonies which colour her work in remarkable ways, creating that freshness and surprise reminiscent of Bill Evans' work. She is the regular working partner for the sophisticated vocalist, Tina May.

Dave Newton has often gained the award as Britain's best jazz pianist and is a sparkling, swinging stylist currently working for one of our most internationally successful vocalists, Stacey Kent, expert songstress of the American Songbook. Dave offers Oscar Peterson and Keith Jarrett as his main influences and insists jazz's priority is to inspire an emotional response in its audience before attempting new innovative instrumental happenings.

Julian Joseph is becoming as well known for his radio and television broadcasting as for his robust, compulsive piano playing. Influenced mainly by McCoy Tyner and Herbie Hancock and valuing swing as an essential, he has achieved wide respect for both his work in small groups and his compositions for big band. He describes the wonder of growing up alongside and playing with Courtney Pine and Branford Marsalis and gives his insights into the development of UK's jazz scene.

Another graduate of Boston's Berklee College is Alec Dankworth, a bass player whose baptism of fire came by joining the band of his parents, Cleo Laine and John Dankworth as they toured the world. He has built on this base, having enjoyed great experiences working with Bill Le Sage, Clark Tracey, Abdullah Ibrahim and Dave Brubeck and running a very persuasive and innovative trio.

Another stalwart of the British bass scene is bassist Andy Cleyndert, ever youthful, but he actually started twenty years back playing Trad. He then quickly established himself on the mainstream modern scene and was in Ronnie Scott's band for many years. He followed that by joining Stan Tracey, where he now plays and records with all Stan's many groups. Recording has a special significance as, in common with a number of bassists, he adds other skills to the mix, here recording and marketing CDs under his growing Trio label. Additionally, he expounds on bass soloing and the role of the rhythm section.

Finally among the basses, there is Geoff Gascoyne, who has moved from jazz-flavoured pop bands like US3 to playing with Jim Mullen and then into Georgie Fame's band. He has set out his mainstream modern composing and arranging stall with three excellent CDs. Geoff also arranges for vocalists - his wife, Australian Trudy Kerr, Claire Martin and Ian Shaw. His arranging and playing skills have in recent years been a major force behind Jamie Cullum.

Jamie Cullum himself cuts a remarkably relaxed figure for one who has made such an impact commercially and emotionally on the British jazz scene. He combines a selection of song material from both established standards and recent pop songs, his vigorous reinterpretations of standards, an excellent voice, pretty experienced jazz (and rock) sensibilities, composing talent, impressively growing piano skills and the ability to combine all these in readily accessible music. Jamie was interviewed just as he was contemplating making the album *Twenty Something* that was to become UK jazz's first platinum best-seller. I candidly had no idea at that time that he would shortly be featuring on CD compilations of the all-time jazz greats!

Jim Mullen left playing jazz guitar in Glasgow to work in London-based rock groups but then found his niche with the widely loved sax player, Dick Morrissey, with whom he founded the jazz-fusion group Morrissey-Mullen, delighting young audiences for fifteen years. Since then he has successfully adapted his gospel-flavoured style to a variety of highly talented straightahead jazz groups. A excellent musician and consistently inspiring soloist.

Kenrick Rowe is a drummer who was drawn to jazz by hearing Art Blakey and by his contemporary jazz friends into supplementing his ska and reggae music credentials with the finesse of jazz drumming as coached by the US veteran Clifford Jarvis. Kenrick has played and toured with many leading lights including David Murray, the pianist Tim Richards, and many British groups including many years with the internationally successful Jazz Jamaica. A fascinating story.

Bill Bruford began successfully with many years in progressive rock bands Yes and King Crimson before evolving to jazz fusion in the Eighties, electronic drums then latterly converting his band, Earthworks, to an acoustic quartet line-up in 1996. In addition to Britain, he regularly tours America and Japan with highly select young British jazz talent. A self-taught musician with a very active musical mind, Bill remarkably composes starting with drums and then the bass followed by the melody – with very successful results.

Clark Tracey has evolved into probably one of Britain's most experienced and sensitive drummers since being launched onto stages with father Stan at the age of seventeen. Five years later, he formed one of the most successful bands of the Eighties, his Quintet which included Guy Barker, Jamie Talbot, Steve Melling and Alec Dankworth. He writes well, has a number of impressive CDs to his credit. He currently plays in all his father's groups and emulates a role-model, Art Blakey, in leading a group of excellent emerging players.

Finally Alan Barnes, a truly multi-reed player, whose playing, compositional and arranging prowess have been recognised through UK awards for many years. His playing on alto and baritone offers glittering communications of beauty and clarity which are a part of all the music he touches. He runs a number of bands and is generally a powerhouse of energy and good humour for the British scene. He makes a strong case that the best jazz players are and will always be the individuals, the characters that communicate through their music.

One question, on the health and future of jazz in Britain brought out quite a range of different perceptions. One view was that the commercial fortunes of jazz here are sound, though always subject to some fluctuation. As Guy Barker commented, if you ever want to hear jazz, you have only to check out what's on and it will be there - in large cities at any rate. Jazz rarely employs enormous marketing effort so you have to look for it.

But players are nevertheless concerned about a shrinkage of jazz venues and the incursions of non or near-jazz into jazz festivals. This impacts on emerging players' opportunities and jazz colleges are providing what playing venues they can.

 A positive historical view of jazz development is that as the original heat of the jazz legends cools in the memory, a wider historical perspective is emerging and a range of influences, not exclusively American, is colouring today's music and this will ultimately culminate in a kind of global jazz – not world music but truly global jazz. This development sounds healthy for the long term.

But in the shorter term, jazz would benefit from understanding better what it takes to grab the attention of new, younger audiences. Whether this comes down to better promotion, marketing, presentation, communication with audiences, greater accessibility of the music without watering down the product, or more public subsidy, is a moot point. Good luck to the promoters, festival administrators, independent jazz labels and players who are working to rejuvenate this most innovative of musical art forms.

One giant step forward would be for jazz to reappear on terrestrial television. A small amount has appeared on BBC4 and Artsworld - more should be encouraged. The notice taken of the video re-issue of BBC2's Jazz 625 in the mid-Sixties should be convincing enough. As is stressed here by many players, jazz is a music to be experienced as 'live' as possible and television easily surpasses radio in its ability to communicate jazz's excitement and the interplay between musicians.

There are many issues raised here by players, about standards versus originals, about what will enable the music to move towards more present day material that a twenty-somethings or thirty-somethings audience can maybe more readily relate to.

One growing development appears to be innovative new trio combinations where chamber-style jazz is producing exquisitely attractive, fully-acoustic listening experiences full of artistry - something certainly in short supply today.

It has been an exciting and demystifying experience to discuss jazz with these players. Short of cornering them at a bar and buying them drinks for an hour, it could be difficult to obtain these insights - and even breaks in jazz sets are not *that* long ! So I hope you are also stimulated by these players' perspectives on the noble art of jazz and then get out to enjoy the experience - live!

Information on Jazz in the UK

What about venues? Besides jazz clubs and other venues, Britain can boast over 140 jazz festivals - an awesome number - where people can check out new players and get closer to their jazz. Along with much else, festivals are described in the bible for the active jazz listener and player at Jazz Services' website, www.jazzservices.org.uk

Where to find the music

Musicians and smaller jazz labels are marketing with increasing confidence via the Internet. Much good music, recorded by specialists and not in high street stores, can be accessed at pretty competitive prices.

First source - the musicians frequently have their own websites, generally supplying biography, gig dates and discography, some selling their own recordings. Website addresses are listed at the end of each player's chapter after the CDs they have chosen as most representative of their work.

Second source - many new jazz labels have sprung up promoting and selling their catalogues and artists on the Internet. The large conglomerate labels cater largely for the vocalists, so it is useful to list here some of the main independents labels.

Independent Jazz Labels

www.33jazz.com

www.cabermusic.com

www.candidrecords.com

www.dunejazz.com

www. jazzizit.co.uk

www.linnrecords.com

www.milesmusic.co.uk

www.provocateurrecords.co.uk

www.ronniescotts.co.uk (Ronnie Scott's Jazz House)

www.siroccomusic.com

www.symbol.uk.com/albums/index

www.zephyrrecords.co.uk

Iain Ballamy

Iain Ballamy, born in Guildford in 1964, is an internationally recognised contemporary saxophone player composer and band leader [tenor and soprano saxes and piano]. Starting on alto sax and self-taught, he learned his craft playing on the mainstream London jazz scene before forming a band, the Iains, which included pianist Django Bates. In 1984 they were both founder members of the innovative and successful Loose Tubes big band which continued until 1990. Iain then became a member of Django's big band, Delightful Precipice and his quartet, Human Chain as well as leading his own electro-quartet Acme. In 1986 Ballamy co-founded Earthworks, later taken over by drummer Bill Bruford. In 1992, he studied and then toured with a group from India – the Karnataka College of Percussion.

Iain's CDs as leader include *Balloon Man* [1989], *All Men Amen*, *Acme* [1996] *Food* [1998], *Pepper Street Interludes* [2000] and Food *Organic & GM* [2001]. The Food group experiment in free electronic-flavoured jazz with Norwegian players included trumpet player Arve Henriksen. His most recent CD is *The Little Radio* with virtuoso accordianist, Stian Carstensen.

Iain has played with many leading American players including Gil Evans, George Coleman, Dewey Redman, Cedar Walton, Kenny Werner, Carla Bley and the legendary Brazilian bandleader Hermeto Pascoal. Among leading British players, he has worked with John Taylor, Stan Sulzmann, Art Themen, John Parricelli and the singer, Norma Winstone.

In 1985, he was given the John Dankworth award for Most Promising Soloist and in 1995 his group was awarded the John Dankworth Best UK Ensemble. In 2001, Iain took the BBC Jazz Award for Jazz Innovation.

What was the first music you heard in the home?

My father always played jazz piano since he worked for the RAF in the '50s. His musical tastes were the likes of John Dankworth, Cleo Lane, the Dudley Moore Trio, plus a number of jazz piano trios, like Oscar Peterson, Errol Garner, some Art Tatum, all mainstream jazz piano music. He's always been a good semi-pro player and knows thousands of songs.

I got started on classical piano lessons and had a number of teachers. I had the sort of nice one when you're six, then the fascist loony, hit-your-hands-if-you-got-it-wrong guy. Then I got a really nice, soft, fluffy, lovely piano teacher lady who was the opposite. So, a few piano teachers and I did a few grades.

I was still playing piano at age thirteen, though by then it was more out of a sense of guilt rather than anything else, as my folks paid for the lessons. The only jazz I really wanted to play on the piano was a bit of Scott Joplin and some Fats Waller I'd started listening to, so I hadn't really had a jazz attack by then.

Then when I was thirteen my Dad said, 'I've got a gig, will you come and operate the tape recorder?' It turned out to be a complete con; he was just having a blow round somebody's front room in Woking, with a tenor sax player called Brian Marret, a bass player and a drummer.

After about three hours, I started looking at the guy playing saxophone and thinking he's quite a cool fellow, I liked the way he carried himself. They were having a lot of fun, joking and laughing, and then I started looking at the saxophone thinking how cool it was. Then after a bit, no, that's *very* cool! It's fantastic!

On the way home I said, 'Dad, I want to play saxophone!' He said, 'They're very expensive!' I mentioned my paper round money. So he said, 'OK, well you have a look round, track one down and find out how much they cost.' So I got the old Yellow Pages out, because I'm quite manic when I get into something and phoned every music shop within a thirty-mile radius.

You found an alto?

Yes, it was a really old one, Selmer Adolphe nineteen twenties, nice old thing but needed completely restoring. In fact, before that happened, Dad said, 'Let's get Brian round and you can try his saxophone.' So he showed me where to put my fingers to get a noise. I went up into my bedroom and half an hour later, it sounded like Coltrane - *Robbie* Coltrane.

Actually it's quite a rewarding instrument, it gives you back a bit early on, the saxophone. I got a horn and a fingering chart and I started to teach myself to play all wrong – double lip, instead of putting your teeth on the mouthpiece. Then when you do put your teeth on the mouthpiece, it's like chewing an electric toothbrush! - unpleasant till you get used to it. It's the vibration of the reed - quite important.

When I got the saxophone, I just went at it like nobody's business until I was getting somewhere – I've never practiced like that *ever* again. All day, every day, all the time. Tears of frustration - and I just went out to hear as many people as I could.

Who had made the biggest impression on you then?

There was a little club in Aldershot called the Night Owls, and my Dad used to play there sometimes. They'd get the Tony Lee Trio down with guests, so I met Bobby Wellins and Dick Morrissey and Kathy Stobart – who helped me choose a mouthpiece. She gave me a couple of very stern, very instructive lessons. I've only had three lessons in my life. She was trying to get me on track. It half worked. In terms of reading music really well, I never learnt that, more using my ears.

That still true?

Yes, still true. I mean I'm definitely not the person to give a flysheet to read expecting it to come out perfect, that's just not my thing. Some people are programmed to do that. But it doesn't stop me reading and writing music. I'm pretty good now compared to how I was then.

time, a little bit older than me. He was already writing his own music and into Keith Jarrett, way ahead of everyone else.

Later Steve Arguelles was in my quartet, so it was Django, Mick and Steve. Pretty soon, we didn't want to play at the Bulls Head anymore because Ted [former member, trumpet] had done weird things like springing off the stage onto the side seating while playing and it was just too weird for the establishment there. The landlord freaked out.

Then Django said to me, 'Why don't you write your own music? This is shit, this stuff.' At that time, I was wanting to play Joe Henderson, Wayne Shorter and Herbie Hancock tunes – jazz standards and I thought they were fantastic. But he said, 'You can write better tunes than that. Why don't you? Instead of this stuff that's all in the same genre and idiom?' I'd never written anything, so I didn't know if I could; I was a bit taken aback really. I went away and wrote out a couple of tunes. We played them and it sounded OK! It doesn't feel the same as doing Body and Soul. I like that song but this felt , not *so* original it had come from the planet Zog - but it felt like *me*.

It always seemed to me like what you did. Not that you'd learnt the history of jazz and you'd learnt how to compartmentalise it so you could show you knew that legacy. For instance, if you study history, you don't have to dress up in bearskins or armour to do it?

I figured that the tradition was that you were turned on to playing jazz, you found out what it was about, studied your instrument, learnt the history, including the British jazz history - there's a long British jazz history since the Fifties and Europe-wide as well. Then at some point, instead of getting bogged down in the soup of jazz history, to output some of your *own* – that's to me what the tradition is. I'm living in 2004 and I'm a white, English middle-class (whatever that is) freak and I'll never be a real American one. And I don't want to be, I haven't wanted to be for a long time, I've just wanted to play music that felt like *my own* in a way, that felt honest.

As a teenager, you formed a group called the Iains?

The governor at the Bull's Head [mainstream jazz pub, Barnes, SW London] gave me a lunchtime gig there and the next time, lunch and an evening slot. They like having a whiz kid in the jazz scene, a young lion. So I cut my teeth there. I got a chance to hear and play with a lot of the good British players - Jimmy Hastings, Stan Sulzmann, Stan Robinson, Art Themen. All these brilliant people were very helpful and kind. And that's the way to learn - on the job, not as a middle class lifestyle choice to go and get a degree in jazz, which is the way it often is now, you know. In some ways that's good and in some ways, that's making a science out of an art. Can be a problem.

I'd met Django on a gig, so I asked him as he already had a great bass player, Mick Hutton, and a drummer, Dave Trigwell. Django was a tremendously talented and precocious guy at the

How did the Loose Tubes band come about?

Well, when I left home, I joined a bunch of guys living at Django's – a big old house in Beckenham - Steve Buckley, Steve Berry and others. It was a good environment for learning and working and we all lived there for a while in the early to mid-Eighties.

Then Graham Collier started a jazz workshop for big band at Lancaster Gate. He put this weekly big rehearsal band together where Alan Cohen, John Warren and Graham brought arrangements. It was a slightly odd mix of people, don't know where they'd all been gathered from, but I was involved because of living with Django and Steve Berry. At the time, 1984, I couldn't read music very well and had no big band experience at all.

It was a twenty-one piece - Django and Steve Berry, Chris Batchelor, John Eacott, Eddie Parker and John Harborne were the most significant ones who started writing charts for the band.

There was a good buzz about this band but pretty soon a strange thing happened. It grew wings and developed a mind of its own, not with a bandleader but as a collective force. It was a bit like the Lord of the Flies, the more outspoken people rose to the top and would bring their own music, then we would say we want to play this, we don't want to play that other stuff. It was always a cooperative, nobody hiring and firing. Whoever was there when it started stayed with it, stayed for years till they couldn't

handle it anymore or there was a fallout or something like that.

It was quite an *incredible* thing for me – like the musical education I never had- learning to play charts in a big band, learning to be in a cooperative and learning the limitations – and advantages - of being in a band that doesn't have a leader.

Weirdly enough, because of the way that band was formed, it was pretty much all white guys in the band and soon some observations were made 'oh, it's racist, oh it's a white thing' and ridiculous things like that. Then when another band called the Jazz Warriors came along, they went 'Just a minute, they're all black' and then this silly idiotic business started. So much so, that people never noticed that in the life of Loose Tubes we had all kinds of people passing through, Thebe Lipere, Andy Grappy was there, Cheryl Alleyne and Mark Mondesir both played drums for a while. It was the beginning of these silly politically correct times that we've got now.

Generally jazz groups start from the organic thing of who's met who, who's heard who play?

Absolutely. There wasn't a choice of five colleges to go to study jazz; it was all word of mouth. I met Django because Steve Berry knew Chris Laurence who was teaching at Wavenden and he said, 'Do you know any good new saxophone players?'

Also you've got to remember that Loose Tubes was one of the first big bands where everyone didn't look like a penguin in a dicky bow and all that. The culture of a big band was very much the uniform but there it was no uniform or leader.

Also I've talked to some of my friends whom I'm still in touch with like John Parricelli and Mark Lockhart and thought, 'We were so arrogant, weren't we, in a way?' We thought it was all going to be like this because we came at a time when things flashed up and there was a revival of interest in England. For years and years there'd been these pretty barren years for Evan Parker and John Taylor, Norma Winstone, Alan Skidmore and many others.

But since then the times just changed globally. Things are so cynically marketed now. Now you can win a competition to become famous, because they know that they can make you famous for a short period of time without having to do anything. It's different.

What happened towards the end with Loose Tubes?

The band kept going till 1990. Different people in the band had progressed at different rates. Some people stayed roughly as they were, other people blossomed and grew. There was less work because we had recession, there was a bit less humour and it had really just reached the end of its natural life.

And then Django, who wrote a lot of the music, started his Delightful Precipice big band which has been hard to keep together. Not personnel-wise but for work, because there isn't any kind of help to subsidise an orchestra that is playing just one person's music. He has a wonderful band, it's like a phoenix rising from the ashes of Loose Tubes.

In the meantime, I'd got together with Bill Bruford and started a band called Earthworks. Effectively Bill joined my band, kind of appropriated my bass player and piano player and we made some records and toured America, Japan. We played in some amazing places where you'd never normally get to as an English guy.

In the meantime, I still had *my* band going. But then in 1988, Jess, the first big love of my life with whom I had been living for 3 years, fell

ill and died – it was all very, very quick and I had a tragic bereavement to adjust to. That changed my priorities and my life quite considerably. Shortly after that, I made my first record, Balloon Man and I kept that band together for a few years.

Earthworks finished for me and Django in 1992. I joined Django's band, Human Chain, in 1992. I've always had a tight musical relationship with Django, especially as he was one of the ones to encourage me, to see if I really had a shell to come out of. I've played on most of his things.

You've played with George Coleman [US, tenor sax]

Yes, I played at Ronnie Scott's with George Coleman. George is someone I really identified with musically and his saxophone sound, and the way he played and everything, always. He's made a big impression on me.

I'd just been fired from a pop band that I'd done a few gigs with – we'd played at the Albert Hall and I ate the mic and made a big explosive note that made everyone jump out of their skin.

After the gig, I went down to Ronnie's. George Coleman was there and said 'Would you like to come and play?' and I thought 'Hell, I can't say no, there may never be the chance again.' So we went into Ronnie's office and he said, 'What'd you want to play?' I'd got this really complicated tune of his that I'd learned and he was going, 'Not sure if I can remember that, man, let's see?' I thought he'd been going to ask me to play a single tune. Then he said, 'We'll start with this, then we'll do that, you do a ballad, then I'll do one,' so he wanted me to do the *whole set*.

The funny thing was, when we were playing together, trading phrases and stuff, I'd play something and he'd do something and funnily it was just about the same thing, very empathetic and we'd hit the same note together! We got on and after that I went to New York and went round to his place and he was saying, 'If you need money or you're in trouble, or you want to know where to go..' He was really sweet, a lovely guy!

When you get to play with someone great like that, it's like somebody holding a light over a fifty pound note to see if it's a dud or not. You know where you stand, you know *exactly* where your strengths and your weaknesses are. That's what I mean about so much of this music being handed down, you can't learn that from a syllabus at college. It was like punching your card, for the hours and hours of experience.

An important thing happened to me in 1992. Charlie Mariano had done a tour with an Indian percussion group [Karnataka College of Percussion], and I was asked if I'd stand in for him. I'd never heard any Indian music before (except what you hear in curry houses!). I went to hear this band in Kiel in Germany with a fellow from the Arts Council. The group had mridangam – like a barrel drum, tavil, ghatam (clay pot!), a wonderful female singer called R.A Ramamani and an electric tamboura for providing drones!

And so I went to India for two weeks. A week to wander around and have my head rearranged, and another to learn the music. They spoon-fed me their music for four hours every morning and then sent me off for a series of gigs in India and Europe. I now believe that was the moment when I stopped being a jazz musician and started being a musician. I don't mean a 'world' musician. But it was when I started being musical and *open* on a different sort of scale. Hermeto talks a lot about 'global music'.

Then in 1995 a John Dankworth Best Ensemble Award.

Now, awards are always nice – but that award was chosen by John Dankworth, not a panel, which he gave to us as a band - Django, Steve Watts and Martin France.

That was good because I discovered early on that the longer you keep a band together, the more organisers say, 'Right, we've had him with this band, *now* what's he got?' In spite of that, we made two records – *Balloon Man* (1988)

and *All Men Amen* [1993]. I'm very proud of both.

You play with both acoustic and electronic bands?

Well, when I'm playing with Food (the Norwegian guys) it's very different to what I've done before because we improvise using sound and space and texture, light and shade - instead of ways in which I was more used to working - writing tunes, rhythms, chord changes – so it's a different palette. Often just making music out of thin air, so it's more instinctive and much more spontaneous.

I realised that Ave [Henriksen] was making such fantastic sounds through electronics with his trumpet that the sound of the saxophone seemed bare. So I got myself a little sonic rig and sampler with a little bit of reverb and gear and started learning to use it in a not-too-slick way. I prefer to take big chances with that stuff and not become a programming master where everything is sanitised. So get in the soup. In fact it's a bit like a ouija board – you get together with three willing people and they're all prepared, so nobody giggles, nobody gets frightened, all get round a table and see if you can have a visit!

Opening for John Scofield [US, guitar] at the Vancouver Centre for the Performing Arts in Summer 2003, we went on stage with no tunes, no set list. We had no plan as to what was going to happen in the gig, no experience as 'Food' of playing a venue with 1200 - 1500 people, and the first lump of music lasted forty five minutes! Afterwards people thought it was fantastic. They were saying stuff like, 'Thanks, guys, that was quite a ride!'

But it is high risk. If anyone was to shout out, 'Rubbish,' it would just ruin it. Or people can say, 'Oh, it's self-indulgent, all this stuff.' But we're just trying to let something happen and it's very vulnerable? I think it stirs up stuff in the audience. There was a programme about Beethoven on the other day, a period drama, and somebody said, 'Ludwig, your music's difficult!' And he said 'Difficult's beautiful, difficult's good, why should difficult be a negative?'

I fully understand that people want to chill out and have a good time, and music does a job for them. But at the same time, I think saying music's difficult should be put on the other foot really. I mean, if I say your music's easy, is that good? Is it good to be challenged a bit by music? I don't always want to listen to really hard-core jazz on Radio 3 but if I switch on and there's something like Chessington Zoo on fire, you know, it always makes me laugh and think, 'Yes, thank God that's on the radio, even if it's a bit too much for some people.'

I've heard sometimes players feel they have to break out of the mould just to show it's not imprisoning them?

Yeah. I think it's so important, I think music's so important, and I think for people to have artistic expression is so important, especially for the world we're living in now where you can win a competition to be famous for nothing. Or you're in an environment where everything's trying to be sold to you or fitted to your profile, or market researched to what you might like, say to find out if Europe's ready for another KennyG, exactly what kinds of rap and hip-hop should be superimposed on it. That really is a bore.

You have to be consistent for your audience so they know what they're getting?

Do I have any choice? I probably do in a way, I could do something else, but I do choose to play this kind of music. I've never done anything where I thought, 'This is rubbish but it could make me a few bob.' I don't care and it seems increasingly unlikely that I would do that, because there's more at stake. Whatever people think of my music, I *can* say that it's made with good will, at least.

People like that beautiful open tone you have on the tenor. How did that come about?

I always liked Stan Getz very much. He had a magnificent, a majestic sound. I always thought that it was right for me not to be a shouty, loud,

cutting player. My speaking voice is, in a way, quite gentle, not much projected, so I suppose if the saxophone is supposed to be close to the human voice...

I actually do love the tenor saxophone, I can't believe what a great instrument I've found for myself because it is like being part of a legacy playing tenor. I've felt for a long time that the rougher or edgier or brighter end of the spectrum's so well catered for that you stand more chance of getting noticed making a *beautiful* sound on it. It's like there's all these fast cars going down the motorway and there's something kind of different, much slower and older, going the other way! Seriously, I always thought it would be good to make a good sound, but your confidence can be questioned at any time, it's always revocable.

But some of the people I like to hear most of all, like Bob Berg, have such a screaming sound, particularly early on. And then you've

got Pharaoh Sanders who just plays one note and you just go, 'Wow! I love him!' It's an instant thing.

Tell me about learning to improvise. In your teens, when you went from playing melodies to jazz, what were the insights as you learned improvising?

Difficult to remember, but let me change it to this. We're having a conversation now that we've never had before. Our language and vocabulary express things, so you could say that music and the idea of being an improviser comes first of all. A lot of people are scared of it but they don't realise that they do it all the time when they try to build a sentence, expressing sentiments and it's the same musically.

Why do you practice scales and arpeggios? Not so you can play in a technical way, but so you can hear what the right things are to play. If you're playing on chord changes or something, if you're using your instrument in an abstract way, in sound and space, that's more of an instinctive thing.

A few weeks ago, I gave a talk and a workshop to a bunch of clarinet and saxophone players aged between nine and sixty and the oldest guy was Head Professor of bass clarinet from a leading Conservatoire in Holland. Very capable musicians these people, but they were terrified of improvising, didn't know where to start, couldn't play things without knowing which scale, that's just how they were wired up. If you can re-wire them, you can give them the confidence to express themselves.

If you give straight quavers to classical musicians they play them, but give them to jazz musicians and they swing them – what that swung thing is, though, is like a mystery you can't notate!

Have your musical influences stayed about the same? Roland Kirk, Charlie Parker, John Coltrane and John Surman?

I wouldn't say they've stayed the same, I'd add about two thousand others and other types of music, I suppose. Quite honestly, my biggest influences are the people I play with and the way I've felt about *making* music, rather than listening.

And your future? Are you getting more experimental or not or maybe having a development of separate streams?

I don't think of separate musical streams; people writing about music tend to categorise, but I don't. I am more interested in the similarities in music, the common ground, than the differences. It's hard talking in an interview, trying to explain something as abstract as music.

One thing I noticed when I was interviewing Wayne Shorter was that he'd start talking about one thing and he'd never finish what he was saying. He'd go to a completely oblique explanation and not finish that. Some people would say, 'Oh, Wayne's a bit of a space cadet' but I didn't find that at all. I found that the points he was alluding to would have three or four different angles pointing towards the same thing, so you knew exactly what he was getting at, he was just giving you a three dimensional view.

You could say about the different forms of music, that people are trying to put you in a bag called modernist, classical etc, then when you do something else, that upsets their preconceptions. If you only do one thing, like say Jamie Cullum, he's going for the young crooner, that's different.

As for the future, I haven't played everywhere I want to, but I have really been away a lot. I haven't got a travel bug. So the idea of doing tours in weird places that are not properly organised... I mean I've got a lovely little baby (Finlay), a lovely wife (Ali), a great house and two fantastic cats! Plus I made two records shortly before Finlay was born in October 2003.

Then I've got film music (*Mirrormask*) to write for Dave McKean [Artist, film director]. I've started work and that'll be a first. There are a lot of firsts in life. You're asked, 'Can you write a saxophone quartet?' And you go, 'Yeah! Er, what do I do here?' 'We'd like a piece for harpsichord please?' No problem. Put the phone down. 'Shit, it's got two keyboards!' You can't say, 'No, sorry, I've never done that before.'

Finally, what about the general health of the UK jazz scene? Or is it doing better on continental Europe?

I think it always has. I mean, it feels as if I mostly work abroad, myself. From what they tell you, the music industry is having its worst times ever, but I suppose I don't feel threatened by that because if anyone wanted to bootleg and sell my records, it'd be a sign I was doing all right!

But the downside is that for people who have had it very good for a long time, when things get worse it goes all the way down the line. Sony came to the jazz awards but they haven't got a single artist signed up, not a winner or a nominee or non-nominee or anyone in the entire British jazz scene. That shows that they don't figure that there's anything there for them. So there are no big prospects except maybe for singers. Apart from that, there are no real opportunities for a traditional recording deal and people will have to find ways to put their own music out and interface with selling it - very difficult. The good news being that the music itself will come out hopefully the way it was intended, rather than the way some A&R guy wanted.

But the danger when you speak to me is you'll get a lot that's positive, because I'm not really in competition with people. I've started to see making music as a very *personal* journey; that there's no point in engaging it against other people at all, it's just to do with people finding their music, *their own* thing. That's how it seems to me now and hopefully it'll carry on in the same way – music is a life force after all!

Selected CDs		
Organic & GM	Food	
		[2001, Feral]
Veggie	Food	
		[2002, Rune Grammofon]
The Little Radio	Ballamy Carstensen	
		[2004, Sound recordings]
Website: www.ballamy.com		

Denys Baptiste

Denys Baptiste, born in 1969 in Chelsea, London, is one of Britain's fastest rising stars, combining the roles of saxophonist, composer and bandleader. He progressed musically via youth orchestras and jazz workshops in west London, coming to the notice of saxophonists Tim Whitehead and Courtney Pine. He then studied music for two years at the West London Institute and in 1993, took the Guildhall's Post-Graduate Jazz Course.

Denys played in Gary Crosby's important Nu Troop from 1992 – 2002, The Jazz Warriors (1993-94) and alongside playing with his quartet and other commitments, he continues to play with Jazz Jamaica.

In 1998 he recorded his first album, *Be Where You Are* which gained the Mercury Music [Jazz category] and MOBO award in 1999. His quartet subsequently toured across Europe and America, including the North Sea Jazz Festival. His second album, *Alternating Currents* in 2001, illustrates the ongoing development of his varying cultural influences as composer.

He has played with many other leading players including McCoy Tyner, Courtney Pine, Julian Joseph, Jason Rebello and Nikki Yeoh, Gerard Presencer, Martin Taylor, Mbeki Mseleku, Orphy Robinson and Cleveland Watkiss.

His latest work entitled *Let Freedom Ring!* celebrated the fortieth anniversary of the famous oration on civil rights by Martin Luther King and was premiered at the 2003 Cheltenham Festival. The album was voted Album of the Year by Jazzwise Magazine.

What kinds of music do you remember first listening to in the home?

As both of my parents are from the West Indies, specifically from St Lucia, I was hearing stuff like calypso, SOCA [Sounds of the Caribbean and Africa] and reggae, a bit of Motown as well and strangely, Country 'n Western – it's quite big in some of the West Indian islands.

At what age did you first pick up a musical instrument?

I was probably thirteen when I picked up the clarinet. At secondary school they used to put up a list every year, asking what instruments you'd like to play and every year I'd put down the saxophone and they'd say, 'No, we haven't

got one.' I settled for a clarinet, grudgingly really and didn't make a lot of progress on it. But when I was about fifteen, I joined the local youth orchestra and they had a saxophone available – a tenor - and so I started on that. It was called the Hounslow Youth Wind Orchestra - we'd do music by people like Souza and Mahler.

You got into the orchestra the same time as starting on the saxophone: sounds difficult?

Playing a bit of clarinet before made it easier as the fingering is relatively similar, so it didn't take me too long - although I found that much younger musicians say eleven to fourteen were much better than me, because they'd been reading from about ten to eleven years old. But it's good to put yourself in difficult and challenging places.

You got to hear Tubby Hayes and Sonny Rollins quite early on?

My first music teacher, a clarinettist, dabbled with a little bit of jazz including trad. But then he was replaced by a saxophone player and clarinettist who introduced me to tapes of Tubby Hayes, at the time one of his heroes. So he'd bring in records like '100% Proof', ' Tubby Hayes Live 1969' and I thought 'Wow! This is what's it's all about!' and it made me even more determined to play the saxophone. So when I joined the orchestra, they said, 'There is a chair vacant and there is an instrument, all you have to do is learn it' – so that's what I did!

What else were you able to develop?

Well a couple of years after I joined the Hounslow Youth Orchestra, I joined an offshoot called the Hounslow Youth Big Band. We'd start doing stuff like Neil Hefti, Duke Ellington, Count Basie – lots of different things and there'd be arrangements by the tutors - that was my *first* experience of playing with jazz.

Then at school, there was a music teacher, a little bit unorthodox. Instead of making us play the classical repertoire, he'd bring stuff in like the Beatles, he'd write arrangements and you'd get little solos. He was really encouraging. He said, 'You've got a good ear for it and should pursue it, you know.' And he was one of the key people that convinced me that I could actually be a performer and an improviser – though at the time, I didn't really know what an improviser was.

In the youth big bands, people don't always take solos, is that how you were at that stage?

Yes, there might be space for a solo, but you don't have any idea of what you're doing, you just hope you hit some of the right notes! The process was very much trial and error.

But then I discovered that my Dad had been

a modest jazz fan in the sixties and he had a few records lying about - Dave Brubeck's 'Live at Carnegie Hall', and a couple of Count Basie and Jimmy Smith records. I remember just sitting down and trying to play along – after some embarrassing performances trying to improvise and not knowing what I was doing! So I sat down to just listen and work out what these people were doing. And I remember learning the solo of a Count Basie tune, 'Evening.' It took ages but eventually I worked it out, note by note, till it made sense.

You were making good progress because you got into the Guildhall School of Music Jazz class?

Yes, I studied after I left school. I left the saxophone for a while because I went to pursue a career as an engineer at the Kingston Polytechnic. But a few days after I got my results, I started thinking about what I really wanted to do as a career. The idea of sitting in an office all day being a manager and telling people what to do seemed really boring. So I thought that I have to have a go at being a musician for a couple of years and if it works out then...I'll see what happens.

There was a course close to me in St Margaret's London Institute of Higher Education with an education course in music, because at that time I hadn't any qualifications in music at all. So I had a bit of catching up to do, at twenty-one, to learn all the basics and theory.

I found a little evening class, like a jazz workshop, run by a guy called John Myhill. He explained stuff on chords, the relationship with chords. Then the most important thing was I met Tim Whitehead, an amazing sax player and a cool guy too. He started doing a workshop in Hounslow, my home town. Once a week, there'd be a group of people, there'd be auditions and stuff, hundreds would turn up! Then they would choose twelve or so people that they thought would get the most out of the course. John Parricelli [guitar], Tim and Martin France [drums] were all there. I did that for a few years.

Another big influence was that, about 1990, I met Gary Crosby, the bass player at the Waterman Arts Centre in Brentford at the same period as all the workshops I was doing. They used to have a jam session at the Centre every Saturday and I met Brian Edwards, an alto player, and Adrian Reid a pianist, playing there. I sat in and Brian came up to me and said 'I'm going to tell Gary about you.' I got a phone call a few weeks later saying to come down to the Jazz Cafe. So on Saturday I took my instrument down and played – it was Gary Crosby with his quintet, Nu Troop. They got me to sit in and a few weeks later, asked me to join the group – the first proper jazz group I'd actually been in. In the end I was nearly ten years in that band. But it was through that, Courtney Pine came along to the Jazz Cafe to check out the new tenor player in town, kind of thing! He was really good, he's always been somewhat of a mentor and a friend, imparting information. He's just really supportive to young players.

The great thing about the Jazz Cafe was that if anybody was in town at Ronnie's or playing at the Pizza Express, on a Saturday afternoon if they didn't have anything to do, they'd come down. One day we had all sorts of people – like Billy Higgins from Cedar Walton's band, Ralph Moore, David Murray. Every week there was somebody coming along from the States, plus great players who lived in London. You could absorb all this music whether or not you were on stage.

You've also jammed with Tim Whitehead in the 606 Club in Chelsea?

He took me under his wing and said 'Just come down to the Club and play with us.' It's quite relaxed there, you know who's playing in the band and if they're up for it, generally you can sit in. In those days we'd stay there till four or five in the morning, an amazing experience –

working with your instrument and with a band at that sort of level. Because if you're studying as a musician, it's very difficult to make any progress if you're playing with people who are at a similar level to you, you need to push and understand how it really works, how a band really *interacts*. I believe that's the most important thing in terms of learning the music – it's playing the music on stage as much as anything.

Next you went to the Guildhall Post Graduate Jazz Course?

Yes, all the elements were coming together for me, making me think I could go to the Guildhall in 1993/4 - go and study jazz properly. It's the one year course where you study improvision, composition and harmony – all the elements that make up the music.

They only take twenty-two people a year, so getting in felt like a real achievement! It was great being around musicians of a similar or higher level, we were all learning from one another and the tutors were great. I was in the same year as Ben Castle - in fact, a number of great people who are out there on the scene now. It was very intensive, but something I needed to do.

So when you left there, you briefly joined the Jazz Warriors?

Yes, it was towards the end of their existence, though they lasted a long time from just before Courtney came on the scene, say 1985/6 to 1993 – but eventually, a bit like Loose Tubes, everyone becomes soloists and bandleaders, gets commitments, so it all gets complicated. Plus logistics and the cost of transporting a large group around can be astronomical. But it was a good experience.

After that you toured with Mbeki Mseleku. He's a multi-instrument phenomenon?

Yeah, he's an amazing musician. It was one of the most educative periods in my life, because he's not just a pianist, he's also a tenor player and he also plays guitar. And he plays them all very, very well!

He's mainly a piano player but he can be seen playing piano and saxophone simultaneously, which is a quite amazing feat in itself. But also in that quartet was Marvin 'Smitty' Smith and Michael Bowie [bass] - the first time I'd worked with guys of that calibre. And I got a good beating every night, but came out a better player. He's now back in South Africa. He's not been well for a few years, since around 1995. It's very sad.

From 1994, I was playing with Nu Troop, it was the mainstay of the work that I was doing. I was also occasionally playing with Tim or I'd be doing sporadic dates with various pick-up bands.

Then Gary Crosby started another group called Jazz Jamaica, a nine-piece band. Although they'd been together for quite some time before, I started getting little dep gigs through Gary and a bit of touring with them across Europe.

Gary's an important figure: his strengths are as manager, arranger plus bass player?

He's mainly really good at thinking of ideas, groups and choosing the right personnel so as to make those things work. Although mostly other people do the arrangements and stuff, essentially he's the person who guides the ship. So he's a Miles Davis or Art Blakey type of person in that respect, a slightly older generation. He's discovered some really great younger players and helped to put them on the map.

There's Jazz Jamaica and the Jazz Jamaica all Stars – the big band retaining most of the original people. But the whole concept [of performance] is different as [now] its mostly written and arranged.

But I just believe that the more musical situations you're in and the more music that you absorb - it can only make you into a better player. Doing that music required a completely different discipline to being in a quartet or playing in a big band – how to structure solos and play the melodies and how to interact with the other people on the stage. So that was a great time!

But there's been a lot of people between 1990 and 1998 when I recorded my first – Nikki Yeoh [piano], a couple of gigs with Julian Joseph, some with Jason Rebello's [piano] quartet. Hopefully Jason'll come and do another jazz album soon, because he's quite missed on the scene.

I've also played with Gerard Presencer [flugelhorn] at the Jazz Cafe. On Saturday nights they'd do a set of jazz with a guest star every week. I was part of the house band so we'd have Jason, and Julian Joseph, different every week. They'd have a set of jazz and then a set of comedy! And combine them like that – it didn't last for very long but a really good idea.

Then in 1998, you got the opportunity to do your own first CD.

To be honest, I had to be dragged kicking and screaming into doing it, really, because especially for a first record, you never really feel ready to say your own piece. Gary approached me and said, 'Do you want to do a record?' He and his partner, Janine Irons, who's my manager, probably approached me first in 1997.

I had a few tunes, and thought I would write a few more, and went into the studio and recorded it. I'd found four guys I'd been watching to be in my group – Andrew McCormack, Harry Bartley, Daniel Crosby and Tom Skinner.

On the album, *Be Where You Are*, the group integrates beautifully, each player has his own spaces to play, or is it mainly written?

No, with that group we did play a lot together beforehand, because I'm not really the sort of player that sort of arranges to the point where it's absolutely pristine and perfect. I like certain things open to spontaneity. So that group that I still play with now, we'll just get together and I

don't even have to call tunes, we just play, so it's the most liberating experience. It's perhaps one reason that that album worked so well because we're used to listening to one another. I don't tell the bass player what to do, I don't tell Tom or Andrew what to do, just give them the barest essentials of what they need to know. Then they do with it what they wish. I want them to shine.

When your second album came out, did you consciously take it closer to the Jazz Jamaica style. What were your thoughts in going from the first to the second CD?

I think it was just the passage of time. I'd written those tunes for a first album because that's what I wanted to say. But over the years I've played so much music, with so many different people, and differing styles. My albums tend to be lots of different things - a bit funky or calypso or avant-garde, something straight-ahead, or in an odd time signature, so it covers all the things between *Be where you are* and *Alternating Currents*.

It had things I'd been listening to and playing with the guys as well. Oh and I'd worked with Martin Taylor as well and that was another huge influence, a guy that doesn't read music – he's just an amazing player. I wanted to put him in a context that maybe people hadn't heard him in much before. It's the mark of a great musician that he can sit in a context and fit in. And he's such a nice guy. I was so pleased that he'd *want* to play on my record! He's world-renowned, he has his own finger picking style that no-one does as well as he does. His solo guitar is, I think, unsurpassed.

I love soul, so there's soul things there with other things but what I *do* want to get across is that it's all *acoustic* – no electric pianos or synthesisers! Which is an interesting challenge in itself.

Your first album won the Mercury Award in the Jazz Category in 1999 and this was followed by many Festival appearances, including the North Sea

Festival where you were the only UK band?

I got a phone call from my manager saying you've been short listed for the Mercury Music prize. To start, I didn't actually know what it was, I didn't realise that it meant you were really one of twelve winners of different categories of UK music and I was the chosen jazz album of the year! Then it was amazing, a roller coaster ride for the next two years - bewildering but simultaneously exciting!

You toured across Europe with the band?

Sure, Germany, France, the North Sea Festival, even went as far as Jamaica with the group. The North Sea Festival is really exciting, because there's just so many great musicians there – everybody from Mulgrew Miller and Al Foster. I would go to the jam session at night and sit in with Roy Hargrove and James Carter and all these amazing players. Really enjoyed that as an experience, soaking up all the different music.

Do you think there's any difference between American players and our players? Are they sharper than we are?

I think they're in a fortunate position where they're at the source of it and I think their attitudes are different as well. There are so many great players in America and to be honest, there are as many really *bad* players in America - a very common misconception, that because they come from America they must be wow, amazing! But there are so many *good* ones that they are *fiercely* competitive, in the way of getting better all the time and there's so many masters there they can learn from all the time. Also the education system is much more mature there.

But in England there are slowly but surely some great players coming out of here, who could quite easily go over there and do very well. Not with everybody but there's a certain prejudice among some American musicians that they feel that we can't play, which isn't helped by some of our media coverage. You get certain jazz stations that'll play mostly American music – well, where's all the British players? There are *hundreds* of players that come out with great records every single year but unless you're listening at four o' clock on a Sunday morning, you're not going to hear, you know?

There's people, I didn't even realise they had made records, you just don't come across them. If they're not being played on the radio, they're not getting any exposure. This means they're not going to get as many gigs, which means as much experience as they should do and therefore not keep up with the American musicians. Quite often people in this country don't appreciate what we have here, not saying for myself or anybody in particular, but just as a scene. Many of the jazz musicians here are of a world quality but they don't get the recognition they deserve. That's the way it is.

I mean we have our own influences in this country and that can make our jazz in some ways more relevant than what's coming out of the States right now. They've got into this quagmire of the tradition, whereas London - England is so cosmopolitan now – there's African people here, there's Asian people, people from all over Europe, so much more fusing of musical ideas than there is in America. They have this fortress of the history of jazz but it rarely moves on from there, though there are many great players. But for the music itself, there's more happening here.

It's difficult for them because there's so much history and they're wanting to play in a certain way, so whole crops of players are all the same. It didn't use to be like that in the early days of jazz, there were lots of different innovators, people wanting to push their ideas out, and being appreciated for it.

One problem is the promotional machine for the players that push forward and get the big record deals. Hence the travel and opportunity to get out there tend to be in the middle ground of what the promoting and A&R people view as something they can sell.

After your second album, your latest

composition is 'Let Freedom Ring'. How did that come about?

I decided to do it a couple of years ago but it was going to require too much time and also be quite expensive, so I put it on the back burner for a couple of years. I wanted to do something that was focused on a specific subject. I'd heard the Martin Luther King speech years ago. My parents had bought a 12 inch vinyl record and on the B side of the Stevie Wonder record was the speech. I remember listening to it, though I don't think I actually understood what had happened with the Civil Rights movement at that time, but I understood it was important. Also that speech just draws you into it, he's a very exciting person to listen to. So I thought, how can I express that particular speech and make some kind of cohesive statement.

So I split the speech into four pieces, if you like, verses and each one is punctuated with a repeated phrase. The first one was ' I have a Dream' and the second was 'With this Faith'. The third was 'Let Freedom Ring' and finally, 'Free at last, Free at last, Thank God Almighty, we're free at last.' So I took those particular elements, some of the rhythms, some of the melodic ideas, because strangely there's actually melodies – that's how he makes it so compelling, I think. He comes from a Southern preacher background, with blues type phrases to it, and I listened to it a lot and also extrapolated my own melodies from it, making it into four pieces.

The message is not that this piece is about the Civil Rights movement but to take the speech out of its context. If you put it in 2003 and say, if Martin Luther King was around now and saying that speech to the world, how much relevance would it have? And you look at it, there's quite a lot - if you take some of the specifics out of the speech, the general message is freedom and justice for people - ideas and ideals that, living in a western country, we take quite a lot for granted. So all it's doing is highlight those abuses of freedom and justice around the world. There are races of people that don't have the

freedoms, there are sexes that don't – so it's trying to make people think a little bit about it.

We recorded it in mid-July 2003 over five days, with my 11 piece band and I'll follow this by a long tour with it in the Autumn.

On the subject of sax playing technique, how do you work on your tone?

As with most instruments, it's the combination of tones within the note that provide its overall effect – it's like the rainbow that overall produces white light! There are tones that give the sound its weight and its fullness, and it's the combination of those elements that creates a sound, good or bad. It's difficult to change your sound very much, because much of it comes from the bone structure of your head! That's why I could try to sound like John Coltrane, I could buy the same instruments as him, the same mouthpiece, same reeds, and I'll still never sound like him, because his skull and mine are different! Perhaps I could find John Coltrane's skull and have it surgically implanted! Only way it's going to happen!

Another factor is your teeth, which is why Sonny Rollins and Coltrane had lots of problems – Coltrane ate too much sugar – and with Sonny it was just neglect, and at one point he basically lost the whole top bridge and when he had false ones put in, his sound was completely different. He took a long, long time to find a way to make him sound right because the teeth are of a different material, they vibrate a different way and therefore create completely different sounds. So sax players must look after their teeth! Mine are my own!

On learning how to improvise, any tips for the young aspiring sax player?

I can only really say how I approached it, over the years. What I've discovered is, first of all, needing to really get to know your instrument. There's loads of books out there to teach you but if you develop a good ear, think of a melody and just be able to play it, *and* be able to relate it to what is going on around you - to play with others is a very important part of it.

As to harmony and things like that, it's the usual stuff like learning arpeggios and scales relating to the tunes and the transcription, making sure you check out all the interesting records — *that's* where all the information is. Then when you've done that, forget all about it, so you can find your own voice.

Now, how about your main musical influences?

For sax players, it started for me with Tubby Hayes and Dexter Gordon. Then with British players there was Tim Whitehead, then Courtney Pine and that crop of players that came up through the Eighties — Steve Williamson, Tommy Smith, Iain Ballamy — I listened, hoping to get somewhere near. Then back over the

Atlantic, it's mainly Sonny Rollins, John Coltrane, Wayne Shorter, Joe Henderson - there's lots of other guys that I've also transcribed but I always end up back at these guys, they're the true masters of what they do, especially John Coltrane and Sonny Rollins.

On your album, *Be where you are*, besides conviction, you seem to have a very clear idea of the phrases you play.

It's as important to say *something* as it is to say it with conviction. That includes having a strong enough sound and enough technique, and strong enough rhythmic delivery to make statements clearly. If you say something to someone without any conviction, they *aren't* going to believe you! It's the same with music - what audiences *do* quickly pick up on is the emotional content and conviction.

You do any coaching or workshops at the moment?

I've been doing workshops rather than individual lessons. What I do is within Dune records, they have their Educational Programme called 'Tomorrow's Warriors' and we do various things with them in different schools and do workshops. We put together pieces of music for school bands for the range from six year olds up to secondary school children.

It's fun and it helps you to understand what *you're* doing anyway, because having to sit down and explain it, you have to think more clearly about what you're actually doing.

And the future?

I'm going to go out and be featuring *Let Freedom Ring* for a year or maybe longer in between doing stuff with the quartet. I think for me, having written this latest piece, I think I'm going to be concentrating on my biggest challenge at the moment, composition. I'm going through a phase of needing to be writing pieces for groups, stuff that's a bit more mature, for my own personal development.

And then trying to be the best musician I can be, so loads of practice and trying to check out as many new people as I can.

One difference between us and pop musicians – though not all of them – our shelf life can be twenty, thirty years whereas a pop musician may get just four or five. And that's one of the great things about doing this music - that the audience is there to follow your progress and see how you develop as an artist – I'm probably going to do some bad albums along the way, but it's still more important to be developing something, whatever new ideas that you have.

Finally, have you ever played the St Lucia Jazz Festival?

Yes, last year. It was really great, for most of my

family were there at the concerts. It was like a homecoming. I'd only been there once before and to be going there a success, as it were, was great! And it's a terrific festival, lovely people and being around all my family – I couldn't ask for anything better really!

Selected CDs

Be Where You Are   Denys Baptiste
[Dune 1998]

Alternating Currents Denys Baptiste
[Dune 2001]

Let Freedom Ring   Denys Baptiste
[Dune 2003]

Website: www.dune.co.uk

Guy Barker

Guy Barker, born in 1957 in Chiswick, London, is internationally acknowledged as a world class trumpeter, combining a wide spectrum of jazz with classical and other musical projects.

Guy developed from school bands to the National Youth Jazz Orchestra and studied at the Royal College of Music. While still a teenager, he met and received lessons and advice from many visiting luminaries, including Clark Terry and Dizzy Gillespie.

In 1984, Guy joined the important Clark Tracey Quintet, staying for eight years, three albums and two tours of the Far East. Since then he has also played with Stan Tracey's Octet, Sextet and Big Band. In 1988, Guy worked alongside Ornette Coleman in a series of concerts of the composition *Skies of America*.

He has toured with the cream of big band leaders from John Dankworth to Gil Evans and Carla Bley and also acted as MD for the Brazilian Hermeto Pascoale's European tour in 1994.

Besides innumerable credits as sideman in the Eighties, Guy produced his first album in 1989 on the Miles Music label, a second in 1991. His 1995 debut for Verve, *Into the Blue*, was nominated for the Mercury Music prize. His second Verve album, *Timeswing*, was released in 1996. His third album, *What Love Is*, was arranged by Colin Towns and released in 1998. Then in 2002 his album, *Soundtrack* on Provocateur was nominated for the Mercury Music Prize. Other compositions include The Amadeus Suite, commissioned for the US Mainly Mozart Festival.

Guy has played with such jazz luminaries as Joe Henderson and Nat Adderley, Tommy Smith, Georgie Fame, John Surman, Sting, Frank Sinatra, Liza Minelli and Cleo Laine. He has been awarded the UK Award for Best Jazz Trumpet four times, most recently in 2001. His band gained the BBC Jazz Award for Best Band in 2003.

Can you remember what kinds of music you first heard in the home?

My father was a fan of Bennie Goodman, big bands and Frank Sinatra and my uncle was a fan of musicals. I remember listening to a record of Guys and Dolls, Gigi, West Side Story and stuff like that.

And, of course, the music from old movies. But when I was about five or six, the thing that probably most turned me on to jazz-inspired music was The Jungle Book, the Disney film — knew it off by heart!. If you listen to 'The Bare Necessities' - I've always wanted to know who the trumpet soloist was, because it sounds like it could be Clark Terry but it's just someone playing like Clark Terry.

Add the Beatles, because it was that time. But my main enjoyment was jazz-inspired music, though I also really liked classical.

When did you first pick up a musical instrument?

I was twelve when I picked up my first cornet in the school brass band. I loved that and had a very good teacher, Eric Smith, a Salvation Army brass band teacher and then Tommy Wilson of the Scots Guards. Because there weren't enough instruments to go round to the kids who wanted to play in the band, he insisted that we did six weeks of theory before we were even allowed to touch an instrument! Then we would have an examination and a test and whoever came first in the test got first choice of the instruments. So you had 35 kids and 19 instruments. And I came second. It was the best thing that could have happened because I had seen the flugelhorn. I'd never seen one before and I thought, 'Wow! that's bigger than the cornet.' And the guy who came first took the flugelhorn! So I got the cornet which was the best thing really because the cornet is the one that has all the hard, virtuoso stuff to play and from the *technique* point of view, was a much better way.

Then a local trumpet player, Ray Crane, who ran a Dixieland band, formed the Harrow Youth Jazz Orchestra and I joined that. It was after that that I joined the National Youth Jazz Orchestra. I was still pretty young – I think I joined the National orchestra when I was about fourteen, so I'd only been playing for about two and a half years.

You'd not been studying anything else like the piano before?

That's right, but I was really obsessed. I remember the National Youth Jazz Orchestra had a rehearsal every Saturday morning and they knew they were going to be short of a trumpet player. Bill Ashton, who ran it, lived round the corner in Harrow. And he knew that I was playing in the Harrow Youth Orchestra, this enthusiastic kid round the corner, so he invited me round to play. He said, 'Would you just come round and play; I want to see if you would be able to do a rehearsal.' I got the cornet out and played all the exercises you had to do for your teacher, I practiced and practiced till I couldn't play another note - and that's when I got the call. And I went round to his house and I was just too shattered from playing. And he said to me, 'Well, you're not really there, so give it a few more years.' I remember being *very* upset.

Then I went on a jazz course that was held in south London - all day for seven days. Maynard Ferguson came and took the big band and I played in a jam session every day and at the end of that was when I got great encouragement from Henry Lowther who passed on good remarks to Bill and said, 'You should put him in the band' - so I joined six months later.

I was in that band for seven years. We rehearsed every Saturday morning, and then we did gigs all over the country. We went to the States, a two to three week tour of California, we played in Russia, in France. At the time, it was the most enjoyable thing I did, it was what I lived for.

It kept a remarkably high standard.

Yes and the standard got higher and higher! I mean, I would listen to the band I played in and then to the band as we developed and I can hear the whole quality of the band improve.

Many people used to say 'Wow, what a band' because you had all these jazz names in, but you have to realise that they were all kids, learning and developing – and it takes a long time to develop. That's the main lesson *I've* learnt in music, is how *long* it takes to get it together. And we're all still learning. If somebody asks me what I do, I say I'm an eternal music student!

Considering there are a lot of good trumpet players around, it seems sometimes that there's an extra expressiveness, maybe a sense of humour in your playing?

You know, the first person that made me want to play the trumpet was Rex Stewart and he used a lot of *vocal* sounds on the trumpet and I was inspired by that. Dizzy Gillespie and Cootie Williams used to do the same thing. I used to listen to a lot of those people, but what I found was I wanted to get as close to the voice as possible as.

But it depends what environment I'm in. There are places where that stuff works and places where it doesn't work at all. A lot of the time, when I'm playing with my septet for example, I don't use as many of those sounds. I

was always taught that respect for the idiom and in some ways there's a lot of truth in that. If you're playing in an environment that requires a certain direction, go with it, don't be so dogmatic as to say, 'This is the way I play and that's it!' Go somewhere else, have a look around because we've all just got one chance so have a look at different ways of playing and different experiences. That's why, when I got asked to do the Bix Beiderbecke concert, I went and learnt all about it, said to myself let's see how you play in this style.

And then I would get a call to go and play with the avant-garde guys. I've played with Ornette Coleman, Evan Parker – and it's all music and part of learning. I understood an awful long time ago that the icons that you look up to, Miles Davis, Louis Armstrong, Dizzy Gillespie – there's only one of them, that's it. I'm not *ever* going to change the way people think about music at all! So for the time that I've got here, it's nice to explore as much of it as I can so I can leave this life saying I've played so many

different things, I think I've experienced music – while doing your *utmost* to have your own voice, because that's the most important thing!

Was there a time when you made a choice to become a professional musician?

Yes, it was on that course, because I asked Maynard Ferguson the same question. I knew I was on the verge of saying this is what I want to do for the rest of my life – I was fourteen – and I asked him, 'Did there come a point for you when you said, 'This is it'? And he said he started working very young but it hit him at a very young age and he couldn't remember exactly, but he looked at me and he said, 'You'll know.'

And as soon as he said that, I thought, he's right, I know now. Because there were so many things I'd taken an interest in but I'd never followed them through. I couldn't find anything that really would grab me. I'd watched my Dad crash cars in movies as a stunt man and seen my Mum act on TV and in the theatre and al ways found that fascinating, but I thought I couldn't go that way. Once I thought I wanted to be a film cameraman, or I would have a hobby or something.

Then when I discovered music, everything went out the window! Absolutely everything, my academic results – I did really well in my first year at secondary school, fifteen A's and they wanted to send me to a better school. Then the brass band really sunk in and I started the second year – it was a disaster purely because all I could think about was music!

At sixteen, I went to an intensive music course at Chiswick Music Centre, just round the corner. I was in this environment when I was studying all about the great masters of music. They had a jazz appreciation class as well. We had a little jazz ensemble, I was in a symphony orchestra. We had choirs, I studied music history, theory, harmony – every class was music. I could not believe this, I just had the *best* time.

And then when I was eighteen, I took an audition to go to the Royal College of Music.

Then I toured the States with the National Youth Jazz Orchestra and when I came back I started the Performers Course at the Royal College of Music in 1976.

It was a three year course and I stayed until my third year, when it all got very busy! I had about a term left to go, it was in the Spring it all started happening, calls for all sorts of commercial work – studio work and jazz work. My father was very encouraging. He came into the College of Music and said to them, 'Look, these people that are wanting to employ him now are the people that could want to employ him for the rest of his life, so I think..'. And he got me off some orchestral concerts and stuff. It was the September of my last year, and I went to New York to study for six weeks. I made some story up, semi-true, that I'd been studying with Clark Terry. He had given me lessons and I'd become quite good friends with Dizzy Gillespie.

When I was around eighteen I made an album with a pop group, a funk band, and with the money I made from those recording ses-

sions, I just got myself a ticket to New York and went and stayed there for six weeks, just breathing it all in. I formed my own band.

I'd already asked the College Director for permission to leave and he'd let me off. Then just when I was to be going home, I got the call from John Dankworth, saying would I come and do the Palladium for a week with Cleo and the band. That was *the* big break at the time. So I got on the plane, had to go into the college and say, Can I have *another* week off to play at the

Palladium? And they could see what was happening, they understood. There were a few eyes raised to the ceilings, where's he off to now? But I did that week at the Palladium and then went back to school.

Then I formed my own quintet with four guys from New York. We got grants from the Arts Council and the Arts Centre. The Jazz Centre Society set us up with a tour, so I was on the road with my own band - that's when I realised I'd left the college. And my teacher, Bob Walton, who was wonderful, gave me his blessing.

Was it then that you formed a group with Chris Hunter [alto sax]?

I'd left college and left the NYJO and just happened to call Chris up, and I asked him what he was doing. He said, 'So good you've called, let's get in a band together.' I said, 'OK, let's do it!' And I introduced him to lots of people, Michael Garrick, people like that. We had a variety of people but we had this quintet, it was the very first time I played at Ronnie Scott's, an amazing experience for a twenty-one year old!

He introduced me to Mike Westbrook, and Chris basically got me the gig with Mike Westbrook so I started working with him. Plus I was doing broadcasts with John Dankworth and I started doing quite a bit of studio work.

Jazz was always my first love but now, I was working, I started making some money and it was enough to get me a flat. When I was about twenty-four, I bought a fantastic little studio flat in Covent Garden.

Then in 1984 I got a call from Clark Tracey who was forming a new band. He said it's going to be with Steve Melling, Jamie Talbot, Alec Dankworth on bass. And this quintet then became my next *obsession*, after playing with the Youth Orchestra. It was my whole life.

A very busy band....

Yes, it was amazing. There we were, five guys in our early to mid twenties, playing all our favourite music. Some of the time we were playing our own but a lot of the time we were playing the music of Art Blakey, Mingus and Wayne Shorter. Then we started adding more tunes that Clark and particularly Steve Melling wrote. But Jamie and I wrote some stuff as well.

That became a really active band and that lasted for about eight years! We made three albums and we toured the Far East twice, went to France. Socially it was fabulous, musically it was fabulous. We had a very good time.

As a result of that, I got my first gig with Stan Tracey. And then because of the quintet, and me and Jamie, Stan formed a band which he called Hexad, a six piece band which was a mixture of Stan's Quartet and Clark's Quintet. Clark was drumming for both bands, then there was me and Jamie and Art Themen, so a mixture. Then I started working for Stan in his Octet, his big band and then there was Clark's band, so it was a really nice time.

You've worked in a lot of big bands. The first time you played with the Gil Evans band in New York, you were standing in.

Somebody had got the call and just wasn't going to turn up. I was staying in New York with Miles Evans, Gil's son and Chris Hunter, all in the same apartment. And I got asked, 'You going to play in Gil's band tonight?' So I went over and Mike Gibbs, the composer, was there.

The venue was downstairs in the bar at Seventh Avenue south. As I stood at the top of the stairs I started looking at the band. There was Lew Soloff, Dave Sanborn, Jaco Pastorius, Mike Stern, Hiram Bullock, Pete Levin, one of Charles Mingus' tenor players! I was terrified, I wouldn't go up those stairs to the band and I walked straight down the stairs! And I just went and sat at the bar. Then it was Mike Gibbs who said, 'I didn't come to have a drink with you; I came to hear you play, get up those stairs!'

So I went up those stairs, sat next to Lew Soloff and his first words to me were, 'Are you staying?' and I said, 'Yes, why?' And he said, 'Well, take off your coat!' I hadn't realised I was sitting in this hot, sweaty club with my coat on - ready to do another runner! But in the end it was a wonderful gig and a real inspiration.

Lew Soloff is also one of the lead trumpet players that Carla Bley calls on?

That's right. I think that Lew got me the gig with Carla Bley. She was creating an Anglo-American band to tour Europe and I think it was Lew who said, if we're going to go to London, get Guy. So I've had a lot of lucky moments like that.

You've played in the Hermeto Pascoale Big Band where you also acted as MD.

There was a wonderful tour in about the mid-nineties. He's just the most phenomenal musician you could ever come across. It was an amazing experience because you had his seven or eight piece Brazilian band and a twenty piece English big band which I had to help put together. And I had to conduct the big band and make sure certain things happened between us – and play the trumpet. It was a lot to do.

When I walked into the room for the rehearsal, the drummer came over to me and said, 'Hermeto wants to tell you something'. So I said 'OK', because Hermeto doesn't speak English. Hermeto had all the scores for all the music in his hands, held in front of him; a big pile of music. He started talking to me in Portuguese. I didn't know what he said and then he gave me the music and put it in my hand. The translation was, 'Hermeto says thank you very much for conducting the band and organising this for me. I'm looking forward to it. This music *was* mine and now it is *yours*. You do with it what you want.' I was flabbergasted.

Every musician still talks about that tour, still saying months afterwards. It was like a dream, I can't believe it actually happened. So I conducted and he played. It was great.

You have so much experience in big bands - useful when you wanted to move on and compose for your own albums?

Oh yes, because all the information goes in. There's a lot of musical information put in front of you, you hear it constantly. Also you hear comments from people saying, 'Oh, that's not very good writing,' so you know what to do and what not to do when it comes to writing. Or you try...

You have worked a lot with Colin Towns, a major British arranger.

Absolutely. Firstly he helped on the orchestrations for the 'What Love Is' album and that was terrific. Then the film director Anthony Minghella heard the album and asked me to do 'The Talented Mr Ripley' – to produce six jazz standards and have my band appear in the film. I've always had this love for film noir and so actually to take part in something, or just observe the creation of a film is fascinating. It's probably really the soundtracks that get to me. Max Steiner and Hugo Friedhofer, Bernard Herrmann and all those amazing composers. Real craftsmen.

In the Nineties you began composing much more.

Yes, when I got a contract with Verve, they asked for two things; 'You have to get a different band together and you have to write original material.' That's when I started writing a lot more. Then I got involved with it an awful lot more and started studying classical music again. I began with a great composer-cum-teacher called Jeffrey Wilson who's inspired a lot of people.

He studied with Messiaen. I spent a lot of time studying with him, creating some chamber music. Consequently when I composed all the music for Soundtrack there was a significant difference in what I was doing.

Colin Towns had wanted me to do an album but he didn't dictate anything. He just said, 'Please take some chances! Don't hold back, take risks, that's all I ask of you. So I changed the band and wrote some stuff and the result is Soundtrack.

Originally I didn't want 'Sounds in Black and White' to go on the album. I thought that it's got a little bit of me I wasn't sure I wanted eve-rybody to know about – that I was a romantic fool who loved the old black and white movies. I thought they wanted me to be some hard-nosed jazzer! But the guys really loved it, so the piece went in and it's been *the* thing that has kept it all going really and given me the opportunity to do things I didn't think I would ever do.

It's a really expressive, exciting piece of music.

It's had a great reaction so now I've orchestrated it. We did a concert at the Barbican and I've completely extended it, added another part, and it's now for the Septet and a sixty-piece symphony orchestra! Anthony Minghella introduced our concert. Then we did it for BBC4 at the Brecon Festival.

Another composition is your Amadeus Suite.

In 1999 I was approached by David Atherton, a great conductor who runs the Mainly Mozart Festival in San Diego and he really wanted my quintet to play. But it had to have a connection with Mozart. So we wracked out brains and thought what can we do? We can't jazz up classics, it sounds awful! Then I discussed it with a good friend of mine, a lawyer, Peter Thompson in Hong Kong, who helped keep their jazz club going, a fan of both jazz and opera. He said why don't you write a suite inspired by characters from Mozart's operas? So he sent me loads of information about what each character was and the story plot - in the end it was a bit like writing for a film. It became the Amadeus Suite and we performed it once in Hong Kong and twice in San Diego.

There seems to be a movement currently for some chamber jazz; without drums or bass and drums? Perhaps jazz is edging closer to classical?

Well I find jazz musicians have *always* been inspired by classical music, in a way. Most of them are huge followers of Ravel, Debussy, Bartok and Stravinsky because they're the masters of composition – that's where you look to.

I always find it funny if you go into a jazz club and you hear somebody say, 'This next *composition* of mine is such and such' ..and it's a twelve bar blues. And it's twelve bars of written music and then off they go! I love them using that term *composition*! And then you look at Stravinsky's *Rite of Spring* and you think, 'Ah, now there's a composition!' Let's get our terminology correct!

Following *Soundtrack* have you got anything you're working on?

Yes, I've been asked to do another album but I don't know exactly what I'm going to do yet. I do like keeping on with the sound of the Septet, but surrounding it with other things. But also, I did take the Underdogs idea, the first piece, which is inspired by a book. We worked with the author and extended that to eight pieces which follow the journey of the whole book, arranged for twelve musicians and a narrator.

We did that at the Barbican and at Brecon. And that was great fun.

So I've been doing loads of orchestrating and composing that has taken up all my time.

I've now completed writing an arrangement for Rosario Guiliani to perform in Milan. Then I go to Siberia and perform all the 'What Love Is' album with a chamber group. Then we're in the States again touring with Billy Cobham's band.

I've got a variety of other projects; there's a singer/songwriter called Chris Difford who played in a band called Squeeze and written many great songs. He said, 'I'd like to write some songs with you if I give you lyrics.' This is a completely different direction and I've started working on that.

Plus I've been asked to do a couple of film scores. There's a lot of different things going on. Now I'm living in this lovely flat with Davina my fiancée and looking forward to getting married - so there's a lot to fit in!

Many congratulations.
Can we move to your main musical influences - the trumpeters?

All of them. The first who made me want to play jazz was Rex Stewart and then Louis Armstrong. Then it's Clifford Brown, Dizzy Gillespie, Clark Terry, Freddie Hubbard – Freddie Hubbard a lot! Miles Davis, Woody Shaw, Terence Blanchard, Chet Baker and Kenny Wheeler. Everybody!

But the most? - it would be Clifford Brown, Freddie Hubbard and Miles Davis.

But the influencers *are* everybody. And I listen to classical music as much as to jazz, because there's always somebody who can surprise you. It never stops. You turn a corner and there's always somebody who's going to surprise you and frighten you – and that's the perfect combination!

Finally, what do you think of the health of the UK jazz scene?

You know, I think it's good. The wonderful thing about the interest in jazz is, nothing's really changed. It goes up and down, up and down all the time and it always has done. Every so often, it's like somebody in the media, on the radio or on TV or the newspapers says, 'Hang on, we haven't done anything on music lately. I know — why don't we say how great jazz is doing in England now, even though they don't know if it is or not. Or shall we do a piece on why nobody goes to see jazz any more in England?

Then they present you with a question and you say, but I went to the Festival Hall the other night and it was sold out! And I went to Ronnie Scott's and it was sold out! I went to the Pizza one night and it was sold out? Or they were all half empty. It's always the same, there are always people who come along and create something new. Say Colin Towns creates his label, that's great. Then there'll be a bit of a lull, then Stan Tracey will have a new project and they say this is fabulous and really healthy! Then they'll say, where is Stan now? Well he's around, he's just doing something else.

I did an interview when Soundtrack came out and they said Guy Barker has 'come out of the wilderness.' I said 'Huh?'. Well, he said, 'the last album you did was *What Love Is* and that was four years ago! I said, 'Well the reason I didn't do it sooner was I was too busy doing something else.'

It's a constantly turning and changing thing. We had the BBC Jazz Awards this year — my band won an award — but if you attend everything, if you go to the London Jazz Festival every time it's run, to everything at Pizza Express and Ronnie Scott's, the Bull's Head and everywhere, all the Festivals, you check them out, you'd conclude that this is the most thriving thing going on.

If you don't go, then it's not forced down your throat. Anything that's on a high artistic level, that requires a bit of active listening, it's something you have to make an effort to do. It's not like where you turn on a radio station and you hear rock and pop things because they are popular. With jazz and classical music you have to search for it! When you do search, you discover it's there. It's all going on and there are always new things!

Selected CDs	
Portraits Plus	Stan Tracey Octet [1992, Blue Note]
What Love Is	Guy Barker [1998, Emarcy/Polygram]
Soundtrack	Guy Barker [2002, Provocateur]

Alan Barnes

Alan Barnes, born in 1959 in Cheshire, is one of Britain's leading jazz artists on alto and baritone saxophone and clarinet. He studied at the Leeds College of Music, obtaining a first class diploma and soon moved down to London. He has since played in the bands of Tommy Chase, Humphrey Lyttelton and co-led the Jazz Renegades. From 1988 to 1998, he led the Pizza Express Modern Jazz Sextet. Throughout the 1990s, Alan co-led a quintet with the trumpeter Bruce Adams, additionally running various bands of his own, including the Cannonball Tribute band and his Latin band. He has recorded many albums for the Zephyr label including *Days of Wine and Roses* with Tony Coe. Alan has also recorded with pianist David Newton on the US Concord label on albums including *Below Zero*, *Summertime* and *Manhattan*.

He has toured in the US with the bands of Warren Vaché and Charlie Watt's Tentet.

Alan revels in humorous communication with audiences. His latest composition, the *Sherlock Holmes Suite* comprises fourteen pieces arranged for jazz octet and narrator. The Suite satisfies both his love of Conan Doyle and also of blowing solos while theatrically dressed up in deerstalker and Inverness cape. The album was released on Alan's Woodville label in 2003, followed by *Swingin the Samba*.

He has won a remarkable 13 Hamlet UK Jazz Awards since 1993 for his performances on alto, baritone and clarinet. He is married to Clare Hirst, also an excellent professional sax player.

What was the first music you can remember listening to in the home?

The earliest was 'Family Favourites' on the radio when we had troops in Germany, Malta etc.. They'd say, 'This is for 'Gunner so and so' - they were playing music like Frank Sinatra and Ella Fitzgerald - so I know all those standards without having to learn them. But what *really* woke my musical imagination when I was about nine or ten was *The Jungle Book* film - all that Louis Prima trumpet playing stuff — that's exactly the kind of music I wanted!

The other thing I loved was Acker Bilk playing *Stranger on the Shore* — which is why I got a clarinet. A year or two later I started to do the music grade exams.

When you became a teenager how was your music developing?

I was into practicing the clarinet, really all the time, because it was the sort of thing that I and nobody else did at school. I got a little semi-bullying about it — I brought an Acker Bilk record to school and remember being cuffed about the head by Deep Purple fans!

Jazz was just different; it was *your* secret, like listening to Humphrey Lyttelton's programme on a Monday night and *Jazz Club* on a Sunday with Peter Clayton. One of the nice things about my life has been that all those people I used to listen to, all the British musicians like Dave Green, Jimmy Hastings - I've ended up playing with them.

And it still feels the same way now. I remem

ber we did a tour with Acker Bilk and Humphrey Lyttelton and it was *knockout*, just being around him. Acker's a great clarinet player with his own sound – which many people are trying to get, few achieve it.

How did you learn music?

Firstly I had classical lessons from a very good teacher, Ann Walker. Jazz started with me playing in a Trad band – my father had some friends in Frodsham called 'Geoff Hayes' Hot Heights' – *all eccentrics.* Geoff Hayes was a chemist developing ice cream whose father had been a hypnotist from the music halls - that was the guy with the soprano [sax] and the white lice in his reed. He would play a couple of dazzling loud scales – 'This drives 'em crazy' he would explain! It was all just great fun.

My Dad bought me an alto - a Selmer -on my fifteenth birthday. I still play it.

They had tons of lead sheets written out in different keys and we'd just play all kinds of tunes – riffy Chicago-type tunes - plus originals. We played every Friday and Geoff wrote one tune called, 'Waitin' around for Friday' – I thought it was incredibly hip.

There weren't any of these jazz educational books about. So anything you did, you either learnt by taking it off the record or somebody showing you what they'd done. Often of course you got fed wrong information, like Chinese Whispers, stuff gets passed along. Not like today.

What about your life outside music?

I was doing A levels in Altringham and I was going to become a reporter – study English at university. But I had a band with a couple of guitarists at school to do gigs - little youth clubby-type gigs, to do blues and stuff.

Then the careers master said, 'I'm sure there's a jazz course in this country at Leeds' - I'd never heard of it. He found a prospectus that was ancient. I wrote to Leeds and got an audition. I'd already been to interviews at universities to do English and I didn't like the stu-

dents I met and I was interviewed by one guy lounging around with his feet on the table. I thought, 'This just isn't for me!'

As soon as I walked into Leeds College, the first person I saw was Bill Charlson [tutor]; he was having a pint, he was dressed great and he's a great flute and sax player *and* a clarinet player. So he sat down and played *piano* for my audition! Just great! All the new applicants had an aural test, which was writing down the French horn line from the tune of the TV theme *Onedin Line*. I got a letter two days later and that was it! *That's* when the parents started worrying!

But that was the key moment in my life when I knew I'd been accepted. It was like in the Wizard of Oz when it goes into colour! I went there and it was fantastic! I was playing in big bands and small groups and if you wrote things, they got played. Like something for strings and flugelhorn, they'd book a room and you could hear what you'd written. Wonderful experience and the best thing I ever did!

One of the great characters in the college was my tutor, Dave Cooper. On my third lesson, I was getting a bit anxious he'd never heard me play and offered to play something. A worried look came over his face and he said, 'Will that be *entirely* necessary?'

Another day a man came into the classroom to put up a large 'No Smoking' sign, with Dave, a lifelong smoker, calmly puffing away, watching him. When he'd left, Dave walked over and put a large picture of Coleman Hawkins over the sign - then carried on with the lecture! So in his own way he taught me that people actually can do what they *want* to do!

At that time was it the only college in the country to teach jazz?

Yes and it was all *professional* musicians teaching, plus it wasn't done by timetables. I remember saying to Bill Charlson – 'I can't sort this vibrato thing out – when do you use vibrato in a big band and when don't you?' And he said 'Right' and we went into this room and he just sorted it out for you – forever - and that wasn't scheduled. He'd expect you to buy him a drink afterwards - but it was good.

So we have your decision to become a jazz musician with your decision to enter Leeds?

Yes, once I'd decided to go for it, that was it! It was going to be jazz and nothing would interrupt this crusade.

Did you get a feeling then that you would turn out to be as good as you have become, probably one of the best in the country?

Well, I don't know if I am! I just *really* wanted to play. I can't compare myself to Art Pepper or Cannonball Adderley, you know, you're always going to fall short of them. A lot of the time, being a jazz musician is a good lesson in being humble.

Also if it doesn't come naturally to you you've got to work at it – if you compare Nigel Hitchcock, music to him is something of utter simplicity. I've played with him half a dozen times in commercial settings – jazz ones - and his understanding of music is *total*. Once we were playing on a jingle in the John Altman Big Band. It was a Latin thing and very hard to place the notes. Lots of people had different ideas on where they should be placed and Nigel just said, 'Think of it like this.' And everybody said 'Oh, yes, that's the key to it!'

It *is* tough playing alto when there's plenty of people like this around. But it's good, it keeps you working and it's good to be part of it.

So you graduated from Leeds in Jazz and Light Music.

Didn't do much light music, in fact, I never really found out what on earth that was!

Neither did Dave Newton.

That was probably the most important part

of the time at Leeds, meeting Dave, bizarrely even the same bedroom. Due to some filing error, we got sent to the same place and had to share for 18 months.

If we could turn to what you once called a pivotal moment early in your career. You were in a big top in Wetherby, Yorkshire and you played Charlie Parker's 'Anthropology' to the unappreciative audience of a knife-throwing act?

Not sure that was a *pivotal* point exactly! At the time I was doing Sheffield Embassy ballroom, as well, six nights a week. And playing in the Sarni circus *and* doing Gilbert and Sullivan and I suppose I could still be doing things like that up there, you know.

But I thought no, go to London - and being naïve helped! I had no idea that when you leave college you're not really ready. You have to see what other people play in gigs and how they handle situations. You get it together when you get down here really.

About a year after you got down to London, in 1981, you joined the Pasadena Roof Orchestra.

It was hot dance music of the twenties and thirties and doing a hell of a lot of touring, all over Europe, plus in the States, when we did a one-nighter in Texas. Wasn't a lot of jazz in it really, just eight bar snatches on the clarinet – I would do a couple of choruses on the *Sugar Foot Stomp*! After I had done enough to buy my sets of saxes and flutes and things, I left.

Then you joined the Tommy Chase Quartet [hard bop] in 1986?

That was fun too, because Tommy's quite a character and it was the kind of the music I was really interested in. Tommy was pretty good and I got some attention with that band, as jazz-dance crazies.

And co-leading the Jazz Renegades 1986-88?

That was similar, it was with Steve White, the drummer from *Style Council*, and I did a lot of writing for that; a lot of Latin things — we had an organ in the band so it was all tenor and organ - a kind of dance-groove band, for good fun music.

And then with Humphrey Lyttelton from 1988 to 1992.

I was replacing Bruce Turner, which I was very proud to do. Bruce was one of the most *original* alto players I've ever heard. I also learnt a lot about presenting music from Humph, about taking your time and how to talk to people and audiences, pacing sets, things like that.

Those are things not done by all British jazzmen!

Probably right. Got to be careful here!

But it is supposed to be a branch of the entertainment industry, isn't it?

No argument there!

Then the Pizza Express Modern Jazz Sextet – it had a terrific line-up.

Sure - nearly ten years there. There was Gerard Presencer [flugelhorn], he was only sixteen when that band started and Dave O'Higgins [tenor sax] was young as well. Mark Fitzgibbon, the Australian, was the original pianist. Dave and I

wrote a book of tunes for it, which we added to as the years rolled by. It was every *Monday* night, eight till one – unfortunately we never got a big crowd. Probably it was the words *Modern Jazz* - that was the kiss of death...

In trying to build jazz audiences, perhaps what the market wants is new formats?

Yes, with some venues, for instance, after you've played there with someone the class of Art Themen, before you come again, they ask you to develop something new. If you're a quartet,

or playing with a trio, they're not interested in booking that. In fact they get quite excited if the jazz element is diluted somehow.

I notice that whenever there's a merging of musical forms, like in fusion, it's the jazz element that suffers. There's a sense that if it's just straightahead swinging jazz, it's been done before. But how could it have been done before? And this over-emphasis on being *innovative*, it's one of the words I hate! 'Oh how innovative!' If someone says that, you *know* you're in for a dull evening, don't you.

Perhaps your musical ear has been developing, so that you can readily understand the more difficult solos. Maybe you can listen to Peter King

[alto] and see what it takes to play something like that.

It's not about knowing what the notes are, it's the *way* it's done and what leads into what. I mean Pete will play a phrase that's going one way, then it goes another way, then it becomes another phrase and doubles back on itself – he's a tremendous intellect, Pete - not just musically. Same thing with Art Themen, same with Nigel, or any of those guys when you hear their minds at work. And you *can* follow it, you know. And you think, 'Oh my God, where did that come from?'

It's like when you hear Harry Sweets Edison and it's so simple, you know what the notes are, it's a sixth, and a fourth, and so on. Then you think, I'll try and do a chorus like that and you can't do it! It's a mystery!

You were part of Bill le Sage's Suite for Genetically Modified Quintet.

Firstly, it is, of course, for *ten-piece* band – that's an example of Bill's humour!

Well, I did lots of gigs with Bill, just bebop gigs, usually with him on piano not vibes, though I know his vibes playing very well. Always got on well with him. He wrote this whole thing when his wife was ill, he had to take her to a day centre – he'd come straight home and just write. I think it's a wonderful suite and we recorded it at the Ealing Festival – a nice CD.

You've also worked with Tina May.

Yes, played in her trio, Nikki Iles, her and me. Very nice, playing a lot of bass clarinet, all the different tone colours, with soprano. I like doubling on instruments. Some hard things to play; Nikki Iles comes up with some *minefields* of chord sequences on tunes - she's an incredible musician. Her method is very harmonically advanced. I think it's really just a different way of playing.

Now, we should discuss the thirteen UK jazz awards you've won for alto and clarinet. You've been sharing the Hamlet Alto Sax Best Player award for

the UK with Peter King since 1993?

Well I do seriously think he should have it every year . I get it by default, you know. The whole awards system, you know, it's nice to get them and the bit of publicity, but honestly, I'm as much embarrassed as pleased…

I see your forward gig dates and you're playing largely in the UK. What happens if you want to play on the continent?

I'm not quite the same pull outside of this country and I've mainly played abroad in other people's bands. I've done things in America, I was with Warren Vaché's eleven-piece band for three months – I wrote the book for that band, so things like that. I've been to South Africa, Japan, and New York with Charlie Watts. But so far as me doing my own thing, I think there's probably an Alan Barnes in every country, wanting to go to *other* countries. Perhaps we should do a rotation! Like rotation farming! I actually feel I've done about as well as I deserve. If this were as far as it goes, I'm happy.

A significant achievement is the number of well-received CDs you've produced.

When I left home, *no-one* wanted to record me, so I put seven thousand pounds of my own money into recording three albums in three days with some of my favourite players – Fret Records put them out, I had a deal with them. I made all my money back and maybe about £4,000 extra. As a result of that, people started ringing me up to do record dates! I believe that you've got a duty to put some of the money back in.

And lo and behold, I've ended up doing it again with my own label [Woodville] – I've invested about £8,000 of my own money in music I believe in and players I believe in, so giving other musicians a chance to record on my label. That is, musicians that *a.* I like, and *b.* have the right attitude to actually selling the product. You have *got* to sell it and the records have to be the kind of thing that will sell. I don't mean compromise, but the kind of jazz that I would like

to buy. I'm hoping to put the Bruce Adams quartet out on it – music like that.

Currently I don't have any definite royalty agreement with musicians, but I'm trying to make my label fair to musicians, so when I see that an album's done fairly well, everyone gets a taste! I won't make any much money myself but at the end of the day, I end up with the catalogue. It's been an interesting process, learning just what's involved in getting a CD out.

It's not as easy as a lot of musicians think - just paying the MCPS [Copyright Protection Society] is around seven or eight hundred pounds, just on the first run of a thousand. You've got to sell a lot of albums to cover that, as there's the studio cost - and of course the high street shops make more than the company does.

But it's useful to see the other side of the business. As long as you're practical about what you spend – for instance, you do an album in a day. I know it's nicer to have three days and do the overdubs but....

How did you come to compose the Sherlock Holmes Suite?

Well, I've always loved the Sherlock Holmes sto-ries. Ever since I was a kid, that perfect bachelor establishment – there's Holmes and Watson, an interesting array of characters and old leather armchairs. The suite's divided up into 14 pieces; some are characters, like there's the 'Tiger of San Pedro', depicting a criminal. There's one of Moriaty, the Napoleon of Crime, one of Sherlock Holmes, called a 'Quite a Three Pipe Problem'. Each section is separated by narrative, some of it by Sir Arthur Conan Doyle directly, but quite a lot of it is me writing about the stories. There's an actor, Alan Mitchell, dressed as Sherlock Holmes. I'm quite interested in *combinations* involving theatrical aspects of jazz; I don't see it as selling out at all. And when the narrator is not around, I dress up as Sherlock Holmes and do it!

There has been so much po-faced music entitled things like - hope there isn't such a name - '*Ubiquity*' – you know what I mean. [er..Roy Ayers' band Ubiquity]. So we want more pieces like 'The Baker Street Irregulars' and 'The Tiger of San Pedro,' comical but serious. I like to present it comically. Like sometimes I go on and say 'Well, here we are folks, two hours of *British Jazz*, what a prospect!' And you can see some people that probably didn't want to come, they've been talked into it by friends or boy-friends, and they think, 'Oh, that's quite funny ' and they'll *listen*!

If I play a tune of mine, I often say, 'And here are those words that strike *fear* into the British jazz heart, ' Now for an *original !*' – people respond well to that and you can take them places they wouldn't normally go. So it lightens the mood without compromising the music. So I'm playing hard-bop dressed in a deerstalker with an Inverness Cape - I really can see this as the entertainment industry!

Now about learning jazz, its rhythms, harmonies, its idioms - what are the main areas you concentrate on?

The two things that I've always found hardest, which I'm still practicing. Firstly – working on my *time-keeping*. If I have any student comes to me for a lesson I say, 'Right, from now on, you never play a note in your life that isn't in time!' I'm not saying, *I've* got great time, that's why I work on it. If you hear a great player like Coleman Hawkins just stand up and do it, it may be rubato style but there's the time and the accuracy. *Time and swing* to me are the essence of the whole thing. A lot of people are doing things apart from swing now, but I'm still fascinated by it!

The *second* area is playing the *melody* and then embellishing it – not changing the melody but adding notes. But also paraphrasing the melody, that is changing the notes but keeping the rhythm or something that keeps people knowing it's still the melody.

It's working on these areas that makes the music unique to me. You come to get a feeling about it, like Art Blakey's definition of jazz - 'the music that washes away the dust of every-day life.'

What about your major musical influences?

The day my father bought my alto sax, the guy, a old former musician there with his roll-up, said 'You want to get yourself some Johnny Hodges records now!' So I got the double album of

Johnny Hodges small bands (1951-55) – I still play it, *Skokiaan*, *A Pound of Blues*, those kinds of things. But that is *still* one of the best alto sounds – unless Benny Carter was playing...

The next record was Sonny Rollins' *Saxophone Colossus* - one of the best albums ever made. Charlie Parker of course. Anything to do with Ellington and Strayhorn. There's the individuality of all those sax sounds – Harry Carney, Paul Gonsalves. In fact, that's one rule about who I have in the band, they got to be able to play, but also be someone I want to go for a pint with!

You've said that jazz has moved from style to style in its development without ever really losing its origins....

I happen to like most of the old styles just as much. Some players would probably laugh out loud if I said that I think Sidney Bechet's as good a player as John Coltrane. I probably can't see some Coltrane followers reacting to that too well. But to me it's the same thing – the life force being poured out through a horn.

It just reaches me. It's irrelevant what the rhythm section's doing. I can't imagine standing next to a force like Sidney Bechet! Looking through John Chiltern's book, 'Wizard of Jazz', every thing Sidney Bechet did was larger than life – a *huge* person in terms of what's inside. His pets – he stood there with a golden eagle on his arm, you know, photo was captioned, 'Sidney cooking at home!'

The same with Coltrane – I've recently done a festival, a mainstream festival, and some musician was saying 'Oh, I hate all that Coltrane'…. And I think how can you not hear that? How can you not hear it's the same as Louis? It's that same *convinced* absolute beauty. If you hear Dexter Gordon, he sounds like a man that means it.

Another feature of your life in jazz, you're married to another notable jazz player, Clare Hirst.

Yes, well we're in different parts of it. Clare's worked in a lot of Latin bands; she was in the pop world for a long while. She was in a band called the Bell Stars – in the 1980s she's had a few number one hits. She's played with David Bowie's band among others. She has her own quartet and she works for that, she's a nice player!

Certainly is. So your future in jazz – what developments do you see?

I'm going to keep on playing, I'm happy with my life, no hang ups, I've come to terms with the amount of talent I've been given! In fact, probably my major talent is that I'm good at running a band and maybe getting people motivated, you know. And at reaching audiences, that's what I have.

I also do a *lot* of arranging, for instance all the ensemble work in the CD of *A Dotty Blues*. I like to do arrangements that come across as *improvised* even though it's written. And the point

– like on the '*Hound of the Baskervilles*' that I've just written, I wanted the point where Mark Nightingale [trombone] stops reading and starts improvising to be blurred, so now I don't think *anybody* can pick out where that is!

Finally, what are your views on how UK jazz is going?

Well, I think the same number of people are going to keep working and they are going to be the *individuals*. And it's not just about playing your saxophone brilliantly. I remember hearing Lee Konitz making a comment about a soloist at the Grimsby Jazz Festival. He said, 'Listen to that, perfect timing, an absolute *flow* of ideas, perfect technique, thank God that's not what it's about!' and I know what he means. Lee Konitz is one *real* improviser. I mean compared to Artie Shaw and Benny Goodman, Pee Wee Russell could hardly play the clarinet, but I still go home and it's *Pee Wee's Blues* I put on.

It's about you playing what you *feel* through an instrument - I don't mind a few fluffs and squeaks. It doesn't matter what tune it is, you've still got to come up with *something*. Every night of your life, you've got to come up with something.

But I do think there's probably more talent now in this country than there's *ever* been – the standard is pretty scary. It brought it home to me when Roy Castle used to bring his son Ben to hear us play on a Monday night, he was about ten and now he's one of the best players on the scene – now *he's* an individual - I could go and listen to him all night! Same with Steve Fishwick on the trumpet, I think he's major! Bruce Adams - a *total* individual! After all, it's supposed to be a *reflection of life* - not some intellectual exercise!

I'd almost go so far as to say that intellectuals *can* be a real enemy of jazz. And that's what scares people off – why there aren't so many *young* people at gigs any more. If it's played with *heart*, young people will come!

It's like literature, Dickens for instance. I wanted to start Sherlock Holmes with some descriptive narration, so I went back and read some of *Bleak House*. You can read *three* pages of close print about fog! I mean, *fog*! And I can't imagine anybody doing it better! So the standards were set years ago.

Everything's so available now. You used to hear Ronnie Scott saying, 'Once a month we used to get a seventy-eight over from America, so we'd go round to Dennis Rose's house and we'd work it all out! So we all knew *that* solo.'

Now I just bought a double CD of Artie Shaw with twenty tracks on each CD, some of the best clarinet playing I've ever heard in my life. But I haven't studied it at all! But if I was given one track that said, 'This is Artie Shaw,' eventually you'd work it out, write it out, all the changes. *Then* you'd know it!

If you're going to play jazz you're coming from a huge line of excellence starting with Louis and Lester Young. If you're going to play something *better* than Lester then Good Luck! You going to get more spiritual than John Coltrane?

Selected CDs

Below Zero	Alan Barnes and the David Newton Trio [1998, Concord]
The Sherlock Holmes Suite	Alan Barnes [2003, Woodville]
Swinging the Samba	Alan Barnes & Art Themen [2003, Woodville]

Website: www.woodvillerecords.com

Bill Bruford

Bill Bruford, born 1949 in Kent, has been playing drums professionally in jazz and progressive-rock now for over thirty-five years and is acknowledged as a major bandleader and drum technique innovator, particularly in electronic drumming. He evolved from a school jazz quartet to progressive rock with the very successful rock bands Yes and then King Crimson, where he began using programmable electronic drumkits. After migrating to jazz fusion with his band, Bruford, Bill formed, in conjunction with Django Bates and Iain Ballamy, the band Earthworks in 1987. He was developing his use of Simmons electronic drums in the band until 1993. Following a period touring with King Crimson, Bill then resurrected Earthworks in 1996, switching to acoustic drums and a totally acoustic jazz quartet format. Earthworks tours around the States, Japan and elsewhere, showcasing high quality emergent and established British talent with Bill's and other members' compositions.

He has also recorded with with many musicians including Ralph Towner and Eddy Gomez on *If Summer had its Ghosts* [1997], with the guitarists David Torn and Al di Meola and the Buddy Rich Orchestra.

Earthworks albums issued since 1999 are *A Part and Yet Apart*, *The Sound of Surprise*, and the DVD *Footloose in NYC* which earned a five star Downbeat rating. The latest Earthworks album, *Random Acts of Happiness* featuring Tim Garland, was released in 2004. This year also saw the combining of Earthworks with Tim Garland's Dean Street Underground Orchestra to form Earthworks Underground.

What kinds of music do you first remember listening to in the home?

Lots of good stuff. My Mum was a great ballroom dancer and my Dad too. We had a huge collection of standards - all the great shows of the day, all the tin pan alley stuff. So I knew the standards pretty quickly - Sinatra, Cole Porter, Noël Coward of course.

My parents would roll up the carpet and dance at home for fun. It looked terrific!

Then in came rock n' roll - I can remember where I was when I heard *Hound Dog* by Elvis Presley. I also had a lot of the three Bs – Barber, Ball and Bilk in their rather anaemic approximation of Dixieland. I practiced along on my drumset. So I started by playing swingtime on a cymbal – not a rock beat.

When I went to boarding school at thirteen, I fell under the influence of jazz. The school had a pretty good jazz quartet. Their drummer, Mike Swann, was leaving so they needed to bring on a new guy. He taught me a bit more about jazz time and what bebop was. We had a huge stack of jazz records. The Beatles and the Rolling Stones came and went. We liked those too, but they just didn't seem as exciting as *Night in Tunisia*, you know?

Had there been anything else that attracted you towards jazz?

That must have been BBC TV Jazz 625. My son has started to give me some of those videotapes for Xmas – they are *great*! Steve Race compering and the quality of the sound, the recording and the filming is brilliant! So aged about fourteen I was transfixed by black and white American jazz stars in that TV show.

...and the drums?

Why the drums, I have no idea. But my sister's boyfriend passed on a pair of brushes for her kid brother, saying swish these around on the back of a record sleeve, it sounds just like a drum. So I learnt that first – ticka-tish, ticka-tish, ticka-tish... then sticks, then a drum, then two or three drums. Then I went up to the loft in the house to practice there.

At school, I was playing pretty average jazz swingtime and trying to find out what jazz was. I'd come into the music mostly through the Californian Riverside label, which had a lot of soul jazz – Bobby Timmons, Lockjaw Davis and the Adderleys. It had a firm backbeat so you could understand where the beat was, closely tied to blues and gospel roots and so an easy way into jazz.

Then I got into Joe Morello. Dave Brubeck's music was everywhere and Morello, as a drummer, was this phenomenon with the most beautiful technique and he seemed to be a master of odd times, which I espoused immediately. Also Art Blakey because he had this *incredible* sound! And the third influence was Max Roach, who just seemed to be so economical and there never seemed to be a wrong or unnecessary note.

When you left school...

I had a place at Leeds University, but I wanted a gap year. So I thought I'll go to London, get famous. Simple, right? So I went to London in '68, did two or three terrible gigs. I hadn't been playing parties and dances or weddings for an audience. I'd just practiced at home and in the school jazz group.

That was the beginning of everything. Within about six months we'd formed this group *Yes*, with Jon Anderson and Chris Squire, which went on to become hugely famous. When we formed that group, I thought it was going to be a *jazz* group. I didn't know it *wasn't* going to be

a jazz group. We didn't really think about that at all. So they started to play their guitars and I played swingtime on the cymbal, I thought that might work and then it seemed better to play straight eighth notes.

There was a very naive distinction between rock and jazz, most of which was being blurred anyway in 1968. You had Mitch Mitchell playing his kind of Elvin Jones with Jimi Hendrix and you had Ginger Baker – a great jazz drummer – playing in Cream. You had Charlie Watts who was a jazz drummer in the Rolling Stones, so it seemed fairly normal that most of the *good* drummers came from a jazz background. Some of them dropped that style and adopted another one or you amalgamated or bent it in some way to accommodate. On the first *Yes* record, about a year later, you can still hear me playing determined swing cymbal, breaking up the time and doing funny drum fills, relentlessly insisting that this should be a jazz group!

We took standards and we extended the standards. We thought we were being awfully clever with them, we wrote extra sections for the music and we played them in a different way. But the convention in rock is that you play it the same way every night. The convention in jazz is that you *don't* play it the same way every night and I think I probably irritated rock musicians a lot by continually changing the parts.

Yes was developing really well but after some years you left to go to King Crimson?

Yes, I created a bit of a shock by leaving *Yes* at the height of its fame but it seemed to me illogical that you should stay with one band forever. I couldn't understand – this is again from a jazz background – my understanding was that the way I would get better was by hearing myself in different contexts and the *huge* drawback to being in one of these rock groups was that you stayed there forever! After four years I'd only played with *four* people in my entire musical career! I was just busting to play with somebody else really.

That caused lots of upset and excitement.

King Crimson was a much more jazzy group, not in the sense that it had more swing tempo, I mean its ethics and its thought were more jazzy, experimental, much darker. And used a lot of improvising! We used to think there was a future in noisy rock improvisation, where there would be no key centre given, no tempo given and we would fashion something out of that. But more from the *European* improvising tradition rather than the Blues pentatonic Afro-American tradition which we weren't interested in at all.

So I learnt a lot, how to function, how not to function in an improvised context and to this day, I really like it if someone says, 'Come on, let's just play. Don't worry about what key it's in, let's just see where it goes'. I'm very comfortable with that, partly because of collaborating with Jamie Muir, [former drummer for King Crimson] who was an avant-garde percussionist and performance artist. A great, wonderful man – we used to scrabble around on the floor with found objects in his apartment in North London, recording squeaks and bumps. Very experimental.

After King Crimson, there were various things until I started to write and record my own

music in the late Seventies – which turned out to be fusion, though I didn't really know that at the time. The first album was called *Feels Good to Me*, then *One of a Kind*; and the third one, *Gradually going Tornado*. And I ran this band, Bruford, and it was great! We did BBC television broadcasts live. I was starting to write now for this and doing quite a lot of writing, but like all young people I thought I knew everything – much too arrogant really! The records sold well, but eventually the band was costing too much money. We were carrying Dave Stewart's Hammond organ round the United States which was too expensive.

You've played with experimental guitarist David Torn in his ECM album called *Cloud about Mercury*

Yes, I did! David Torn – a wonderful guitar player from New York City, a jazz player essentially. It was a wonderful record and I was thrilled to play for Manfred Eicher. That was great.

Now by this point, we'd arrived at the electronic drum set, now *that* was a shock, because suddenly – this is a bit of a diversion but basically electronic drum sets arrived in 1980 and I spent about fifteen years with that pretty complicated instrument.

Then they were kind of toys but that's because nobody had ever used them in an interesting way. The great thing about King Crimson is it *loves* new tools and toys to express itself with. So there was big encouragement in the King Crimson of 1980 to use the new sounds of the day – Roland guitar sound synthesizers, stick bass, electronic drums. I started to play tunes on them. You can pitch them, all different, a little like a marimba. But then on the press of a button, it can turn into anything else you want. But of course, the musician always wants the wretched thing to do something that's on the outskirts of its design capability,

or usually, beyond. So the machinery breaks down, causes mayhem.

But I had got a lot of mileage out of that with King Crimson, and by the time we got to 1987, the instrument had become sufficiently robust and interesting, now with sample technology as well, and the ability to play tunes *and chords* off pads, that I decided to form a group based around this instrument. The drummer would play the harmony! Brilliant! And I'd hire three single line jazz players from the newly emerging British jazz scene - very hot at the time in the Mid-Eighties with Django Bates and Iain Ballamy and Loose Tubes. Whatever I do be-

hind them, they won't sound like they usually sound because, I assure you, this drum kit does not sound like other drum kits! And that was called Earthworks.

We made some genuine progress in that area through to about 1993. Earthworks played all over the world including the 1993 Montreal Jazz Festival. I can remember playing there in front of the drummers Jack DeJohnette, Bernard Purdie and Max Roach. They've come to hear this thing called the electronic drumset because I'd said I think we can take this seriously now, it's no longer a toy. Let's try and use this in jazz. I saw the looks on their faces, this poor guy Bruford suffering up there with his intransigent, intractable kind of instrument that wouldn't really do what you wanted it to do - it's *not* a piano! So they admired my efforts and thought, 'Good for him! He's exploring this, we needn't! Let Bruford do it!' That happens a lot in the drum community.

Earthworks got quite a long way with that and we recorded using the electronic set. Three or four CDs – *Earthworks*, *Dig*, then *All Heaven broke Loose*, a variety of compilations and stuff until 1993.

In 1994 I went back to King Crimson for a little period and used the electronic set there until to about 1996. At that time, I thought, enough of this rock business now. I'd just done a nine week tour and I was tired of nine week tours. That's six nights a week and the point is I was out of the country and I had a young family. So enough of talking about jazz - I really wanted to do this jazz thing full time.

But the public or the promoters will only take you seriously if, in as much as you have given up one, you espouse the other. Otherwise they just talk of you as one of these rock guys playing at jazz. I suffered from that in the early days, but *fifteen years* in, most people now probably realise I have something to contribute in the jazz arena.

Things went up a gear in the mid-Nineties when I formed the second edition of Earthworks and brought my composition much further. Dropped the electronic drums, reverted

to essentially the standard format of saxophone, piano, bass, *acoustic* drums, the reason being that I couldn't stand another MIDI patch change! What had happened with electronics was that the musicians, including me, were forever changing the characteristic of the timbre and the sound and no longer paying any attention to the notes.

Instead, let's settle for a bit. When you see a piano, you know the sound that's going to come out of that instrument, so you can relax. A drummer with a cymbal and drums, you can see what he's going to give you - no confusion,

there's clear authorship. That's what I particularly like about jazz is *authorship*. What I particularly dislike about multi-tracking is *loss* of authorship.

What I particularly like about jazz is *performance*. What I don't like about rock is the absence of performance, digital data, the pro tools, it's the dickering around. Rock's forever being manicured until its perfect. So now with jazz, I'm a realiser of the art of performance on record, not of continual editing.

How about your compositions; you began in Yes and King Crimson..

I was almost pushed into writing by Jon Anderson in Yes, who kind of composed generally by shouting at other musicians until they came up with something really good! But his idea was that the real person, the main man, is the writer, while the musicians are mere functionaries. I don't subscribe to that idea at all, but nevertheless I did catch the writing bug. I wrote a lot for electric guitar and electric bass and so forth, round my Seventies group called Bruford. I wrote much of those records.

But when it came to Earthworks, the first Earthworks was really based around this electronic drum kit and I didn't do a whole lot of writing. My writing essentially was the configuring of the series of patches which were interesting timbrally. You'd play that then to Django and Iain and say, 'I don't care what you do, but I'm going to play this.' And they'd say, 'Oh, great, then I'll play this.'

By the time we get to the second edition of Earthworks, there really were notes on paper, proper tunes, proper form, shape, improvising and quite a lot of attention paid to drama and dynamics. That's maybe something I brought from my art-rock, or prog-rock background

Jazz conventionally uses 4/4 time and musicians swing within that. Your compositions generally feature special time signatures and the function of the drums, where the music gets complex,

is really to guide the ear to understand all the changes you're making?

I think you've said it admirably . I think the composition often comes from the drum first, I often write from the drums up. Oh, that's a nice rhythm, this is something which works. Here is a pattern of eleven notes, it's a cycle. I can see that if I broke it this way it'd be different again. Let me add some really dumb boring bass notes

and some really stupid chords. Oh right, this is where we could place the chords and how the bass could move. OK, let's write some better harmony and we'll need some melody fragments here. I often build up from the bottom and that generally is successful.

My ability with harmony is average. That's ok and sometimes my work is revised by Steve Hamilton, a trained pianist, who thus becomes a co-writer. It's quite difficult for a drummer to write something interesting for a Bates, a Hamilton or a Garland because their sense of harmony is quite advanced. They are often able to suggest a better way of moving the music from A to B. And the other thing I learnt over the years is to try to get and stay out of the way, not to trip the soloists up, so they have agreeable places they can take the music and the music can go there.

So the music does not have to be completely written out?

Certainly not, it's an aural tradition, after all. In my early days of writing, in the seventies, I tended to *overwrite* and I boxed the musicians in too much. People like Allan Holdsworth complained bitterly. The problem was I didn't know how to extend or how to free the music up, suggesting the music harmonically just enough. So lacking that information, I tended to overwrite. I'd write sixteen bars and not know what happened next so I'd write another sixteen bars, and then another. What *should* have happened was an extrapolation of the first sixteen bars.

Do you write using the piano?

Often that is what I write on and that gets to some MIDI machine or other, then you do a demo. Recently with Tim Garland in the band - he's a terrific composer, much better than me - so I have no incentive to write whatsoever. But I can give him an interesting rhythmic pattern and bass part and fax him that and I get a symphony back the next day, based on the possible rhythmic variations abstracted from the nucleus I've given him.

Writing is something I originally developed to get four musicians into a room, an excuse to get people to play. If you pick up the telephone and invite four good musicians to play, you suddenly get awfully nervous and feel you ought to produce something for them to play – that's how it happened with me. Sheer terror, and making it up as you go along.

I'm not a college-trained musician so I picked up music as I found it lying about. I learned a bit from Mike Swann when I was thirteen, fourteen. Every band I've been in or formed has always had musicians who are more advanced technically than I am, which is great. So you just ask Django Bates or Allan Holdsworth or Tim

Garland, they'll tell you. Musicians are great at telling you. I've picked up a lot in that way just as an excuse to get people in a room. I like that type of collaboration - so I like groups.

Going back in time, how did you learn jazz, its forms, chords, harmonising?

With no formal musical education, I listened, copied, transcribed, played along with, in the old style. I listened well, I hope. Jazz is becoming really so complex that it's now very hard to do that. *Particularly* on drums, they need constant instruction from about the age of thirteen onwards to be any good at all, such has been the increase in technical capability – just like tennis players – they are all so well trained now.

But you've interested yourself in composition and harmony; a drummer now has both to develop his expertise on the kit and learn harmony?

Preferably, he'll read drum music, he won't pretend to read ordinary music. But absolutely he should be able to bang his way through the standards on piano and know what a II-V-I [chord pattern] is and 32 bar tune is, etcetera, so there's a lot for the drummer to learn.

Can we discuss pitch and timbres? What I notice in listening to Earthworks is that the drums are careful not to distract from the melody.

I am very careful about the orchestration of the drums and maybe if this passage has been on metalwork, then the next passage will be on drums; if its been on drums, the next will be on rims and so on. Certainly drumming is about the drama of the instrument and its power to direct the dynamics of the band. So where you apply your weight and where you *reduce* the weight is *critical* in drumming, it's what it's all about really. I do think about that a lot. I think I'm quite a *tidy* player in the sense that I sort of know *why* I did something, why that instrument was played at that time.

Often you start a tune with drums..

Yes and since you wrote the tune, you can tell how it's going to work with the melody and so forth. So you can set lovely things up for yourself – something is going to work in thirty seconds because *this* is happening now.

Can I ask what you wanted to achieve in the selection of the second edition players for Earthworks? [In 1995/6 Patrick Clahar [saxes], Steve Hamilton [piano] and Mark Hodgson [bass] joined the new Earthworks.]

I think I was trying to get some youthful vigour

from them, which is always helpful, some enthusiasm. People who aren't too formed, too set in their playing style. If you use [relatively] anonymous, highly talented, quite unformed musicians they're prepared to go a number of ways. Then Earthworks is a vehicle which tours internationally. There they can find out what it is they want to do.

The only requirement is that whatever it was you did before you joined Earthworks, could you please not do it in Earthworks. And be prepared to change while you're in Earthworks. *You're* looking for change, *I'm* looking for change. In the end you have a vocabulary and a set of techniques and ideas that you didn't have at the beginning. That's the point of joining the group. Not for the lousy hundred and fifty quid you get. So it is a vehicle for change - particularly my change.

Patrick Clahar and Tim Garland are very different, but these are all good quality players of comparable standard to their American counterparts. They now no longer consider themselves inferior to their American counterparts. When I grew up, most British guys *thought* they were inferior to the Americans.

A number of American reviews of Earthworks are highly enthusiastic, reckoning that Earthworks is a decidedly world-class band...

Oh yes, they would consider it world-class, with no problem at all. It's to jazz's sadness that there are still some people who think that white musicians can't play jazz, incredibly. Still people who think that *European* white musicians can't play jazz. Jazz has this amazingly conservative depth in the States which makes it hard to break through and even though I have good reviews as long as my arm, the last thing I need is good reviews. They get you absolutely nowhere.

It needs a change of attitude?

A change of attitude and that probably comes from twenty-five years of active service!

Do you do any teaching, any coaching?

I teach a course in Contemporary and Cultural Perspectives in Twentieth Century Popular Music at degree level in the ACM [Academy of

Photo: Earthworks 2004

Contemporary Music] in Guildford. I do hands-on drum kit instruction at Kingston University.

What do you think of the general health of Jazz UK?

It's such a big question this. Well, there are some givens. The standard of jazz musicians has risen enormously. There appear to be plenty of people coming out of the Royal Academy, Guildhall School of Music and various drum schools of one sort or another who are prodigiously well equipped.

They want to play *some* kind of a performance music that's not all to do with computers and the only word we have for it is jazz. It's a *terrible* word! It's the worst word anybody can think of. It sounds something to do with the 1940s or 1950s – those words 'gig', 'man', all that nomenclature from the Fifties is dead baggage. You say 'jazz' to my students who are twenty-two years old and they look at their feet and they shuffle and get embarrassed and they don't know what you're talking about. Are you talking about Kenny Ball? Or Ornette Coleman? Kenny G, Acid Jazz ? Nobody knows what it is.

But there is in the human spirit a desire to get up on a stage unplanned, unprepared with another person and say, 'You play that, I'll play this – it'll be fun!' That's not what rock or pop music is or what classical music is, so we need a word for that spirit and the only word is jazz. So do I think jazz in Wynton Marsalis' definition is alive and well? If you want jazz to be in a museum, I think there's going to be a problem.

I believe in live performance. Four guys on a stage with two hundred people, I think that's great for live music. Ronnie Scott's.

Who do you reckon to be the typical jazz fan or Earthworks fan?

Is there a typical Earthworks fan? – not really, I don't think. Young guys whom I can seduce into coming to hear the group are always astonished. Young people have no idea that jazz comes at you with the velocity and the intensity of a Tim Garland or Steve Hamilton. Or of an Earthworks.

But they think it's going to take them thirty years to learn the instrument - which it is. That's another problem. It takes rather a long time to learn to become a good jazz musician, it's a very skilled profession and the young are increasingly associated with instant gratification.

You've said Earthworks is a chameleon-like beast and that genre purity doesn't bother you.

From a drummer's point of view we here in this lovely island have almost no rhythmic tradition at all. So we go at this rhythmic thing by bor-

rowing from everybody else – I listen to Japanese music, Chinese drummers, Brazilians, Americans, see what the Africans do – I'm like a jackdaw, stealing a little bit from everywhere, making a bit of this and a bit of that. You put it through your own system and you come up thinking this is how my drumming can go.

Our attitude to jazz is a bit like that , we take from here and there. We add in a Northern brass band sound, we use some British music hall humour, whatever, we have Loose Tubes. Some satire, some poisons, some parody. I think jazz depends on this *local* way of doing things. Like Garbarek has a local *Norwegian* way of doing things, Django Bates has a local *UK* way of doing things. That's the charm of jazz that it can accommodate that. So we don't play anything pure in Earthworks at all. It's all an imaginative reconfiguration of more or less well known elements.

And what you reconfigure it to be is hopefully very attractive, interesting and individual, personable and in our case, very British. I prefer to use British musicians for Earthworks!

Selected CDs	
Cloud about Mercury	David Torn [1986, ECM]
Earthworks	Bill Bruford [1987, EGCD]
Random Acts of Happiness	Bill Bruford's Earthworks [2004, Summerfold]
Website: www.billbruford.com	

Ben Castle

Ben Castle, born in Beaconsfield, Bucks in 1973, is a fast rising performer on tenor and soprano saxes. He also plays alto sax, bass clarinet, flute and clarinet. He operates across a range of musical genres but loves playing jazz. Ben has worked with many leading musicians in rock/soul including Sting, Mica Paris, Carleen Anderson, Steve Hackett, Brand New Heavies and Culture Club. He works in the larger groups of the highly praised jazz singer and pianist, Jamie Cullum.

Ben has played with most of the leading jazz artists on the UK scene including Stan Tracey, Peter King, Art Themen, Alan Barnes, Tim Garland, Julian Arguelles, Don Weller and Lawrence Cottle.

His first album in 1994, *Big Celebration,* with his father Roy Castle written for big band was followed by the similar *Breathe Easy* album in 1998.

Ben leads two different style jazz groups – Four from the Madding Crowd (album issued in 2000) and also an acoustic quartet. His other album credits include Jamie Cullum (*Pointless Nostalgic* and *Twenty Something*), Geoff Gascoyne (*Autumn* and *Songs of the Summer)*, John Etheridge and Michael Garrick. In 2002 Ben recorded with Carleen Anderson on her album *Alberta's Daughter.*

Ben also composes and arranges for big band, orchestras and other small groups.

In 2001 Ben gained the UK's Award for Best Rising Player and also was nominated for a BBC Jazz Award. In 2004 he won the jazz section of the US International Songwriter's Competition and released his CD *Blah Street.*

What kind of music can you first remember listening to in the home?

When I was young, I remember my Dad had lots of music like jazz and Frank Sinatra. But the first tape I bought was the soundtrack to the film ET because I loved the music. Then my cousin taught me how to play the Deep Purple solo from *Smoke on the Water* a big guitar riff but very easy, when I was seven or eight. Later on I listened a lot more to Deep Purple – which had jazz influences - it had a huge effect!

What musical instruments did you pick up next?

When I was seven I started learning the clarinet. My Dad had bought one for twenty-five pounds, so I got his cast-off and had lessons at school. A couple of years later, I picked up the sax, alto to begin with – it was something I could hold!

Your Dad was a musician who practiced around the house?

Yes, there were always loud trumpet noises round the house. On piano, he'd play *That's All* and I can still remember how he'd change the harmonies around a bit.

You were a pretty musical family?

My older brother played trombone and my older sister played trumpet and piano. My other sister started but didn't really follow through on music.

But we had a front line all sorted out. Sometimes we were a horn section doing gigs with the local band, my Dad, brother and sister and I – *The Castle Horns* - it's great to be doing those kind of things.

And Dad got me on stage with him from about the age of nine, playing and doing comedy routines as well. This got me used to playing in front of large audiences and got rid of my nerves!

In your teens you played music at school and with other groups?

Absolutely. I've always been into loads of styles of music. I became the unofficial school session musician, so if somebody needed an instrument to be played in a group, they would ask me! I would find myself learning bass for a gig, then a bit of guitar or keyboards. I dread to think how awful it would have been, but good experience.

I also played in the school orchestras, jazz bands, big bands – plus the rock thing which was our own initiative and where I played drums. I thought I was good till I started working with *really* great drummers then I thought, 'OK, time to put the sticks away!'

I'm a big believer that these experiences all go to mould your eventual sound. All the different styles of music you play or listen to – it all works towards the bigger picture.

There's things you hear that you aspire to?

That's right. What drew me into Deep Purple was the sound of the Hammond organ, plus the drummer was a huge fan of Buddy Rich - you can actually hear it in his playing.

And in your teens, your Dad took you along to hear the Pizza Express Modern Jazz Sextet.

When I was about fifteen, we went to see the Pizza Express Modern Jazz All Stars and my Dad was absolutely gobsmacked by Gerard Presencer [flugelhorn]. You see, Gerard's only

a year older than me. I personally was blown away by Dave O'Higgins, it was the first time I'd heard him and of course, Alan Barnes. I can remember Dad saying to Gerard, 'How can you be so good, so young?' Gerard told him it was through listening to a lot of Clifford Brown [US, trumpet, 1930-1956].

Well, my Dad had stacks of Clifford Brown records at home and I just went through them. It was a huge turning point for me. I just kept listening to him for ages after that, because I saw how much good it had done Gerard.

But the main turning point for me had come when I was thirteen and my Dad took me to hear Buddy Rich at Ronnie Scott's. I'd seen them on TV playing *Birdland*. My Dad knew Buddy reasonably well because earlier there'd been a famous moment when Buddy played on my Dad's hands! At one stage, Buddy asked for requests, I shouted out 'Birdland' and they played it. I was transfixed by the drumming but also by Steve Marcus the tenor sax player - who also had *big* hair. And that's when I realised that's what I want to do! So now I've got the playing together and I'm working on the hair!

After that, you were playing more and more music?

Absolutely! It just seemed to take over. But I had known from the age of nine that I was either going to be a musician or an actor. My school teacher had asked us what we were going to be when we grew up. And I said these two options. And he said, 'Right. I can guarantee you that none of you will end up being what you've just said!' So if he's reading this...

You were doing commercial gigs around the age of seventeen.

To start with I was playing in pubs, or background music at parties, weddings. It was nothing terribly amazing, but building up contacts.

When I left school, I had to put together a band for my friend's wedding and it was the biggest stress of my life! I'd never done a whole function for dancing, everything. So it was a real eye-opener for me and a really scary time – I lost sleep because I didn't know a lot of musicians then, I didn't know a lot of tunes.

What instruments were you playing?

Well I'd already found that sax was my main instrument but I still love playing clarinet and will fight its cause because there don't seem to be that many people around playing it in a modern jazz context.

Around the age of eighteen, you decided to do the Guildhall Post Graduate Jazz Course.

Well, I had always wanted to go to the Guildhall. It was probably the best known course for jazz at that time, but I was told by Scott Stroman, the course leader, that I was probably a bit young for it as a postgraduate course.

Though I did look at the classical course playing clarinet, when I got into the jazz course, it was great. I learnt so much. Even eleven years on, I'm still filtering all the information! On the course, they weren't saying, 'This is how you need to play jazz', it was more, 'Here's something you can work on,' something about harmonies, about arranging, or about voicings – an awful amount of information in a short space of time!

What areas do you now find most useful?

As well as classes, I had one-to-one lessons with Pete Churchill on piano voicings but also about song writing and arranging. That was definitely good – he's got such a clear way of describing things – each lesson I'd have a revelation. If I was trying to do something and piece various bits together, he would say something to help. He'd make it sound so obvious and second-nature.

When you came out from the Guildhall course what happened?

Throughout my time at the Guildhall I was doing gigs, and a few recording sessions.

The gigs were a mixture of jazz and back-

ground ones and recording sessions for people who needed a sax and it was good for me to learn about playing in a studio. Initially you go in and think that the more notes you play, the more impressed they'll be. I remember one I

did and somebody came back on the talkback – 'That sounded a bit like jazz!' – as if it was the *worst* thing I could have done to play a bit of jazz there! So you soon learn that that's not the be-all-and-end-all of music.

You try to work out what they want, even though they *often* don't know themselves – so it's about trying to get to that point as quickly as possible.

Then in 1994, not long after my period at the Guildhall, I was able to do an album with my Dad, *The Big Celebration*, which is actually out of print now– which I'm not entirely displeased about. I'll always treasure having done one with my Dad because it was just before he got too ill to record and yet also when I was old and good enough to do it! I do sometimes listen to it and cringe, but it was an amazing opportunity getting a chance to write and arrange music for the recording.

Basically it was an album of hymn tunes that

we did in various styles. So I did some arranging for it in big band style and we did a couple of Dixieland and some more modern and some soul style jazz pieces, plus some originals. At the time I was only nineteen or twenty so it was great to meet some very good musicians through doing the album and they've remained in my regular band ever since.

Then in 1998 you did another big band album called *Breathe Easy*.

It was for the same record label and with a similar kind of idea. I did the arrangements. We did about eight big band tunes and three small band tunes, some of which I wrote. It was great at helping me find what I wanted to do and I used a lot of what I'd learned at the Guildhall.

Is writing and arranging a growing part of your work now?

Yes it is, for various projects. I either write for myself or for others or with others and that's definitely influenced a large part of my sound because I learn so much about harmony when I write music.

I've done some arranging for television, mainly incidental music for drama or documentary shows and video clips. Although I do enjoy studying a new style to write in a particular vein, it's generally commissioned by people who know other music of mine.

You've played with a wide range of fine pop acts including Mica Paris and Sting who comes from the jazz world.

He's still a massive jazz fan. I did a handful of radio and TV appearances with Sting, when he was promoting his last live album. The video was cool and I rather liked the song. Sting used Branford Marsalis and Kenny Kirkland and people like that in his band and I was hugely influenced and impressed by them. He's very talented as a songwriter and musician.

The band when I was in it featured on bass Christian McBride, one of my heroes. Before the broadcast, we did this duet in the changing room. We struck up this blues together and we just clicked. Also Jason Rebello was playing and Guy Barker. It's excellent to be working with those musicians. There's a few times when I've thought back to when I was a child and I've been listening to these early albums, as a fan, and now I'm actually playing those tunes with that band and it's such a great feeling. I sometimes have this great beaming smile on my face while I'm playing!

You've played sax in two Geoff Gascoyne albums. He's becoming an arranger of some note now.

Yes, I think he does arranging for Georgie Fame, Claire Martin, Ian Shaw and Jamie Cullum as well. I think Geoff and I have clicked musically. I have this funny thing with bass players, I seem to be in about fifteen bands led by bass players - there seems to be some kind of affinity. The problem is most of them write *really* hard music, because it's their one chance to inflict it on everyone else!

But I love playing in Geoff's quartet, because some of the music, you really have to get your teeth into. It was probably the first band I was playing in regularly where there'd be quite tricky forms and unusual time signatures, it wasn't your usual 32 bar forms. So it was a really good thing to do.

Who else in the jazz world do you specially appreciate playing with?

I've been playing recently with Stan Tracey, and we're just about to do an album together as a quartet. Hopefully we'll do a tour sometime next year. I find his playing great, both to listen to and to play with. We've been playing recently, usually a quintet with Bobby Wellins or with Guy Barker.

But the trio with Clark and Andy Cleyndert - they've been playing together for such a long time, they've got a great rapport and so I really look forward to these gigs. Certain people are just there for you. I love Stan's minimalist approach to accompanying and soloing. You just know that in everything you play, he'll be there for you while leaving the space to play. It also pushes me in different directions as well, which I love – I just get inspired during these gigs.

It came after I'd been doing more pop-influenced work, and after some local gigs. It was terrific to be playing with a truly great band. When I wasn't playing, I was dancing at the side of the stage – just for the release of it!

Andy Cleyndert commented that he reckons Stan is the great improviser - never the same twice.

That's right and his playing is so very infectious, it draws you in to listen to it.

About your quartet, Mark Edwards, Jim Watson and others.

I've got two bands really, a quartet called 'Madding Crowd' and then a sort of straight-ahead quartet. Because I'm influenced by so many styles of music, 'Madding Crowd' is a way of exploring those. We're all jazz musicians in the band but we've all come from different backgrounds. Tim Harries, the bass player, was in Steeleye Span for thirteen years and he plays with Brian Eno as well as in heavy metal bands. He got me listening to Charles Ives and Schoenberg - he's just an amazing musician. He and Mark Edwards who plays piano and keyboards have totally changed my attitude towards music. They were both on the Big Celebration album, with Phil Crabbe on drums. In fact I'd done a load of arrangements before meeting any of those guys and when I met them and heard how amazing they were, I just changed all the arrangements!

You're using Madding Crowd to take your music in a new direction?

Hopefully in a unique direction. Certainly it's going to have its own sound because of the different influences we all have and bring to the music. My ideal is to make music that I truly believe in – and I've thought a lot about this – and I would want to listen to because then it's honest and true and should have longevity.

At the same time, I'm hoping to use the acoustic quartet do a jazz album at some stage.

I've spent a long time finding what I like in music, taking up the bits I like and discarding what I don't like, whether its jazz or rock music, folk or classical. And I've found the bits that I feel

comfortable with, gradually finding my own sound.

Your most recent CD is Blah Street.

Yes, I've got a new album with Madding Crowd. We recorded most of it about two years ago and I was recently approached by somebody who's starting up a new label and he is really into the music. That's what I like - rather than being with a huge label - to get some enthusiasm about what I'm doing so there are no problems if it doesn't quite fit into categories.

Can you remember back to how you learned jazz, in particular how to improvise?

When I went to the school along the road, they

had a jazz band, and I was really nervous that I'd be made to improvise because I'd never done any before. But there were written out solos with chord symbols above so you could play these. Gradually I started to feel a bit more comfortable doing my own thing and I can remember my first ever improvised solo was at the Purcell Room. My school had taken it over to do a concert with the orchestra and the jazz band. That was the first time they took the music away and I had to improvise and solo. Gradually I got more comfortable and I started to get a feel for it.

Then I did the Summer School at the Guildhall, the two week course. Simon Purcell taught me the II-V-I [chord] progressions and that gave me something to practice outside of a blues scale - but with regard to jazz language, I found practicing II-V-Is very helpful because it incorporated so much of the language of so many of the tunes in jazz. It's very descriptive of the harmony. So I would practice II-V-Is in all keys. I'd start very simple, just playing part of the chord notes, and then something more complicated. So that was a huge help. Then I'd go through the *Charlie Parker Omni Book* and see what he played over that progression and then play *that* in all the keys – again very helpful.

Also I had lessons from some people whose playing I really rated. My Dad used to do gigs with the BBC Big Band where Iain Dixon was playing – I absolutely love his playing - he's pretty underrated. He sat me in a corridor in the BBC Studios in Maida Vale and made me play one note for half an hour and if ever I veered off that note ....

Sax training includes playing long

notes against a wall and evaluating the sound coming back?

Yes, some do and some don't bother with it. But a lot of the greats just practiced one note a day. Dewey Redman would practice one note for about eight hours and just find all the nuances in that note! All these guys have amazing sounds. I'm sure Sonny Rollins must have done that because he's got a *huge* sound. You can tell they've really put the work in. Sometimes I will play a note for an hour and it *really* does help the sound of the horn – but it drives you mad!

Iain Dixon in that one lesson also taught me some things about intervals and he made me play a pretty complex tune, *Donna Lee*, in all twelve keys. But again, it was hugely helpful because the tune is descriptive of jazz harmony, kind of bebop ahead but in a soloing style. If you can hear the tune in all twelve keys rather than try to transpose it, it'll be very good for your ear. So all this in one lesson!

Who are your main musical influences?

In my own instrument, the obvious ones are John Coltrane, Wayne Shorter, Sonny Rollins – but one of my *first* big influences was Michael Brecker. I kind of did it the opposite way round to everybody, I started with Michael Brecker then into John Coltrane then Charlie Parker then Stan Getz, Lester Young, Coleman Hawkins and then Louis Armstrong and Jelly Roll [Morton]. So I went from the modern players back to the 'classics' to the point where I wasn't that interested in sound. At the Guildhall I was Brecker-mad; Denys [Baptiste] and I used to talk about Michael Brecker all day and every day to everyone's annoyance – my nickname at the Guildhall was Bennie Brecker – then I just got fed up of everybody trying to sound like Michael Brecker. I thought I've got to find my own thing.

It was remarkable that I'd built up all this technique playing through Michael Becker's solos, playing along with him – then you hear Wayne Shorter who hasn't got nearly the same technique, but can rip your heart out with two notes, that's more what I want to do. Michael Brecker is an amazing player but I had to stop listening to him.

The current players I still enjoy listening to are Branford Marsalis and Joe Lovano. With Branford, I know that I'm going to love all his albums – some he goes a bit more out there than others – but I know it's going to be hip. With Joe Lovano I absolutely love his playing, but I don't always love his albums, though every album is different which I consider a good thing. And I love Iain Ballamy's playing – so many of these great players are in England – Julian Arguelles and Iain Dixon, Stan Sulzman and that's just some of the sax players.

You come to realise there's more to music than impressing people from a mechanics point of view. It's more about engaging people's *imagination*, developing a thing of beauty. I'm much more interested in doing that than being a monkey doing a trick for someone. But inevitably if you do a solo that is very fast and has all the fancy bits in, it gets more of a reaction on a gig. So it can be very difficult to do something that you personally believe in more.

This phase, 'running the changes' is about a player doing fast runs up and down the scales but paying little attention to the melody? Is that a correct explanation of what he's doing?

Yes, I suppose it is. I can catch myself going through the motions and I have to shake myself out of it but if I'm really tired and the rhythm section doesn't work that well....

I feel improvised music should be the absolute cutting edge so I've been keen to find ways that will connect with an audience that will keep them happy but also bring people in. That's something I'm passionate about - because I know there's an audience there for jazz and creative music.

I do gigs on music festivals – not jazz festivals - where people come up to me and say, 'I didn't *think* I was going to enjoy it but I did.' People who don't believe they're into jazz see the interaction between the musicians, they hear the *energy* that they don't get from a record. Or they've only heard avant-garde jazz or Trad jazz from their local pub and they've thought, 'That's what jazz is!' and reckoned they don't like it when there are all these different types.

And so I love playing at festivals that aren't jazz festivals, because you've got people coming with an open mind. A lot of jazz audiences have pre-conceived ideas of what it should be. So if you don't play *Stella by Starlight* – I mean, I love those places and playing standards – but I love people to come to the music as music, not 'That's no good because it doesn't fit my criteria.'

How do you think the market for jazz is going these days?

I don't know. People keep saying that jazz is coming back, though it's difficult to see evidence of that, but bands such as Radiohead are incorporating jazz - they're very influenced by Charles Mingus. Also a lot of bands now will cite Miles Davis as one of their heroes, and it's more Thelonius Monk and John Coltrane or Mingus – the people who have their own unmistakable voices and a bit of 'attitude!'

That in turn has influenced me. I find that people involved in pop music go right to the *heart* of the music, more than a lot of jazz musicians do, because their music has to make clear statements and what they do is on record and a lot of people listen to it.

About the general state of jazz, it has changed recently because people are embracing the music of their *culture* within jazz – so Soweto Kinch has been doing a bit of rapping on his album which has impressed some critics and not others. But it's very much part of his personality and part of what he has listened to. A lot of people are embracing that - and also trying to find *more venues* to play jazz.

It can be very difficult. At one club, I'd just been doing a tour to about 600 people each night with my band but not playing to jazz audiences and it had gone down a storm. But I did one jazz club at the end of the tour, and we were playing really well together and I said 'This is one of my own tunes now' and I actually saw a man in the audience shake his head and then put his head in his hands! In fact a lot of jazz clubs are like that. They like what they know, and every week they want *Autumn Leaves* and *All the Things you are.*

Sometimes this can be an older audience, maybe Third Age?

Absolutely! This can be the problem because all of these people say, 'I can't believe there's not more young people coming to the clubs'

and they're saying it because this music is vibrant and there's *young* people playing the music.But often the young people at those gigs are jazz students or musicians of some level themselves. What I would say to someone who's not a jazz aficionado is generally at these clubs the music being played is *culturally irrelevant* to

younger people - because they haven't grown up with the *musicals* that the songs come out of. They're not going to know *Stella by Starlight* or any of these tunes.

Jamie Cullum made that point. He's known the Radiohead tunes he does longer than the standards..

Sure, I grew up with *both* because my Dad would play standards on the piano and I love standards, playing to those who love them - but I sometimes get embarrassed when young people accidentally walk into a gig and I'm playing old-fashioned music. But I *want* to be playing music that's really on the *cutting edge* and that really attracts people. I want to take bits of Radiohead or Bjork because those are people who've made quite experimental music but made it popular - getting anything like that in the charts is absolutely fantastic!

I think that these artists have opened people's ears to something a bit different and I have got frustrated in the past that not many jazz musicians are doing the same. Not making the music that's now and cutting edge. People have done albums recently with electronics but it's still their jazz album and they just thrown a bit of electronics in to say 'I'm current!' And it doesn't work - you've got to go to the heart of every music that you're trying to master.

You do some teaching in Bracknell, along with players such as Peter King, Gerard Presencer...

Teaching isn't a huge part of what I do now but a few years running I took part in a workshop weekend in Bracknell which was good fun and great to be with those musicians, say with Julian Arguelles - always one of my heroes - and Pete King. Plus I was teaching a group with Art Themen and it was great because we both came at it from totally different ways but saw each other's point of view.

We'd teach during the day and then there'd be a jam session in the evening. The students would be seated with their arms folded, like they were saying, 'Right, come on, you've told *us* what to do, let's see what *you're* made of!'

How do you see your future? What are the main things that you will concentrate on ?

Firstly I love writing music and collaborating with other musicians – so that's one element I need. And I do a bit of production as well, though I really have to believe in the music before I do because it's quite a commitment.

Also I just learn so much playing with other musicians, with *their* music! But ideally I'd like to be doing a lot with my own bands so I can really do *my* thing and make my own statements!

Selected CDs

Blah Street	Ben Castle [2004, OT RecordsRIZCD]
Songs of the Summer	Geoff Gascoyne [2001, Jazzizit]
Twenty Something	Jamie Cullum [2003, Universal]

Website www.bencastle.com

Andy Cleyndert

Andy Cleyndert, born in 1963 near Birmingham, has for two decades been acknowledged as one of the UK's foremost jazz bass players. On leaving school, Andy turned professional in 1981, first landing a regular gig in Manchester as part of the house trio at the George Chisholm Club, supporting such leading players as Art Farmer, Charles McPherson and Peter King.

Moving to London in 1982, he joined bands led by Bobby Wellins and Don Weller/ Bryan Spring among others. After taking a degree in maths and psychology, Andy joined Ronnie Scott's band with which he played and toured extensively for five years. He has until recently been a member of Celebrating the Jazz Couriers, a band commemorating the famous Ronnie Scott and Tubby Hayes group that won the 2002 British Jazz award for Small Group category.

Other major performers he has played with include Gene Harris, Benny Green, Annie Ross, Stacey Kent, Kenny Wheeler, Junior Mance, Joe Temperley and Gerard Presencer.

Following Ronnie's Scott's retirement, he has been a member of all Stan Tracey groups and his recordings since 1995. He is also a member of the Don Weller Quartet which he has recently recorded for his Trio label, a successful and growing recording and marketing venture.

What kind of music can you remember first listening to?

I was brought up on classical music. My mother would have been a professional musician if she'd had the chance, so she made sure all of her six kids had a go at something. She played violin and piano but was interested in singing as well. Everyone went to choirs, so there was lots of church music.

What instruments were you picking up?

I started off with violin, piano, bit of recorder and I did some singing.

Were you a keen student of those?

Nope! Actually yes. I seemed to be able to pick up an instrument and naturally get into it quite easily – but I never liked lessons and I never enjoyed practising. Always a good starter... except that I later took up the bassoon and was more interested and went a lot further with that. Then I picked up the bass eventually.

At what age was that?

Briefly at eleven. Someone came round and gave a lecture about the bass and asked if anyone wanted to learn. I wasn't there but my younger brother was and he said, 'my brother would like to learn' - so one Monday I was called into a bass lesson! That was in the last year of primary school, so I did it and then left. I picked it up again some time later when some friends were getting into jazz.

Had you studied much on the bass?

That year in primary school was enough to get the basic hand position and show you how to play it up to the thumb position, which is a different thing altogether.

So if I needed anything technical I just sat down and worked out how to do it and then the rest I basically learned on gigs. I didn't really study the bass properly until a lot later.

As a teenager, I practiced by sitting at home in my bedroom, playing to records. Probably more than anything else, I developed my ear then, just from working out what the chord sequences on records were.

When did you start doing gigs?

When I was fifteen I started doing Trad gigs. We'd moved to Bishops Stortford by then and there was a local Trad scene, with someone called John Peters up the road in Harlow, whose girlfriend used to play the bass with him. Then she quit and I did a gig with him, and he said, 'Do you want some gigs?' - he did lots of gigs up in London. One of these gigs was with Cy Laurie, a big name then in the Trad scene, when it was Trad versus Bop in the sixties! I remember the first gig I did with him.

He came over to me afterwards and said, 'That was really, really good, now whatever you do, don't practice!'

For maybe the last two years at school, I got in with Julian Stringle, the clarinet player, who had a Dixieland band, and through him I met Alan Barnes who had a little bebop quintet. Every weekend I used to go up to town and play with them – then on Monday mornings, go back to school.

I got through 'O' levels and then was not sure what I was going to do – but my life just revolved around music at that time. When I left school, I still didn't have a clue what I was going to do, but then I just started getting gigs.

Much later, you specially took years out to do a degree.

Yes, because I'd just fallen into music, I never actually made a decision to be a musician. Eventually I thought I'm not into the music enough to want to sit at home and want to practice all day, though I enjoy going out and gigging. So I could be wasting time.

I re-did my A levels part time and I found I actually really enjoyed it - Maths and English - got a buzz from both of them. Maths was good, void of any emotion and so the perfect foil for English and my continuing career in music. Through studying English I started to enjoy reading for the first time. So I just carried on to do a degree continuing with maths but dropping English in favour of Psychology. That was fine. But it wasn't till I'd finished the degree that I thought, 'Actually - I really want to be a musician!'

So when was your decision to be a professional first made ?

At eighteen when I left school - I was getting gigs, working a lot. There was only a handful of bass players then, probably literally half a dozen players in my generation. I started working with Don Weller and Bryan Spring when I was nineteen or twenty – and at that time the band was really popular, we were doing about two gigs a week for just that band.

An early residency was at the George Chisholm Club in Manchester.

When I left school, I was doing odd gigs now and then with Julian Stringle and his father managed to persuade someone at a health club to open a jazz club. The basic idea was to have lots of visiting Americans plus a local rhythm section – they offered me the bass chair in the house rhythm section, so off I went up to Manchester and that lasted about six months. That period was great, playing every night, learning from playing with Art Farmer, Joe Newman and Pete King.

It was pretty mainstream so it wasn't too difficult – probably some things were a shock – but I used to check out their records before

hand, what Art Farmer and the others did, so they went ok.

Other players have spoken about working with Americans Art Farmer and Charles McPherson.

Yes, Charles was another one, he has a reputation for giving people a hard time, which means occasionally giving people a very fast tempo, so he can give them more of a hard time!

He's been over here so many times. Probably fifteen years ago, he just took me to one side after a gig and completely trashed my playing! [Laughter] He wasn't particularly being nasty but he gave me his lecture which was actually very constructive in a destructive way! Then, fortunately, I saw him do the same thing to someone else very soon after, so I didn't feel that bad! And then years later, Ernie Garside said to me, 'Charles really likes working with you'. I replied, 'That's nice because years ago, it wasn't quite like that!' And I jokingly reminded Charles

of that. He just turned round to me and said, 'So it did some good!'

After about six months in Manchester, I came down to London and got this gig that every bass player in town had been through at one time or another - Les Ambassadors on Park Lane, a posh restaurant gig, six nights a week. That was good, as the pianist used to write out good changes and I learnt quite a few tunes in that six months. But I was the first bass player to get sacked from that gig for not taking enough interest!

After that I started working with Don Weller, Bryan Spring and the Bobby Wellins quartet.

Who stands out among all the American players you've supported - Bud Shank, George Coleman, Ray Bryant, Gene Harris and others?

Gene Harris by miles. I think he's as much a blues as a jazz piano player. I wouldn't say he's the greatest improviser – in fact, I would say that Stan Tracey is the greatest improviser I've met - but Gene was amazing. To explain, the first thing I latched onto in jazz was the Oscar Peterson Trio, so I used to listen a lot to Ray Brown. Then I thought, 'Who else has Ray Brown played with?' – so your listening fans out as you listen more widely. For a long time, Ray had Gene Harris in his trio and I liked his records but I wasn't that knocked out. Then Martin Drew and I got to play with him one night at the Pizza Express, Dean Street, during the first UK tour he did and it was just an absolutely amazing night - probably one of the most swinging nights I've ever had! As that went so well, he asked us both to do the next tour, and I thought, 'This is easy, this is swinging like Ray Brown and I can do Ray Brown'.

When we got on this tour, I suddenly realised that Gene Harris had such a huge presence, his playing, such strength, this huge mountain, and such an amazingly strong groove in his playing -that not many horn players or piano players have - such a strong time thing going on in their playing that as a rhythm player you can latch on to.

It's normally about horn players thinking that the rhythm players take care of the time and they just play over the top. In my opinion it's not that at all, I feel that everyone should be part of the rhythm section, including horn players. Gene had the strongest groove in his playing of anyone I've worked with. The shock came after he'd just played an amazing solo, and then comped another great solo out of Jim Mullen who was also on the gig. When it came round to me, it went from this great juggernaut of groove to this sad little bass solo. I discovered I had next to no independent groove at all. I think it

was then that I realised what Ray Brown was really about. Jim played great with Gene, although he was maybe frustrated slightly by being limited to the blues, after having widened his own playing style. But Jim is fantastic at the blues and Gene Harris brought out that side of him completely.

What is 'doing Ray Brown' all about?

His sound has a real percussive front to it, as well as a very warm sound behind it. And also I think he just plays the best walking lines of them all really. In some ways, I think the Oscar Peterson Trio was really the Ray Brown Trio. Although Ray was just playing a walking line, some of the things he was doing were more harmonically interesting than Oscar's. That band definitely revolved around Ray.

He was a great champion of the bass and the bass player. There's a really interesting series of interviews, I think by Alyn Shipton, that were on Radio 3 a while ago. He asked Ray why he chose the piano trio as the vehicle for the Ray Brown band. Ray replied, 'It's not a piano trio, it's a bass trio!' Alyn carried on and said, ' But it's really a piano trio', and Ray stopped him again and said, 'No, it's a bass trio!'

Depending on the writing, can you have the bass as the most controlling feature of the music?

Yeah! Ray was a very strict bandleader and he completely controlled what went on, it was very highly arranged. You can hear him on the record giving out the commands on what is going to happen next shouting, 'Shout Chorus' or whatever.

Thinking of solos, how does a bass player construct a solo? Do you ever sit down at the piano to work things out?

No. Basses are really hard instruments to solo on. If you're a horn player you've got a bass giving you harmony and rhythm. You've got a drummer adding to the rhythm.

You've got a piano player adding to the harmony – so you've got this lovely bed just to lay on – and if you've not playing, you got this luscious rhythm and harmony going on underneath you, so you don't have to play all the time, just a phrase here, a phrase there. When there's a bass solo, most of the time the drummer will stop playing a ride cymbal, so you've lost that nice striding feel, so it'll come down to probably clipping a high hat, and that's it. The piano player, especially if it's Stan, will just stop, so there's nothing going on, nothing accompanying you.

You still have to point out what the harmony is, so you're still stuck around this basic harmony, and you've got all this space with lit-

tle going on behind you, you can use the silence, but only so far, so it's tough.

It's quite restricting and my favourite situation for bass soloing is a guitar playing four in a bar. You've got the groove of the four and you've got the harmony – it makes so much difference, because you're released from those restrictions, so it's possible to improvise and play more interesting phrases.

Other than that, it's good to have a drummer playing with you rather than just tapping out some inane time. Clark [Tracey] is great to work with since he really listens to where your playing is coming from. He's predicting what you're going to play next, there's more than just the basic rhythm going on, he actually accompanies and lays down a groove.

How about your period playing with Ronnie Scott?

When I had finished my degree, I decided, yeah, I wanted to be a musician. I had kept working while I was doing my degree, but more gigs in hotels rather than jazz gigs.

So when I finished my degree, I realized I'd slightly sidelined myself. Then out of the blue, I got the call to do Ronnie's band and I did that for about five years, until he stopped playing. When I joined, it was a sextet with Mornington Lockett, Dick Pearce, Ronnie, Martin [Drew] and Critch [John Critchinson, piano]. Then eventually Ronnie decided he just wanted to play as a quartet. I had a complete ball playing in that band! The band used to work a lot, so I was doing that full time and it used to pay well, as Ronnie just used to split the money equally. We toured abroad quite a bit. It wasn't always the most musical of bands but the standard of playing was exceptionally high through playing so much as a band and it played the fastest tempos I've ever heard! It took me at least four months of playing with them to even get close to their tempos!

As part of the gig, at the end of the first set Ronnie would take a tune, everyone would take really quick solos, then – bang – everyone would walk off and it's a bass solo for ten minutes! You're left there on the stage with this hall-full of people on your own, so that was a challenge as well. I mean, you couldn't just sit there and improvise round and round on the chord sequence you'd just been playing – and anyway it was one of those super fast tempos – so there's no way you'd get close to soloing at that tempo, so you just had to take the music to a different place, work out a separate little solo bass piece to fill the time - and hope they're going to come back!

It was also very special being on the road with Ronnie Scott. He was always a lot of fun - a fantastic bloke and extremely funny.

These days we also have Humphrey Lyttleton as a great audience communicator - Alan Barnes reckons he learnt a lot from Humph.

I sometimes think that Alan doesn't quite like the fact that he's so good at repartee as it takes the attention away from his playing a bit. At the Appleby Festival he did the narration for his Sherlock Holmes Suite and it was absolutely hilarious. After that however, he got an actor in to do the narration for the album and follow up gigs. He wanted to concentrate on the music.

Do you see a difference between the players of Ronnie Scott's era who had to learn their jazz from liners crossing from the States with 78s and your own generation?

Yes, Ronnie used to say there was a golden age for jazz. In his formative years it was a fresher language, which everyone was trying to get to grips with, and now it's definitely not a fresh language any more, however much people try to pull it in different directions. So in some ways it's a lot harder to make your mark, to be original.

What did you find you had to learn when you started playing with Stan Tracey?

I remember the first or second gig I did with Stan; it was a newly formed quartet with Gerard [Presencer] and someone came to review that

gig. The comment was, 'Yes, Andy Cleyndert, very good, but hasn't quite found where to play yet' – which was exactly how I felt. Stan's such a complete player and has a very strong left hand – very strong everything – so initially I felt quite boxed in.

I was not quite sure how to approach it – I'd heard him play a lot with Roy Babbington and Roy's lines used really to reflect what Stan was playing. He used to play bass lines the same way Stan would play solos, I think, and it would have been possible to approach the gig in that way.

If Stan's a complete orchestrater, maybe that gives you more freedom?

Yes, eventually it did! I realised you can play what you want with Stan – I mean you have to respect your place in the rhythm section, but everyone does exactly what they want to do.

Possibly Stan plays fewer notes as he gets older?

No, definitely no! I've got a box of his master tapes from all his recordings and I've found this one of the trio with Dave Green and Bryan Spring from the Seventies, and he's playing as much, as well, as creatively now as thirty years ago. It's just that he's a real true improviser, not one that learns lots of licks, then plays them in different orders. Every time you go on a gig with Stan, you rarely hear the same thing twice! Maybe Clark does but I haven't played with him quite as long!

Have you ever tackled any arranging or composing?

Not yet – I might if I ever get it together to have my own project.

In the album, *Sing the Line* which you co-led, you had long extended sections of bass playing?

Yeah, I did that just at the end of the period with Ronnie's band. It had just finished and I thought, 'What am I going to do now?' I felt the urge to start getting something together myself. And I didn't want to plump for being a bandleader straight off so I did a couple of projects – one was the trio with John Donaldson and Dave Mattacks. That was definitely a three-way project. We all brought three pieces in and discussed how we were going to arrange them. So everyone had a lot of input.

And the same thing with Colin Purbrook, which turned out to be his last recording – the *My Ideal* album. That was with Colin Oxley as well, he's fantastic. Again, everyone had a lot of input.

How did you come to join the Celebrating the Jazz Couriers band?

Mornington had the bright idea to get together a band dedicated to the Ronnie Scott period – he'd had a ball in Ronnie's band as well – it was really good fun. And Mornington - in fact everyone - had a really high respect for Ronnie as a musician and a person. So he wanted some form of tribute to Ronnie and Martin wanted to do the same. It's been very successful and we've

put out two albums on my Trio label which have had really good critical reviews.

For a bass player, there was plenty of solo space in that band, though some gigs can be more open. Bryan Spring's Trio with Mark Edwards has got free-er and free-er the more we have worked together and the music will go all places and is always highly creative and inspiring. However, you can play in the most restrictive bands where you're really tied to an accompanying bass position, where no one's particularly interested - provided you're playing with good time, not playing wrong notes. But if you're playing with the right people – such as Gene Harris - that can be just as good as a gig which is more open.

What bass players do you count as influencers?

Everyone. I picked on Ray Brown as an illustration but everyone has had something to say. Charles Mingus had his own voice. Charlie Haden I find interesting because he uses so little and does so much with it - he plays with such conviction that he makes very little sound amazing. He seems not to have a great deal of technique and doesn't use a lot of harmonic knowledge in what he does - but he sounds so strong.

Did you ever go back to study Jimmie Blanton?[Ellington bass player]

I have those duet recordings [of Blanton with Duke Ellington] and then the recording that Ray Brown made with Duke Ellington, emulating those early recordings which I love. So when Stan and Clark got this Ellingtonia band together, I stupidly suggested I should do one of those duets with Stan. I thought, 'That can't be very hard?' Actually – it is. Technically it's not very difficult at all, but to project it and make it sound good is hard! Then I started listening seriously to what Blanton was doing and he had such a big sound and so articulated. Put him against the best players today and he'd still sound amazing. So definitely a challenge.

Do you do any teaching or coaching in jazz?

Occasionally, I like teaching but only to keen students. I do think teaching is really important but mainly for feeding enthusiasm. When I went through school, I'm not sure that I had even one good teacher in that respect. However my last English lecturer had total enthusiasm for the subject he was teaching – which should be the basic foundation of teaching! It was a real revelation, he's interested in what he's teaching!

I've already done some workshops at the Jazz Academy and the Royal Academy. So if anyone's interested, I could be interested in teaching.

Do you play any classical music?

Well, when Ronnie's band ended, I thought, 'Help!' because that was a full time band and I wasn't doing anything else. So graveyard for you! I also felt I hadn't got that much together up to that point. I had got into practicing a lot more but still not really enough.

So when Ronnie's ended I did go and find a decent classical teacher and got into that. However I quickly realised that to be in that side of things you have to have been doing it forever - as long as I've been doing jazz!

Classical music I do find really fascinating. On the performance level classical soloists have to have so much command and so much together before they can start to put their own colour on a piece of music! Just to be able to play the piece in the first place is a life's work! To rise above that and be a real true soloist with your own interpretation is just staggering! However I sat down for three or four years and started working with the bow, which improved my technique and sound tenfold, I would say.

I wasn't that far wrong technically with my playing, but just a few adjustments made a big difference. On gigs just after a month or two, my sound became just *huge* compared to what it was. And that was just working on the technique of the left hand, nothing to do with plucking the string. A revelation!

What about all your non-playing activities? You're a sound engineer, photographer, designer and you've started Trio Records.

Trio springs from early times, when I inherited my grandfather's old reel-to-reel. I used to fiddle with that, try recording things. Then when I started playing on recordings and broadcasts, I would think, 'Oh, don't like that sound, why is it like that?' So I wanted to find out how to make it sound better. I started recording gigs, initially just with a stereo mike, eventually expanding to a more professional set up. It was just a hobby, an extension of what I was doing as a musician.

Latterly however, it has become clear that there is not much the recording industry can do or does for jazz. So a hobby has turned into a small label.

I recorded a load of gigs, for example, with Junior Mance [piano] on the first tour I did with him and I thought, 'OK, surely someone's interested in releasing that' – but in the end I didn't find anyone. So I printed up some albums myself and we sold them on the next tour. That worked so well I did the same again.

I've also done the two Jazz Couriers albums, as well as two for Stan, including a new recording of his classic *Under Milk Wood*.

What sort of numbers of CD pressings are we talking about here, broadly hundreds or a thousand or so?

I think most people do a run of one thousand and get rid of them and have a reprint of 500 and normally that's as far as it'll go. It's very easy to work out the economics of it and very easy to work out that the only way you're going to make a modest amount of money on recordings is to produce them yourself and sell them on gigs! Basically cut out all the middlemen.

Do you see your future in that area?

No! I don't want to be a sound engineer! I actually only enjoy doing it if I'm there playing on the gig. Taking out the gear and setting it all up, then listening to music you're not that interested in ...and coming home and having to mix it for hours and hours! No thanks! For all the hours you put in, you don't really make enough money. So it's got to be a project you're really into!

And also worthwhile. The latest trio album with Stan, *Zach's Dream*, has sold very well, with

really good reviews. Plus I've finally got Don Weller to record a quartet album, which is the first of his quartet since 1979, I think, and that has turned out really well.

What about the future? Some are concerned about the new generation of players and where they will play.

Personally I just want to keep the ball rolling.

I think that rather than look to musicians for the future, we really need to look at who's listening. You've got more musicians than before but less and less places to play. The audience is the same one I was playing to twenty years ago, except it's twenty years older. It's different in cities where there can be a younger audience but generally it's sad because there hasn't been a fresh generation of jazz listeners.

Selected CDs	
My Ideal	Purbrook Cleyndert Oxley [1997, Trio]
Zach's Dream	Stan Tracey Trio [2002, Trio]
Seventy Something	Stan Tracey Trio [2004, Trio]
Website:www.cleyndert.co.uk	

Jamie Cullum

Jamie Cullum, born in Reading in 1980, is an acclaimed new singer and pianist who produces fresh, updated jazz-influenced interpretations of the American Songbook alongside his originals and covers of contemporary songs by bands like Radiohead, Jimi Hendrix and Jeff Buckley. He is a largely self-taught musician with impressive vocal skills and an exciting, percussive jazz piano style and is a high energy attractive performer.

He began by playing guitar in rock groups but then started to enjoy jazz by Oscar Peterson and Dave Brubeck. Jamie was also playing piano and got seriously involved after his singing performance got a great reception at a local jazz pub. Later during his degree course in Film & Drama, Jamie was gigging regularly. He performed with the Pendulum Band at the major Brecon Jazz Festival where he started his collaborations with the leading bassist and arranger, Geoff Gascoyne.

After graduating, Jamie began preparing tracks for an album. The singer Clare Teal encouraged Alan Bates, boss of the Candid label, to sign him up for the album that in 2002 become his successful label debut *Pointless Nostalgic*.

Following his million pound record deal with Universal in 2003, he has been touring widely across the US, Canada and Europe, frequently selling out major venues. He provided the closing concert at the Royal Festival Hall at the London Jazz Festival 2003.

His latest Universal CD, *Twenty Something*, has broken jazz records by selling in excess of 300,000, three times ahead of Courtney Pine's record set for British jazz in the early Nineties. [This interview just predated his Universal contract.]

What music can you first remember listening to?

It's difficult to remember because I was in the kind of family where there was always music on. My parents have always been music fans - my mother sings a bit and my Dad sings and plays guitar. They're not professional or schooled musicians. My older brother [Ben is 4 years older] started having piano lessons when he was younger, so it was just very natural for me to want to copy him. I had radio and TV influences, so I remember the Sixties rock and roll show that Dad had on every Saturday morning.

When did you first pick up a musical instrument?

I tried and failed at piano lesson between the ages of 8 to 10 - that never worked – I was told to give up - so I did!

Then it was a matter of copying my elder brother. He went through a heavy metal phase and so did I, and then he became interested in musicians who played very fast, so it was natural that we should get into listening to Oscar Peterson. One of the first I listened to was *Night Train* by Oscar Peterson – it was very bluesy and by that time I could understand the blues, feeling my way round the piano a bit better, and some guitar just to impress the girls.

This was around 14, when you're a bit more unsure of yourself and I started playing things, only to myself at that stage. I was then playing guitar a lot more as it was pretty popular.

I discovered Harry Connick Jnr and the piano as he was young too. Then I got into Thelonius Monk, John Coltrane and Miles Davis. I got books on these people and they were so cool in their groovy suits. I was also interested in black guys too, as my granddad was from Burma and he looked a little like Nat King Cole - I wanted to look cool.

When did you get into more serious gigging?

After A levels, I needed to spend some time just doing music, because I'd been trying to do it between home work and course work and this got *very* frustrating. So I took a year out, deciding just to play piano and travel and try to teach myself a lot more - get myself gigs and things like that. Sometimes in groups - all this time I played in a hip hop band and a funk band, and a rock band, piano, guitar, drums all kinds of things, just to keep involved in music. I wasn't very confident and it helped me get involved with other people – it was easy to communicate with people through music, easier to relate.

At this stage it wasn't voice, it was always *instrumental*. I wasn't really singing, just doing a bit of backing vocals - but I didn't have the confidence then.

In that year out I played a lot of piano at home and saved up to go away. Then I discovered a local pub that had weekly jazz. The piano player defaulted one week 'cause he'd split up with his girlfriend, so they asked if anyone could play anything. My friend put my hand up, so I went up and played a couple of tunes. They screamed for more and I sang a tune ' Do you know what it means to miss New Orleans'. They invited me back after that to play every week. So I had to learn a new song every week - I learnt a lot of new songs that year!

I also got involved with a lot of older jazz players who had come up through the dance band era and they knew every tune. They'd be able to point out if I was doing anything wrong,

if I didn't have exactly the right changes. That was a very useful association. And I'm still in contact with all those people - still do gigs with them. They're in their sixties and seventies but they're just great jazz musicians.

Then I went travelling in Europe for a while, went to Paris, was supposed to be for two weeks

and I ended up staying there two months, playing in cafes and bars. I met a girl, learnt more piano out there, and when I came back I felt a bit more like a musician.

I went to university when I came back, to study English literature initially. I was quite academic at school, but I realised two months into it that I enjoyed reading too much to enjoy studying it at that high level - unlike at school, where you read books, talk about them and that's it. At university we had to read far too much criticism, which I thought was a bit anally retentive – I'm sure it isn't – but it just didn't connect with me. It's like people who are interested in hi-fi technically rather than listening to music, or people who are interested in cameras rather than taking photos.

Do you find playing in front of audiences a challenge?

Well, it *is* more of a discipline, but funnily I saw the Michael Jackson documentary last night and he was saying, 'You've got to feel it.' If you think about it too much it won't come out right. I really identify with that, because I'm not a trained musician and a lot of the things I do, some people have studied three years in front of books to learn. I've just sat at the piano and at gigs and worked it out. So you've really got to *feel* it. That's how it works for me. But I would love to go back and study music one day, if I get the chance, the money and the time, get into the intricacies.

You were in the Film Studies Department at University?

There was a notice on the board saying musicians needed for the production of *The Cherry Orchard* and I went to the audition and got a main acting part. I've always been greatly interested in drama and film, and got heavily involved in the film side and made a number of shorts. My flatmate is an amateur filmmaker and we are often working at scripts and things like that. So I'd like to do something someday, as a writer.

But at university you kept gigging.

I was always doing gigs at the university, started off doing just one or two a week. Then by the third year I was working in Oxford, Reading and London five nights a week. And doing a degree *and* my exams – I did gigs the night before most of my exams!

This was just because I didn't want to turn down gigs, mainly pubs, weddings and bars and stuff. But that's where I learnt to do it in front of an audience, playing songs and also putting on a show, not just sitting there and bashing out a few tunes.

How do you learn jazz?

I study records. Also I've read a lot of books that didn't make much sense. Really it was mostly just copying stuff off records and literally learning on the stand. I did a lot of work with guitarists at that time. In these bands where I was singing, there were no other male singers, so I didn't have to play all the chords, I could play the ones I knew - so I would ask and someone would show me. Gradually it just started to happen. Mind, I still see chords I don't know be-

cause I haven't been through it methodically - not in the Bill Evans building-block kind of way. If I saw a thirteenth I might not know the chord but I'd know it in the context of the song - it is all an *aural* thing definitely.

Who are your musical influences?

It definitely started off as Oscar Peterson and Thelonius Monk and Harry Connick Jnr. Bill Evans was the one I really got obsessed with through my late teens, listening to every record and read his biography and meeting people who knew him, trying to know everything about him. But of course he came through the classical tradition and that's nothing like what I came through.

Also Miles [Davis], Coltrane, the Big Six you know, but more recently it's been people like a Chicago singer called Kurt Ellings, I'm a big fan of his. And Chicago singer-pianist Patricia Barber, Mark Murphy and Jon Hendricks.

The non-jazz people are too numerous to mention but people like Stevie Wonder, James Taylor (for the guitar, say, in Fire and Rain,) Jeff Buckley, Bob Dylan, good songwriters, or songs that say Elton John has done.

Plus Joni Mitchell, her jazz phase with Mingus. Mingus is a really good album. I also have a lot of her albums and the best hits with Wayne Shorter, the London Symphony Orchestra and Herbie Hancock – it's just so beautiful.

How do you choose material?

It's a mixture of old classic ballads like 'I can't get started' and more modern material like 'High and Dry.'

How are you going to manage that blend in future?

I personally would put those songs in the same category, because I only heard *I can't get started* about three to four years ago and *High and Dry* is a song by RadioHead that I remember from my teens at fifteen or sixteen. So if anything I feel *more* nostalgic about that song!

It's just a beautiful song that I wanted to play

really. And the funny thing is - young people who come to my gigs, ask me, 'Oh, did you write that song, *I can't get started*? And the older people ask, did you write that song *High and Dry*? So it's a meshing of the two and I like when that happens.

It's just how I feel and a question of good songs really. It's just a song I wanted to play and I don't think 'Oh, I'm doing a pop tune now'. It's just a tune I really like and that comes quite-naturally.

What do you think of some other ballad singers?

Claire Teal - I'm a big fan of hers. She is the person who gave my initial CD to her label – I made an initial one just with my own cash at university - some money from my grandmother - and Claire was the one who gave that CD to Candid and said, 'You've got to sign him up.'

Ian Shaw - I've got to know him since moving to London. He's great, soul-influenced in his earlier career but a lot more interested in the technical side of singing than I am, with fast tempos and odd time signatures. But he's always on the quest for interesting songs - as is Claire Martin actually – she's introduced me to listening to a lot of records of tunes and things I haven't heard of. So I think the *British* singers are the ones that take a few more risks with repertoire.

What about Jane Monheit?

I did hear her when I went to listen to music in New York, saw her before she was signed, at a nightclub at three in the morning. She was amazing, with beautiful long hair, did *Body and Soul* then left - it was like, 'God, who was that?'

And now I see her on these big stages and I think, maybe she doesn't know how to handle herself on stage – I don't know. My flatmate went to see her and said it was like a Long Island beauty pageant. And they dissed her because they said we don't believe what she's singing - about love and so on. I was thinking she's older than me - so people are quite likely to say to me, how can you sing *I can't get started* – and I must admit when I hear her as a singer I don't fully *believe* her, it doesn't touch me on a gut level. Got a beautiful voice, lovely technique, everything, [but] it doesn't really hit me where it should do.

I feel *you* really achieve a realistic interpretation of 'I can't get started' - that rueful edge to the voice.

I'm glad you think that's put across. If you notice on the album, every song I choose are ones I've been doing for a long time. Ones that mean something to me, including 'I can't get started' - and it's just a different perspective to what a fifty-four year old Sinatra would give it.

But I don't think I would try to sing a song like 'Lush Life' yet, for example, - love the tune but don't think that I could bring anything meaningful to it yet. So I do pick tunes pretty carefully.

In the future are you going to continue with the combination of rock and jazz?

I think I'm going to carry on as I am. The great thing about this record ['Pointless Nostalgic'] is it's got a lot of attention and at certain venues, I'm getting a much younger audience than jazz people are used to, because of the numbers 'High and Dry' and 'Pointless Nostalgia' which my brother and I wrote. The interesting thing is I'm leaning towards possibly doing a big Nora Jones type record, and *maybe* I could. I'd like to continue doing the mixture of old and new, fresh and different - that kind of mixture. I would not try to make it a commercial pop album but if I had to make a slightly more accessible album I wouldn't take any shame in that because I believe that's as much of an art as making an intense Jarrett pipe organ solo record!

You see a greater need for some jazz players to communicate with audiences?

Jazz people moan a lot actually when they do a gig at the Bulls Head and only two people turn up. And sometimes they wonder why that is.

And I think, 'Do you want me to start listing you the reasons?' – no doubt you're playing amazing music but you've got to do something to promote it and bring people in - some sort of gimmick, because that's the sort of world we live in - if you don't like it, then play hip-hop.

For some people, straight music works, but what I try to do is put on a show as it were and make a bit of a fool of myself – not acting out but don't hold back basically. People enjoy it and say it has a lot of energy and it's part of going to one of my gigs – is he going to leap around like he did last time? - and I don't mind that. That's just how I am - I get *terribly* overexcited. Sometimes it works and it gets them into music.

What about piano style development in the future? You said you liked Bill Evans?

My piano style couldn't be much further away from Bill Evans really. I love listening to his playing but I haven't tried to copy it so much. I'm still absorbing it, record by record - if anything comes out of it, I'll be very happy.

Are you setting out to be part of a jazz vocalist revival in Britain?

I have seen a lot of singers including Stacey Kent with a lot of reserve. I call them the 'storyteller' type singers that I love very much, but I consider myself outside of that.

A major radio producer said to me the other day, 'When you make your next record, the more polished and three minute radio-friendly you make it, you've got an open door for this show.' And that's great to hear, but I'm not a polished person and I don't really consider myself in that tradition. I mean there's this new guy, 19 – 20 in America - fantastic, he's a piano player/singer, everyone saying he's going to be the next craze and how are you going to combat this - this guy goes to school in a *trilby* and a suit. I'm *outside* that tradition, trying to pretend it's the Fifties – I can't do it really.

I invest performing with as much *energy* as going out on Friday night with my mates, that kind of thing - *shamelessly* if I can say that!

Selected CDs	
Pointless Nostalgic	Jamie Cullum [2002, Candid]
Twenty Something	Jamie Cullum [2003,UniversalCJ]
Songs of the Summer	Geoff Gascoyne [2002, Jazzizit]
Website: www.jamiecullum.com	

Alec Dankworth

Alec Dankworth, born in London in 1960, is one of Britain's most prominent double bass players and leads his own trio. Starting with classical clarinet, Alec then exchanged his bass guitar for the double bass and took the Jazz Course at Berklee College, Boston. Immediately afterwards he toured internationally with the band of his mother, Cleo Lane with John Dankworth as musical director.

Alec was part of the successful Clark Tracey band from 1984 to the early Nineties. In 1997, while based in New York, he played with the Duke Ellington Orchestra and toured with the legendary pianist Dave Brubeck whom he remembers with particular affection.

Alec has worked with a wide range of notable instrumentalists including Abdullah Ibrahim, Julian Joseph, Alan Barnes, Peter King, Jean Toussaint, Tommy Smith, Michael Garrick and violinist Nigel Kennedy. The many vocalists he has worked with include Cleo Lane, Tina May and Jacqui Dankworth.

With his father, Alec co-led the Generation Band, a big band venture showcasing a blend of new and older talent that has produced two CDs. He has twice been awarded Best Bass in the British Jazz Awards (1995 and 1997).

He currently writes for and manages his own trio (Julian Arguelles [sax]) and Phil Robson [guitar]) which released a CD *if you're passing by* in 2004. He also performs regularly with the Tina May and the Jacqui Dankworth bands.

What was the first type of music you can remember listening to in the home?

I was very much influenced early on by my parents' really extensive record collection. They would be listening to what was of interest to them at the time. Actually I seem to remember having a little rebellion against jazz in a way because that's what they were listening to most, so I did my utmost to find things other than jazz. My contemporaries were not into jazz, so I was a big fan of people like Elton John, Stevie Wonder, James Taylor and some rock bands like Yes.

Your father is well known for his

composing and saxophone abilities, but did he always play jazz or was he in classical music before that?

I think his love was always for jazz, though he went to the Royal Academy of Music as a classical clarinet player. I studied clarinet class ically as well. So we both studied for all the grades in the same way.

What was happening when you were in mid-teens ?

Well, by that time I was playing classical clarinet and saxophone officially at school. I'd started on cello – that lasted around a year – but ended up with clarinet and sax, rather in father's footsteps really.

But I was playing electric guitar as well and I formed a rock band out of school, playing rhythm guitar. Then the bass player of the band left and there was a bass guitar lying around the house. It seemed natural for me to pick it up.

After a while, I realised that I didn't want to end up in an orchestra playing classical clarinet, also difficult to do that as there were so few orchestras and it was more fun playing bass guitar anyway. So I switched – after I studied classical clarinet at the Guildhall School of Music. After less than a year, I took my bass guitar across to Berklee College in Boston.

It was a good place to get a jazz orientation at that time in 1977. Nowadays there are jazz courses proliferating in this country but then Berklee was definitely *the* jazz course to go to worldwide. And also there was a good friend of the family, Mike Gibbs, as composer in residence, so there was a connection there and maybe they reckoned I couldn't get into too much mischief!

Did the course enlarge your horizons?

It certainly did. I'd been on the periphery of jazz. Even with my parents' influence, I'd not been wholeheartedly into jazz music, though I wasn't playing in a rock band any more. Still there was a lot I hadn't heard, probably because I'd only listened to one collection of music – my parents'.

So when I got to Berklee, with its 2000 musicians, half of whom were guitarists and half of whom were probably jazz musicians, I had to listen to music from many different walks of life – one friend listened to Wes Montgomery, and I became a fan. I also liked George Benson, that kind of music, up to the contemporary stuff like Chick Corea's *Return to Forever* – lots of jazz fusion which was developing at that time. Nowadays, it's not that often that you buy something recorded right now. I'm still buying records that were made forty or fifty years ago!

What did the course teach you, as you were still mainly a classical musician by training?

I already had a good amount of classical training in harmony, plus I had studied jazz harmony, mainly through playing it, I think, having a Real Book [jazz standards in chord form] and getting some jazz lessons from my father. Whereas Berklee was designed to cater for the absolute beginner almost.

So I started above some others, but there was still a lot to learn about being a bass player and professional musician. The course was pretty structured and a good place to learn – very good harmony, arranging and ear-training classes.

You returned from Berklee and immediately started touring with your father and mother's band.

Yes, a highly professional band that included some top British jazz musicians – Kenny Clare on drums, Bill Le Sage on vibes and piano, Paul Hart who is an extraordinarily multi-talented musician – I was thrown right in the deep end! So an accelerated learning process for me and I learnt a lot from them, especially Bill Le Sage. I got a huge vocabulary of tunes from him over the years. I had a residency in an Ealing restaurant three nights a week with him on piano – he would start new tunes without turning round to tell me what the tune was, or what key it was in! But that was really good!

Was there ever a time when you might not have become a professional musician?

Not seriously, no. There was a story that John liked to mention – I wasn't the world's greatest practicer and he would say he never attempted to teach me in a serious way or get me to practice regularly - because they were generally charging off round the world, they would say either you practice or you're going to have to go down to the local petrol station and get a job as an attendant! Then I'd get straight down to the practicing!

You mentioned that some of the other people you've interviewed were just so obsessed with their instrument around the fifteen to eighteen years old period that they really couldn't consider anything else. Because music was around in our household from the beginning, for me it was a natural process, like a gradual osmosis thing.

You then moved on to Tommy Chase?

Yes, that was probably my first experience of an out-and-out hard-bop jazz band, where I met Alan Barnes.

I learnt a whole new repertoire of music there, a whole lot of Art Blakey and Sam Jones tunes. I wouldn't say I'd been a hard-bop fanatic really up to that point.

You were also part of Clark Tracey's Quintet in the mid-eighties?

Yes, I'd been aware of Clark, as his Dad was a contemporary of my Dad's and they knew each other well. It was the fulfilment of a dream of mine at the time, I remember, being asked to join. We did a hell of a lot as it was a very busy band at that time, as near as you could get to a full time band – not as full as the Miles Davis Sextet in the Sixties who worked seven nights a week without fail – but we did long tours – four week tours of the Far East a couple of times, plus Yugoslavia.

Over in the Far East with Clark Tracey, I found there's such a different reaction there to jazz to what we were experiencing back home, I suppose, where the audiences are more experienced and knowledgeable. By contrast, in the Philippines or Indonesia, you'd either end up playing to a group of expats glad to see anyone from England, or a huge university where you'd get two thousand teenagers turning up to hear some hard bop and their reaction was quite incredible – so enthusiastic, they'd clap all the way through, not just at the end of solos! If you did a fast lick, the place would erupt! It was really inspiring.

Because it's generally, well, not youngsters who turn up to most British gigs and it's nice to see a cross-section. Maybe it's this country but young people consider jazz as old fashioned music I suppose.

We had about four or five dates in the former Yugoslavia and we were a bit apprehensive about these unknown venues. But it ends up we're appearing at two international jazz festivals and touring round with David Liebman and his band, playing to huge audiences of all sections of the community, all age groups turning up in their finery! Their musical event of the year!

If we weren't travelling abroad, we were charging up the M1 doing all the jazz clubs up and down the country and recording as well. So a busy period for that band. That band included

Guy Barker on trumpet, Jamie Talbot on sax, Steve Melling on piano and me.

Was it more possible in those days to keep a band together and keep it playing regularly?

I think there was probably a bit more work around in those days. We did a number of Jazz Services tours in those days. Nowadays they fund a tour that *you'll* have got together, whereas in those days they organised the tour as well. They'd provide the gigs, a bus, the driver, a PA system and I did quite a lot of those kind of tours with Clark and other bands.

You've also played a number of times with Julian Joseph.

I first worked with Julian in 1990. He'd just come back from Berklee himself. I actually met him one night outside Ronnie Scott's and he said, 'Are you busy? Do you want to join my band?' So I was in his band for a number of years with Jean Toussaint and Mark Mondesir and that was quite a departure. Julian's music is always innovative and certainly I found it very exciting stuff and I really enjoyed that time.

We did a lot of work with that band – trips to the Montreux Jazz Festival, trips to Sweet Basil's in New York, always exciting stuff, people always enthusing about his stuff. Generally very arranged and unusual, odd time signatures.

One session for the BBC was particularly interesting. We went into the studio and he was given four brown envelopes – he chose one and there was the lead sheet to *Body and Soul* and we

had all day to re-arrange it. He sat at the piano for about half an hour or so and then called us all back in, handed out the parts. There was a version of *Body and Soul* you'd never recognise from what was on the paper! So he's always very creative.

You also played in the Tommy Smith Quartet.

Yes, I was in that for quite a while with Clark Tracey on drums and Jason Rebello on piano. It was a really good period as I like Tommy's music – challenging again but with a European approach to jazz, I guess, a bit minimalist and more emphasis on the sound quality.

Tommy went to Berklee as well, and pretty much immediately afterwards joined the Gary Burton band and toured with him. We did a lot with Tommy, including a six part TV series. We went to Montreux as well, so a pretty busy band.

You have toured with Abdullah Ibrahim?

Yes, that was probably the first of the international groups that I was involved with. The first thing we did was a tour of the UK with a string quartet, then a tour of Europe and South Africa.

But his music was different again and quite a bit more spiritual than most of the jazz. It seemed like they were communicating not just music but another meaning. Sometimes they were songs and would have lyrics, say about something that had happened in his childhood.

Each tune had a story that had some significance that went along with it, as opposed to the abstractness of jazz. He'd been in exile, living in Switzerland for a long while during the apartheid era. So it was quite different from someone of my generation just being excited by bebop. I still play one of his tunes in my current band.

Let's get to when you started your own quartet - Robin Aspland, Mark Taylor and Andy Panayi.

In 1993 I started my own band and that went for quite a few years. We also did a world tour with my sister Jacqui with that band. We did five concerts on the Hawaiian islands and then went on to Indonesia. Unfortunately we never recorded a CD with that band, quite a shame, though I've got a few cassette tapes. Maybe we should release them sometime.

I also did a lot of work with Tim Garland later on, after his period with Lammas, in his quartet and I was into his style of playing, fairly similar to Tommy Smith, quite European, I suppose, like the ECM style, northern Europe specifically. Probably less swingy music, less straight-ahead bebop related, bit more open, not so diatonic jazz harmony, more modal, a bit more adventurous.

And I was introduced to Phil Robson [guitar] through Tim who's in my current band, my trio. We did an interesting tour of Syria with Tim. At the time I went to Beirut with my own quartet and Jacqui as well, so I was getting lots of Middle Eastern flavour!

You also worked a lot with the Tina May group. How different is it supporting a vocalist?

I would hope I learnt the skills from an early age in my Mum's band. You have to play, even more than in an instrumental band, in as minimalistic way as you can really, as they're to be the centre of attention. Though that's my philosophy for all musical situations that I play in. I try mentally to put myself in the audience, be objective about what I'm playing, trying to

support whoever is the focus at any one time, so just playing the harmony and the root [chord]. Then when you *do* have the room and the time to do something else, they'll notice it a lot more!

You have some great long introductory passages to play on Tina May's album. Do you write those yourself?

The harmonic arrangements are generally done by the pianists, in this case Nikki Iles and Robin Aspland, both did arrangements. Then you get into the studio and someone says, 'Who wants to take a solo on this tune?' or 'Shall we start this off with just bass and voice?' or 'We've got too many solos!'

On the gig, it's normal to do more soloing, but on the record you cut it down a bit. So the solos are decided on the day, the harmonies beforehand.

Can we discuss how you run your group?

Firstly I get myself playing a few more melodies and that's good! Other than that, with my trio, which is a drummer-less trio, generally it's sax, melody, guitar, rhythm and I look after the bottom end of things. But it's easy to experiment as there's only three of us, so I've written out a few harmonies and we can take different parts on some pieces. We *all* can keep the rhythm going really, it's just an organic thing that develops between us over a lot of gigs. There's not much rehearsal.

As you get older and more experienced, you all want to run your own groups, so there's a natural breaking away from the people you used to play with?

Yes, there is. I haven't been as prolific with bands as some. But you do want to be running your own band and all of those that we've discussed have been individualistic bands, not particularly playing standards. Whereas the run-of-the-mill gigs that I've done over the years as a bass player, have been almost jam sessions, you just play standards with much the same solo order and off you go. But I can get away from that by forming my own band.

Your trio plays a mixture of standards and originals.

There's more of my tunes than standards – often the ones you wouldn't have heard of – so not *Autumn Leaves* – though occasionally we do *Cottontail* or a Dave Brubeck tune.

You've actually played with Dave Brubeck; often those have unusual time signatures and aren't what you might call regular standards.

Yes, though that wasn't what I generally played with him, though we would play *Take Five* every gig without fail! Apart from that he's really quite a straight-ahead player really. He's steeped in the history – he loves playing stride piano, for instance, that's his roots. Plus he got into jazz in the Forties, so I learnt some really old tunes while I was in his band like, 'Twas only a shanty in old shanty town.' And he took great joy in reciting the lyrics one time. Must get the lead sheet again!

Tell me about the Generation Band you co-led with your father John. How did that start?

My Dad said one day, how do you fancy forming a band? He was interested in doing something afresh with the big band which he's been associated with over the years – his earliest was probably in the late Fifties.

I said I'd like that. He suggested using an unusual line-up of instruments and I chose the musicians from my contemporaries. We made up some new arrangements for it and it had some great talent – Guy Barker, Gerard Presencer, Tim Garland and Jimmy Hastings from my Dad's generation.

You did the albums *Nebuchadnezzar* in 1993 and *Rhythm Changes* in 1995.

At the time, John had a residency, a week at Ronnie Scott's, so that was the main gig of the band and the venue for recording those records.

We followed this by a number of gigs around the country. Plus a few concerts with Cleo singing as well. I did some arrangements for it, as did a number of others in the band, which had a number of composers including Mark Nightingale, Andy Panayi, Tim Garland, Stewart Hall on guitar and violin, so a pretty eclectic group of arrangements there.

It's contemporary big band writing from all of us really. Andy Panayi may have written more straight-ahead kind of arrangements, though fiendishly difficult, then Stewart Hall wrote some very contemporary, eastern European arrangements – one of them is called *Pig's Head Copanitza*, based on a Bulgarian wedding dance! And that *was* in 11/8 time, again really difficult!

Then in 1997 you moved to New York.

My wife and I decided to move to New York, partly on the encouragement of English drummer Mark Taylor, to my parents' apartment over there.

It was like starting from scratch, even though I'd had a number of contacts – people I'd been accompanying as visiting acts in the UK. So I did a lot of hanging out in the New York jazz clubs and really paying my dues all over again. Meeting a whole new younger group of musicians who'd just come out from Berklee and also from all over the world. New York is just so excitingly cosmopolitan, in fact I felt more a part of Europe in New York than I did in London. I'd be playing with musicians from France, Germany, Austria as well as Russia, Australia – in fact all over the world, on a daily basis.

It's still the world centre for jazz?

Yes, the Mecca of jazz. It's no longer what it was in the Fifties and Sixties but it's still definitely part of the NY way of life – definitely jazz on the streets!

I did a lot of trio and quartet gigs in restaurants where the proprietor would agree if some bandleader walked in off the streets with a jazz trio asking, 'Do you fancy giving us a go in your restaurant?' And the chances were he'd say yes, because it's not such an alien music form there. Here it'd be, 'Can you do a good version of the latest Madonna tune?'

It was there you played in the Duke Ellington Orchestra.

I did. We had a residency at Birdland and that was very exciting for me. I'd been meeting all sorts of interesting people and having jam sessions but all of a sudden I had a regular gig

with a well-known band and I was meeting seventeen people at once instead of two or three!

I remember the first gig I did with them, I was given the bass pad of tunes. It was huge and I started to scramble though it, wondering what the play list was going to be, and then finding the relevant parts. Then the pianist said to me, 'If I were you, I wouldn't bother trying to find the parts, better off just busking them.' Which is what I did! Any other band that would

be an impossibility. But every tune *was* a standard! *A Train, Satin Doll, In a Mellow Tone* – you couldn't call yourself a professional musician if you couldn't busk those!

There are hundreds of tunes that a professional knows and can turn his hand to in different keys.

Sure. Plus because of the amount that I've always relied on my ear, I've never had too much of a problem in transposition. The way I memorise a tune is not related to the key but more to itself and its harmony. So you need to be able to hear intervals and I always hear the intervals of the bass line in advance.

I also need the melody to remember the song. Once you've got that, you get what the harmony should be, though melodies can be ambiguous and then you learn it by rote.

Then after a year in New York, I got a call from Dave Brubeck. I knew Marion McPartland and she'd helped me out in my moving over there, so when she heard Dave needed a new bass player, she recommended me.

Most of the time, it wasn't what you imagine as classic Brubeck. That was mellow with the Desmond [alto sax] sound, whereas this was a harder bebop band. Quite often I find myself on stage in Carnegie Hall or the Hollywood Bowl, the Kennedy Centre, or the National Cathedral in Washington. All these were amazing gigs, I sometimes had to pinch myself.

You look out there and there'd be a sea of faces, sometimes the same age as Dave, and you'd wonder how everyone's digging this instrumental music so much! But there were always youngsters in the audience as well, so somehow he has attracted a range of generations all through his career.

One of the tours I did with Dave was his Fortieth Anniversary Tour of the UK. During the gig at Brighton, some of the guys from REM the pop band, one with bright orange hair, the other with blue hair, arrived and they were so pleased to be in the dressing room. In the end they got a ride back to London in the band bus. And in Park Lane, we dropped them off at the Dorchester! Dave's music has been so accessible and it just continues to inspire young musicians to get into jazz.

A lot of jazz pianists say that Brubeck was one of their first influences. Rhythmically that *Time Out* album was very innovative for its time. I pair it up with one by Wynton Marsalis called *Standard Time* which also dealt with unusual metres against standard tunes - quite revolutionary. I think it's remarkable that there's around forty years between these two albums. Sure there's been other albums using odd time signatures but these are the two that people remember.

I keep my time in Dave's band very close to my heart. Also he's such a nice person – I don't think he ever told me how to play bass the whole time I was there and I know from being a bandleader that's such a difficult thing. But his only control was to write the piece and after he handed over the lead sheet, it was out of his hands. So I felt free and confident to experiment myself and let my own musical judgement decide what would work in each piece – which was much appreciated and good for music making.

Who are your main gigs with at the moment?

Jacqui's band is one, Tina May is another and my Mum and my trio are my main groups at the moment.

And Jacqui's just formed a new quartet with me, Mike Outram on guitar, Roy Dodds on drums. It's quite an interesting new experience working for my sister as bandleader, something we haven't done before. But she's an amazing singer with quite mellow versions of standards and originals. And her record's come out on Candid and at the same time I did my first re-

cording with the trio, also out on Candid – so a double release!

How did you make the selection of tunes for your trio?

Well there are about eight originals, written over the years, so not designed to appeal specially to a single type of audience, though about three

were written specifically for the recording and, unlike Madonna, I did not have my marketplace firmly fixed in mind! I just wrote them for my own pleasure, but hoping they translate into something that other people enjoy as well. None of it's normal bebop or straightahead jazz. It's taken from a wide variety of musical influences over the years, the bands I've been in and the bass players I've been listening to.

It's played with guys I really respect and enjoy playing with, Julian Arguelles and Phil Robson. Some of it's quite European in flavour. Then we do a couple of standards, a Brubeck tune then an Abdullah Ibrahim tune.

You touched on musical influences. Are there any you have particularly admired?

The late Ray Brown along with Oscar Pettiford, probably his predecessor, Ron Carter and Eddie Gomez, and of course Dave Holland, the British bass player I respect. Some of my tunes are influenced by his composing.

Besides bass players, who do you admire?

Miles Davis, Sonny Rollins, Coleman Hawkins, Bill Evans and Keith Jarrett. I have done a lot of listening to other instrumentalists, so these are the guys that I transcribe and attempt to play on the bass! Normally with dire consequences!

And your future? It includes working with the trio?

Yes, certainly and in the future maybe manage a larger group. I do want to do more composing. It's something that I've not been prolific in doing over the years given my heritage, so it'd be nice to do some more there.

So there's all those areas to be developing but also my own career, rather than being a bass player in other people's bands.

What about the health of jazz in the UK?

I'm a little concerned about it in the UK because there doesn't seem to be a replenishment of audiences, though this varies a lot from venue to venue and some are very healthy. But often the audiences are of a generation or two above myself, so it could mean a crisis of audience in the near future.

Having said that, London's great as a city and jazz centre - there's probably more jazz going on in London than any other European city! While some venues are closing down, others are opening up, so there's a healthy number of venues. Certainly also there's no shortage of new, young musicians coming through.

As for creative musicianship, all over Europe there are wonderfully creative things going on. A lot of records are being produced, not that will make people rich but this demonstrates that there will always be people interested in the music and its history. It's still a young history, so we shouldn't give up too soon - *I* would expect jazz to be evolving in *all sorts* of directions.

Selected CDs

if you're passing by   Alec Dankworth Trio
                                    [Candid, 2004]
Nebuchadnezzar   Dankworth Generation
                                    Band
                                        [Jazz House, 1993]
'Fortieth Anniversary Tour of the UK'
                            Dave Brubeck Quartet
                                        [Telarc 1998]
Website: www. alecdankworth.com

John Donaldson

John Donaldson, born in London in 1955, is a modern jazz pianist, bandleader and composer of eclectic musical tastes. In his teens he played in various pop and jazz–fusion bands, till he took a break to travel the world. Back in England, he took a classical music degree at Anglia University and while in Cambridge was a member of the house band at the Cambridge Modern Jazz Club that supported many leading visiting players. This band entered the 1980 San Sebastian International Jazz Festival Competition where John was awarded the prize for Best Soloist.

In 1982, John moved to America and later stayed ten years on the West Coast, playing in and around the Bay Area, San Francisco, California, with such notables as Eddie Henderson, John Handy, Red Holloway, Larry Grenadier and Jeff Ballard.

John returned in 1993 and has since played with many leading performers including Alan Barnes, Iain Ballamy, Clark Tracey, Buddy de Franco, Jon Gordon, Ingrid Jensen, Don Weller and John Etheridge. He has accompanied Norma Winstone and many other vocalists.

He has performed at the Monterey Jazz Festival several times and regularly performs at many of the major British jazz festivals including Swanage and Appleby. He is the regular pianist in Alan Barnes' Latin Band and has toured several times with Don Weller.

John has recorded a number of CDs, including with Clark Tracey, *Full Speed Sideways* in 1994 and with Alan Barnes, *Cannonball* [ASC 2000] and *Swingin the Samba* on Woodville in 2003. He has also produced three CDs as leader or co-leader, *Meeting in Brooklin* in 1993, *Sing the Line* in 1996 and *Septpiece* in 1997.

What is the first music you can remember listening to?

Like most kids, I was into the pop music of my youth – the Beatles, the Stones and others. Jazz seemed like something very exotic, something I didn't know much about. My earliest jazz memories are of people like Duke Ellington and Count Basie on television, looking hip and always smiling. I remember seeing Miles Davis with Chick Corea and Keith Jarrett on a pair of Rhodes - probably filmed at Ronnie's. I found that I liked the music because it had that energy, like a rock band. I went out and bought a couple of jazz records - *Miles in the Sky* and the album

John Coltrane Quartet plays, his album after *A Love Supreme*.

I started going to jazz gigs. I went to Ronnie's and saw Weather Report – it was the band that recorded the album *Sweetnighter* around 1973 with Zawinul, Wayne Shorter, Miroslav, Eric Gravatt, Dom Um Romao - when I was about seventeen or eighteen. Then I heard Monk and Mingus at the Hammersmith Odeon. I also saw Ornette Coleman and Cannonball Adderley there.

Mingus and Ornette Coleman could be thought as quite advanced music; were your ears comfortably open to these players?

Mingus' music was always relatively easy for me to get into. One of the first jazz albums I heard was *Live at the Jazz Workshop* with Clifford Jordan and John Handy. The music was really of its time and had that X factor.

Ornette's music was initially harder to get into – the band I saw was Don Cherry, Ed Blackwell, and Charlie Haden who I remember had a wah-wah pedal attached to his bass. But even so, at that time there was a vibe in much of the music that caught the mood of the times and drew you in. It seemed to have relevance to what else was going on and that made the music more accessible for me and easier to relate to. It seemed a bit underground, the sounds were fresh and not clichéd. There was anger about the Vietnam War, Civil Rights and so on and some of the music back then spoke to that very powerfully.

I saw some other great gigs at Ronnies' - Sonny Rollins quintet and Ben Webster playing with Stan Tracey's trio made a huge impression. They were playing opposite the early Soft Machine with Elton Dean, Robert Wyatt, Mike Ratledge and Hugh Hopper. They had some very adventurous programming back then. That band and a number of other crossover bands were great in that they were a kind of stepping-stone for my generation into other stuff like Coltrane, and electronic music.

Did your parents try to steer you between classical and other music?

Not really. Sometimes they might ask me to learn a tune. They paid for piano lessons and let me go my own way. Neither of my parents played an instrument but my aunt gave us an old upright piano. When I was about eight, I started playing it and taking lessons. The only music I heard early on was from the radio and T.V - but everyone sang. I was into popular music and influenced by the classical music I'd heard and played. I saw all kinds of gigs and didn't really compartmentalize all the different music I heard. I checked out as much stuff as I could.

I had lessons from a local piano teacher and got to Grade 8. Later I became interested in

jazz. I heard that Stan Tracey was teaching at the City Lit [a London College], so I went to his classes for a while. These consisted of Stan writing tunes on a blackboard, the class copying them down and then we'd ask him questions and he'd play. I took this class for a term or two – there were maybe just a dozen people. Stan should write a book about how you learn jazz - structure, harmony, improvising.

He has huge knowledge and experience, plays great and always sounds like Stan. Everyone respects him because you know the music is honest and has great integrity. I don't know if you can teach that though.

The only other jazz education I had was when I went to the Barry Summer School [South Wales] for a week; the teachers there were John Taylor and John Birch. John Birch taught me the Circle of Fifths and John Taylor encouraged me to mess around with sounds I was discovering – so that's probably the extent of my *formal* jazz education.

And your classical piano?

I kind of stopped playing classical piano when I was about fifteen and started playing in some bands. There was quite a bit of fusion around, this was in the late Sixties or early Seventies. So I messed around with some fusion bands, played on a few pop singles. Some of the time I was with a band led by Sammy Rimington that used to do gigs at the Speakeasy, Marquee, the Rainbow, places like that. We did a tour and a record. I also played with Viv Stanshall's old band Big Grunt for a while. I did a bit of touring abroad, in Germany and Scandinavia, mainly playing a Hammond L122.

Then I just stopped doing all that and went travelling. I became an inveterate traveller for a couple of years, hitching round Canada, the States, down to Mexico, all over Europe. I played when I could and made pocket money by playing in piano bars. During that period I heard a lot of music. The first time I heard McCoy Tyner was in Vancouver: I don't think he'd played in England since Coltrane's death. It was the band with Alphonse Mouzon [drums] in the early seventies and I heard that band every night for a week in a half empty club in Vancouver.

When I got back, I decided to stay put for a while and went to college. I did a straight classical music degree at Anglia University, as it's now called, in Cambridge. I got a grant and this meant really that I had three years just to practice. I shared a house with a couple of other students called Chucho Merchan and Nic France – both have gone on to do a lot of jazz and pop music. We became the resident band at the Cambridge Modern Jazz Club which was run then as it is now by Joan Morrell. So for the best part of three to four years, we played behind all the visiting soloists – Don Weller, Martin Taylor, Jim Mullen - people like that - a great education, terrific experience. We played with a local sax player, Trevor Kaye. He taught me my diminished scales!

Then as a quartet we entered the 1980 San Sebastian Jazz Festival competition where I won a prize for best soloist. Mercer Ellington presented the prize in front of a stadium full of people. It was a very surreal experience. The largest audience we'd previously played to was at 'The Man in the Moon' in Cambridge! There was television and radio coverage – we hung out with Freddie Hubbard's band and Art Blakey's band and they were encouraging – this experience was really important in giving me the confidence to take it further.

Then you moved to California.

Before that I spent a year in the Appalachian Mountains. I was now married and we went out there initially for a year. My wife had a job doing stained-glass work on a church. I picked up a gig playing in a resort and did some sessions at a studio in Franklin, North Carolina.

Then we decided to drive out to California and visit some friends before coming home, and ended up staying there for ten years. I played mostly in the Bay area – places like Santa Cruz, San Jose and San Francisco, Monterey and St Luis Abispo.

How did you find the jazz scene, compared to Britain's?

In terms of players, there are great players *everywhere*. In terms of gigs when I arrived, I lucked my way into a few good ones straight away. People were very welcoming, even though I'd had relatively little playing experience. The scene in '83 was still pretty good—but the number of live venues there has diminished over the last twenty years.

My first forays into 'professional' jazz were in California. And the first gig I was on out there was backing Eddie Henderson. It was a live radio broadcast, big band and small group, a sort of baptism of fire. Then I played with a lot of local guys who included well-known players like John Handy, Richie Cole. I gigged with the bassist Paul Jackson, played latin-jazz on gigs with great players like Pete Escovido, Louis Romero. Brazilian music is very big there and I played with Helcio Melito, Claudia Villela, Laurendo Almeida. I played with Larry Grenadier and Kenny Wollesson before they left for New York. Jeff Ballard, too, in fact I met Jeff on that first gig with Eddie Henderson.

Sometimes players would come across from New York.

Yes, just like in London, you'd play with guys from New York. In fact many musicians moved out there looking for a more relaxed lifestyle. When I met Joe Henderson, for instance, he was doing low paying gigs, before his big rediscovery, when he did those albums in the Eighties. He was doing a lot of teaching and gigging with local musicians.

I was out there ten years. We had to move back to London for family reasons at the beginning of '93. There were only a few people I knew back in London, but I soon met people like Clark Tracey, Dick Pearce, Geoff Gascoyne, and Gerard Presencer. Iain Ballamy whom I'd met before I left England and later when he was touring out there was very supportive, gave me a week at Ronnie's – later he played on a record that I did in the States.

Yes, you and Iain played at the 1993 Monterey Jazz Festival in California. But en route, you stopped off in New York to record a CD called *Meeting in Brooklyn*. You had a really classic rhythm section, Ray Drummond and Victor Lewis.

Before I left California I'd been in a band that

had a manager who also managed Ray Drummond. So when the opportunity to do this album came along I asked Ray to do it. He suggested Victor and that's how it happened. That was a really interesting experience – we flew over, did the record live to two track in six hours. We took the DAT tape back to London, Oliver Weindling listened to it and released the album on his Babel Label. Koch Jazz released it in the States. It did surprisingly well.

On the album, you performed the Kenny Wheeler song *Nobody's Song but My Own*, which has become a classic.

Kenny's written many great tunes that have interesting changes and I've always loved his writing. I bought *Gnu High* around 1976 when it came out and played it to death and I've been a fan ever since. I think it was the first ECM album I bought. Kenny's a true original. I once did a standards gig with him and it didn't matter what the material was or how the trio played because everything he played was so strong and had its own unmistakeable sound and character. Just a great player.

Another CD on which you were co-leader, was *Sing the Line* [Red Dot Records, 1996]

Yes, that whole album was very much a joint effort. It looks like a trio album but is more of a collaboration between Dave Mattacks, Andy Cleyndert and myself. Dave got us some studio time, we came up with a list of tunes and some arrangements. A friend of Andy's called Jote Osahn is a fiddle player and she brought in her mates and we had strings on some of it. Andy Panayi played on some tracks and Agatha Coffey sang 'Wild Mountain Thyme.' It's a weird collection - there's some originals, a folk song, songs by Kenny Werner, Don Weller, Steve Swallow, Abdullah Ibrahim and Bill Evans.

You are a regular in most Alan Barnes' bands: what do you like about playing in those bands?

Oh, Alan's great - he just re-invents himself all the time – we've got a band that does all-Monk tunes, we did a band of Cannonball material, and there's his Latin band. Alan is one of those guys who is very comfortable doing lots of different styles, seems to know every tune that's ever been written, plays God knows how many horns but always sounds like him. He's an amazing communicator, great leader and very passionate about what he does.

You've worked with Norma Winstone over a number of years: how did that start?

It was about 1995 when Norma phoned me out of the blue – I think Stan Sulzman had given her my number - and she offered me a couple of weeks' work at the Pizza on the Park. I was a bit awestruck, but this was great and that's how I met Norma!

Did you need to adjust to accompanying such a singer who performs like a wind player?

She's a fantastic musician who just happens to be a singer. Her time and musicianship are amazing and she's also a great person who treats her accompanists as equals, unlike some other singers I've worked with. In 1997, we went to the Monterey Jazz Festival and played there.

She was a hit there?

She was! Many people there were fans of Norma, she has a kind of underground following so it was a treat for them to hear her live. I remember that gig very well, within about a minute of the start of the gig you could hear a pin drop. She's amazing.

You've been touring with that beautiful sax player and bandleader, Don Weller.

Yes, I've played with Don for many years now; another unique player. I first saw Don play at Eel Pie Island when I was a teenager in a band called Boris. Jamie Muir played percussion. It was pretty far out - but one of those gigs you just don't forget. I first played with him years later when I lived in Cambridge and he came up many times to play as a guest. But it's been a real thrill to work with him regularly. I play in the Cannonball Band and do deps with his Quartet.

Plus I also play in the Electric Octet he's brought together. We toured recently, starting at the Bulls Head and played venues up north for about ten days. In the band I play Hammond, Fender Rhodes. They're not actual Hammonds and Fender Rhodes anymore, but what's called a modelling keyboard. It sounds almost as good as the real thing and it weighs only about twenty pounds.

Like MIDI keyboards?

Yes, 76 notes, the B3 even has the Leslie speaker effect. Don had a funk fusion band in the Seventies or Eighties called Major Surgery and he was thinking of calling this band Relapse. He's reworked some of those pieces and the sounds on this particular keyboard seem to suit the music. You get the Wurlitzer with a wah-wah and so on.

All jazzmen tour a lot. How do you find the jazz clubs up north?

There's a very good Arts Centre at Darlington – Wakefield, Halifax, Sheffield, Huddersfield, Newcastle, Lincoln, the list goes on. Mostly clubs are run by dedicated local people above and beyond the call of duty who keep an audience coming back for more. A lot of them have good pianos! Many of the gigs in London don't have decent pianos. But all over the country there're good gigs.

Do you personally have a main style, or major style of playing?

I'd like to think so; but I'm like a lot of musicians, a bit chameleon–like which is the result of years of playing different types of music. I don't change style consciously. I listen to a lot of different stuff.

As for piano players, I love McCoy, Monk, Bill Evans, Herbie, in fact just about every piano player, but the stuff I listen to is pretty varied, classical stuff, pop music.

In terms of style, some guys don't compromise at all – they play exactly as they want all the time – but frequently they don't work very much. I suppose that's the ideal to be able to survive, playing just the music you want, but everywhere musicians have to be flexible to survive. In the States I think, there are less stylistic barriers, musicians have always done different music. Partly it's cultural, partly it's economic, the safety net there is thinner than it is here. To play jazz exclusively, for most people has become a luxury.

Since returning to Britain you've worked with many visiting Americans such as Freddie Hubbard and Art Farmer.

Yes and some younger players too. I've toured with people like Ingrid Jensen and have played with Jon Gordon over the past few years when he's over at Ronnie's or the Pizza Express. I've done tours with mainstream players: Buddy de Franco, Duffy Jackson, people like that.

How stimulating is it to play with good, different players? Does it bring new things out of you?

You play better with certain players where there's chemistry obviously, and playing with musicians who are playing at a high level does inevitably raise your game. Great players seem to be able to do the impossible with minimal effort and

can read what other musicians are doing instantly. But basic things like feeling the time the same way and having similar approaches to harmony helps.

How do you think you learnt how to play jazz?

Firstly through those classes of Stan Tracey and John Taylor. But mostly from records, other musicians. Somebody can show you just one simple thing and it opens doors and it's like 'Oh, is that how that works' on jazz harmony and other stuff. You just pick things up as you go along, you stumble onto things.

The decision to become a professional musician – when did this happen to you?

I never really took that decision, although that's all I do – I just play music and in order to grow and keep my jazz habit going I have to go out and play in bands and to audiences too. The two go together. I mean, for me it was never a calculated thing. Some people are very career orientated. They have a career plan with all the angles they're going to bring into play but…. I'm pretty disorganized about that, but I do want to do a recording fairly soon.

What about the increase in more formal jazz education that's happening now?

Nowadays, people go to college, get a very well

rounded education and know everything by the time they're twenty – they're frighteningly accomplished. It's a mixed blessing, because as the standard goes up, the audiences diminish. Look at New York, great musicians can't get arrested. A degree in marketing is what you need to work!

At its best – some of our most original creative players have come through one of the colleges, but at its worst, making jazz 'legit' - like there's a correct and incorrect way to play - you know, there's always more than one way to skin a cat. If you define something in terms of academic targets you kind of control it too. Part of the attraction of the music for me has been the sometimes incorrectness of approach of many great players and particularly their unique vibe. Young people should be allowed to be young and their imaginations uncluttered by exams and tests. The idea of the institutionalisation of jazz seems odd to me.

I think education in the broad sense is great and raises the general level of players incredibly – it's just the spirit of the music might get hi-jacked along the way. There's the danger that you get people thinking there's only certain ways to do something and everything else is crap – a kind of jazz totalitarianism.

How do you see the future of jazz?

Who knows? Maybe there'll be a new Coltrane or Charlie Parker, but now there are so many strands to this music there is a danger of jazz futureshock– so much of everything. There's not a *huge* audience for the music. I saw Wayne Shorter play to only a half-full hall in Brighton last week and last year I saw Brad Meldhau play in Poole to a tiny audience. Gigs in London of course are the exception.

This music is hard for most people to hear. Most people want and get wallpaper for music, there are not many people who really want to listen. But whether there's an audience for it is almost secondary. You just become addicted to playing and so that's what you continue to do.

You say musically you are still learning.

After two decades of playing jazz, what are you still learning?

Where do I begin – new shapes, colours. Over time you hear more, I mean you hear more possibilities. And the stuff you've been listening to, you go back to after twenty years and you hear it on another level, you hear what they are playing rather than what you thought they were playing. And the longer you play the more you hear. It works at different speeds for everybody, different levels for everybody – some guys hear the guts of the music very quickly, others don't. Some people can hear paint dry but perhaps don't make an *emotional* connection to the music.

How do you see the health of jazz in the UK?

There are great players everywhere of all generations, with some real originals, so I'm optimistic. In the ten years since I've been back in London many really talented younger players have emerged, and while they take your gigs, the great thing about this music is that it's multi-generational - so they do inspire you to reconnect with all the things that attracted you to this great music in the first place!

Selected CDs
Meeting in Brooklyn - John Donaldson, Iain Ballamy
[1993, Babel Records]
Sing the Line - Donaldson/Cleyndert/Mattacks
[1996, Red Dot records]
Septpiece [1997, Red Dot records]

Tim Garland

Tim Garland, born in 1966 in Essex, is one of Britain's most internationally acknowledged tenor and soprano saxophonists, also playing the bass clarinet. He is equally known for his considerable strengths in composition.

Tim studied Composition at the Guildhall School of Music. On leaving, he formed the group Lammas with poet /guitarist Don Paterson and singer Christine Tobin. When only twenty-three, he joined Ronnie Scott's band and with them toured Britain and northern Europe. He has much experience composing for and playing in big bands including the London Jazz Orchestra, the Dankworth Generation band and the BBC Big Band and smaller groups such as Jim Mullen's band.

In 1997, his first swing album *Enter the Fire* was issued and well reviewed. It interested Chick Corea, who later invited him to tour worldwide in 1999 with his sextet Origin.

Tim's later album, *Made by Walking* (1998) also earned plaudits. His sextet then reduced to his current Trio with Geoff Keezer and Joe Locke. He also runs a nine-piece band, the Dean Street Underground Orchestra, currently combined with Bill Bruford's Earthworks to form Earthworks Underground.

Tim has also played with Stan Tracey, Peter King, Kenny Wheeler, John Taylor, Ralph Towner, Gary Burton, John Pattituci, Tommy Smith, Jim Mullen, Clark Tracey and Ben Sidran.

His musical interests extend outside the normal boundaries of jazz to include classical and hybrid written/improvisatory formats, such as his recent composition, Concerto for Saxophone and Orchestra. At Newcastle University he is a jazz Composer Fellow in residence, the first appointment of a jazz composer at a major UK music college.

What music can you first remember listening to in the home?

There was always lots of classical music, mainly the romantic era at home. My Dad was an amateur cellist, my elder brother and sister both played other instruments.

What instruments did you first play?

I started as a piano student and took the music grade exams. My favourite composers were then mostly the Romantics, but I was also getting to really appreciate more modern composers like Debussy, Ravel, Bartok and Stravinsky.

Then you entered the Guildhall School of Music to do a degree course in composition.

It was during the course that I started to treat the saxophone as my main instrument for improvising. I'd been playing piano for a long time but somehow I'd never felt completely comfortable playing jazz and improvising on it.

I was commissioned as a student to compose the piece I called, *Points on the Curve*. The title is taken from a piece by Berio, a composer I really admired. When I came out of college, I heard the kinds of jazz that most people were playing and I got to where I felt the need to be constructing something a bit different.

That led to the start of the group Lammas?

I'd been really impressed with the classical guitar and was looking for a guitar player when one day Don [Paterson] just turned up on the doorstep. He played an intriguing blend of jazz style with a lot of folk music influence. The fact that he was a poet as well made up the building blocks that we combined to construct Lammas and what the group would be all about.

Not having a bass player in the group did give us much more musical freedom. But additionally, the guitar was tuned with extra low notes on it as a substitute. Operating as a trio also meant more freedom, more space - both musically and in the car!

We had Christine Tobin singing in Spanish, Irish and English. One of the most important things for a group is to get people who really have their own voice - that was the whole point of Lammas, really. And I think that's what we achieved. Everybody grew a lot through that band and remarkably Lammas ran for ten years.

I was also playing with other bands at the same time. There was my period with Ronnie Scott. [Tim was invited to join the Ronnie Scott band in 1990 and toured the UK and northern Europe with him.] At the same time I was playing various kinds of swing music. Also I was going to a lot of festivals and played in a number of big bands, including John Dankworth's.

You've played for a while in Jim Mullen's band?

Yes, I was playing with Jim's quartet for about three or four years in the mid-nineties. He's a wonderful player with a great sound and he's probably undervalued.

Then in 1995 you put a number of your pieces together and two years later added your Suite 'Enter the Fire' to produce the album of that name?

'Enter the Fire' started in earnest in 1995 and came out in 1997 as a kind of broadening out on what I felt I could do. Before that I hadn't felt ready to make a swing album - I've always been against this *museum-culture* way of looking at things. I didn't want to do a swing album early on, because my influences would have been so obvious!

I was always keener on the *writing* side of things and the playing caught up over the years, really. I was always more confident as a writer than as a player. But with 'Enter the Fire' it became more an equal footing!

Then in 1998, Chick Corea called.

Yes, the 'Enter the Fire' Suite had been added to round off the album and Chick was the first person to notice. He said that some of the tracks sounded like they'd been recorded at a different time. I thought that was very observant, as he'd not read the liner notes! Initially he'd been interested in issuing my album 'Into the Fire' in the States, but it was already signed to a US distributor. Then I remember a whole year when nothing really happened.

After that, all of a sudden, I was asked to join his sextet Origin and we toured for the best part of a year and a half together - we did about one hundred and fifty concerts over thirteen months. And since then I've done a quartet with him as well, so we got to know each other really well. I mean, even though Lammas was around for over ten years, I'm not sure if we've done 150 concerts!

This was a lot of music and of course there's nothing like it for getting your playing right up, it gives an enormous boost to your confidence. You're playing in the best venues all over the world. So it was a dream come true really.

It was an interesting contrast - after the time with Lammas and part of that to do with something *not American*, but coming from where *we* are. Then all of a sudden, I was in one of the most American bands there is. But Chick's attitude is just that people should come to the music from *their* personal angle — whether it happens to sound American or not is bye-the- bye, you can always tell when someone has the music first-hand, just honest and spontaneous.

That's what we strive for – with varying degrees of success.

Chick Corea seems to be a player with a really quicksilver mind.

Yeah, he's so full of ideas that you never get on very well unless you're prepared to dialogue - and that's one of the things I've always wanted to do. I reckon that's one reason why he liked me, because this interaction was one of the central components of the music.

He never wants to stay still, he's had countless different bands varying from very electronic

things to way-out acoustic things. And as time goes on, the musicians are becoming more and more adaptable and he can revisit all these areas of the music that the musicians around him grew up with. So *they* are also able to participate and the horizons are actually able to *increase* as you get older!

His sixtieth birthday recordings lasted around three weeks and celebrated the bands of his past. It was exciting to see how many different bands he was able to get together with the original personnel, like the Three Quartets Band with Eddie Gomez [bass], Steve Gadd [drums] and Michael Brecker [tenor]. And his

stuff with Bobby McFerrin! My part in the recording is really quite small – though I'm very happy to be on it, nevertheless!

One of your current bands is the Dean Street Underground Orchestra.

Yes, that happened because I find New York is such an important place to keep passing through and it has a tradition of large bands playing in not so large clubs. They actually sound amazing because the sound's so fruity and big. So I talked to Peter Wallis at the Pizza Express about getting a group of about nine musicians together, because that's about how many you could fit on the stage, inspired by that Monday night session thing because at the beginning of the week it's easier to get the musicians. And two and a half years later, we're still doing it! I like it to be a bit of an international platform so I could fly people in occasionally, which is exactly what we've done. Although there are so many fantastic musicians in London, I didn't want to limit it, so we can get Perico [Sambeat, alto sax] over from Spain, Keezer sometimes comes over, Jeff Ballard [drums] of course did for the record – he lives in New York.

And it's a great vehicle for my writing. As a resident band, I also wanted it to be not over-serious, something that people would want to come back to again and again and create a balance between something original and things where the guys can just loosen up and have some fun. You don't want to write some magnum opus about the state of humanity, it just wouldn't work.

Instead we just breathe life into pieces where the tradition is already well established, hopefully setting in motion a chemistry between the players, where everyone is inspired and the word 'entertainment' should be in there, it shouldn't be banished. The word 'artistry' should be there

too. I'm quite a sociable person really, so I love being up there with the guys.

I have a New York version that occasionally meets and they're amazing too, but it does mean a lot of telephone calls!

You'll still be spending quite a lot of time playing in America?

Well, as long as I can. I've had a work permit for about four or five years. Jazz is a extremely cosmopolitan and eclectic music. You learn maybe much more by playing with a drummer who is from Brazil, or maybe a saxophone player from Sweden or somewhere. They will feed in something completely different and open your eyes. New York is one of those places where you're most likely to meet this sax player or that Brazilian drummer because everyone goes there - it's still the Mecca of the music.

Another group you're in is Acoustic

Triangle, with Malcolm Creese on bass and Gwilym Simcock on piano.

Well I know Malcolm through working with John and Cleo. He has quite a wonderful sound, he's incredibly appreciative of new music and excited about doing something totally acoustic. We often don't have any microphones for anything, not even for announcing. We just choose the right venues. It seems so natural and right.

Sometimes the audiences have been small and sometimes quite the opposite, but it can feel like you're on some *quietness* crusade – wrong word to use, but you know what I mean. There's so many screaming bands where the drums are too loud - and all you actually want to hear is beautiful sounds. We've got this young guy, Gwilym Simcock, he's only 23, and he's just a *phenomenal* piano player and his time is amazing. I taught him a bit at the Academy. I would say he's probably one of the UK's strongest pianists, probably ever!

The music's got a lot of classical influences in it as well, with arrangements of Ravel and a bit of Poulenc. Hopefully without getting too arty or removed, we can actually mix these worlds together!

And finally, your Storms/Nocturnes Trio with Joe Locke [vibes] and Geoff Keezer[piano] ?

That was a result of my release on Stretch, *Made by Walking*. I'd known Joe for years anyway, but then when I got together with Geoff Keezer - he's a wonderful writer as well – I love that sense once again, an acoustic sense of the chamber music format. Joe is such an absolute dynamo on the stage, it's very infectious. Some people were expecting this trio to be maybe a bit whimsical, but they come and hear it and are blown away by the rhythmic power of it, so that's great fun.

Geoff Keezer on piano is remarkable - he really analyses tunes.

He can tear them inside out. He's able to go off at tangents and has an amazing left hand. So you've got all that facility, which does bring the music inevitably slightly closer to classical music, but he swings and we have quite a good time doing swing-influenced pieces. It's a good vehicle for my writing and I play quite a lot of bass clarinet in that trio.

The second album has just come out - hopefully it and my other trio will co-exist. Storms/ Nocturnes uses amplification and can play on the regular circuit, whereas Acoustic Triangle tends to be a little more rarified, playing in churches and, say, converted theatres.

Some of it, I have to say, is about finding the right drummer and if you don't find the right drummer to play with, all you want to do is not have one. After all, everyone's got a good sense of rhythm in these bands, sometimes you don't need one.

Because it does mean you have to set up a load of PA, and half the time the audience just don't need that volume, I don't think. That's my take on it anyway!

You also play with Bill Bruford's Earthworks.

Indeed. Earthworks has run for about fifteen years now I think and I've been doing it for two years. Again, I think he wanted some fresh writing and we've toured the world actually with that band!

Bill [drums, formerly of Yes, King Crimson, Genesis] is one of the few guys of his generation who've made a point of really keeping up to date. He's completely his own man, but he has endeavoured to broaden his own parameters where some others of his generation have closed them off and I respect him a great deal for that, especially as he was one of my early heroes. That rock side is also very much part of *my* upbringing in the Seventies - I'm not a stranger to that at all.

So I love it all, the fact that I'm in two bands that have a very obvious lack of a drummer, then I'm in Bill's band - you've either got someone very personal and energetic and totally committed with something to say on your instrument or you're not anywhere!

When you were learning jazz, what early obstacles did you face?

One of the main ones would have been, in the early days, not hearing the music live or seeing it played. It was the result of someone coming into my school and playing live – I was about twelve - then I could see the spontaneity of it and the interaction and the energy of it, as well as hear it.

I've always had a soft spot for that jazz education side, to give people a chance to *see* musicians play, because normally it's just sterile, produced and compressed on MTV and it's not particularly real any more. If people can see a saxophone player playing, six feet in front of them, for the first time ever, they can feel the air coming out of the horn, it's incredible and always worth doing.

How did you learn jazz's harmonic side?

All the classical training I'd had up to that point must have helped. When I first started to play the sax I could see in my mind's eye a piano keyboard and that would help me through. I don't anymore so that was obviously one pictorial way of understanding harmonies.

And I slowly worked backwards from Coltrane as many people do, getting back into bebop land and starting to appreciate Dizzie Gillespie and Charlie Parker, Bud Powell, Wes Montgomery – in those days when photography was in black and white!

But I came to it through whatever was going on, through Seventies funk, English rock and all the classical stuff. I worked back and it probably wasn't until I was about twenty, or twenty-one when I really started to enjoy what Miles Davis was doing, because it wasn't in my upbringing, what my family listened to. So I worked into it slowly.

But definitely, the live experience was the one that turned me around. Everything made sense after that. It was rather like the difference between reading poetry yourself and going to hear someone good reading and *delivering* the poem.

I found this with Don Paterson in the ten years with Lammas. He's a great poet so we'd go to poetry festivals and play for a bit. He would be reading and some of the other poets would also read and I realised how much I'd got into poetry through the fact that it was performed.

If you ask the majority of people how did you get into whatever music you're into, they won't say because we heard it *live*. They'll say because of this record and 99% of it is recorded. – and that's nothing to do with *performance* anymore. So that's what I fear we're in danger of losing.

On soloing, you stress getting interaction within the band?

Yeah. You can't do it on your own, if you're talking about *building* a solo, it can sound extremely contrived if you try to raise some artifi-

cial climax. You have to be kind of *goal-oriented* in your ideas, you should make sure you don't stay on one level, and you should think to lead the band at various moments where you want to really *assert* your own personality and they should all be listening to you. And then it's effortless.

But you leave space, space for *dialogue*. It's always a drag when soloists, no matter how good they are, are not leaving any space for others to comment on it, so it just sounds a bit like those play along records. That bores me – *I* have been responsible for it myself, and that's one reason why I'm so hot on it now because I can hear myself on record, doing it! It took me a while to understand.

Good drummers will work with you in solos. They will match the level of density with what you're doing and will egg you on at the right moment. It's wonderful working with great drummers and I think Jeremy Stacey is a real natural. I've only recorded once with him on the 'Enter the Fire' album. Jeff Ballard is probably my favourite of all, he's quite incredible.

What about creating the element of surprise, of finding something new in a solo?

Yes, well you have to know the background material well and that's perhaps where this paradox of practice and repetition comes in. So you play things a lot of times until it's really in your blood. Only then can you kind of break out of the box and say, 'Oh, I'll do it this way!' because you know the foundations are so strong so you can seemingly utterly destroy them, but then you can come back because they're there, so you don't get lost.

I do worry sometimes when I hear people break out into very free music and perhaps if they're influenced by the kind of Coltrane aspect. You knew it was ok with Coltrane because he was writing pieces and had done it before. Like that tune, 'Twenty-six Two', it's Coltrane's sound and he's just so on the money with the swing, you know? So then when he comes to the later stuff, you can believe it all! But when someone takes it up from *just* that point, I can't believe it! It just sounds like an excuse.

Who are your main influences now?

Well, a lot of the music I got into as a student I still love, Berio, Takemitsu, Messiaen, Debussy, Ravel and Bartok and Stravinsky's amazing. I mean I know something like the 'Rite of Spring' - sounds hackneyed to talk about it but the orchestration is incredible. Messiaen - piano pieces like *Isle de Feu* are just terrific. They're new sounding even if they are not new any more. So classical music, that I started on within the family, has become a lasting influence and I look now towards different ways of synthesizing different elements of classical music.

Saxophonists-wise I don't think you can get much better than Joe Lovano. I've known him for about twelve years now. He's so lyrical, a bit like the great Italian tenor! He's grounded incredibly well in the history of the music and I'm glad that I'm able to take a lot of the influence of what he's about as a musician. And Joe Henderson, talking of saxophone players.

Another influence is Jan Garbarek. On the album *Belonging* , there's a piece called *Blossom*, which is amazing. It's about that need for lyricism. They're the long standing ones that I *always* love listening to.

But I also loved things that really, really swung, so early Art Blakey and being blown away by that. It's just his sense of energy! It's all the things that you sense are really on their own home base. That's convincing.

Jarrett seems always to have been one of those people. Also Kenny Wheeler, a lot of John Taylor and maybe others I haven't heard so much of.

And obviously I should mention Chick because now the influence is first hand. I love his stuff, especially the acoustic things he did with Gary Burton, so that was a very strong influence. One reason I have the vibes with the band Storms/Nocturnes is I'm sure because of Chick and Gary.

What about teaching and coaching in jazz?

If you get someone who's really ready, is committed and really looks like they're going to go on and be a professional, it's a joy, because you both grow. I've had the good fortune to have about three of four really top notch players and you can tell, week by week often, how much they've absorbed. And then you can hear their personalities develop, completely separate from your own.

For most, it's formulating and putting things into boxes, and trying to make it as understandable as possible; but nearly all the time , it all comes down to how well you can perceive things aurally, like if you can recognise an interval very quickly. The better your ears are, the less you have to rely on formulas.

I think one of the *best* things about teaching is that you're not trying to turn everyone into a star player, but their own appreciation of the music as a *listener* grows immensely, so you're creating educated audiences that love what they hear.

Some jazz manuals suggest that good

jazzmen can play every tune in every key? Do you do that?

I could probably have a good stab! But George Coleman, he's amazing at all that. He's one of these practice devils and can probably do all that – he frightens his rhythm sections by playing well- known tunes in a key they haven't practiced before! It's very good for them and I'm very glad I haven't been humiliated!

No, all of that is great - all you are hoping for in the end is the maximum amount of *freedom*. If your fingers are just playing patterns then it's not the maximising of freedom. So by playing things in different keys, you're perhaps being more creative by making different choices. So it's a great idea. I wouldn't necessarily recommend *all* twelve keys, more like five or six. Life is already short enough...

What do you see as the elements of your future development?

I'd like to create a greater understanding in myself — a real working synthesis of the strands of music that I love. Looking at different forms of structured composition and doing that in slightly more orchestrally oriented music, with jazz elements, for example. That in a way, it seems to me, is the music of the twenty-first century.

We've had so many decades of Afro-American influenced music which has worked its way right into the heart of what we traditionally call Western Music. Some of the most interesting music coming out now is that way inclined, you know, and that excites me a great deal.

Will it be improvised?

For instance, I've written a saxophone concerto where half of the solo is improvised and half of it is written out and it's up to the intelligence of the soloist to work in suitable improvisations with the textures of the orchestras. I hope to write a string of these concertos, one for piano,

vibes or flugelhorn or whatever. Working at Newcastle University will hopefully afford that opportunity with the Northern Sinfonia.

Also I can also deepen my own sense of purpose on the instrument. I think probably my best stuff is yet to come in both performing and composition. I mean I haven't reached some sort of plateau, like prodigies when they're twenty-two!

Another hope of mine — a few years ago I worked with John Taylor and he was just like this child at the piano. Chick as well, looking at the piano with fascination and think what shall I do now? But those guys are about sixty, so I want to be like that when I'm sixty! It's like a temporary amnesia so you can come to the music for the first time again and again. That's what I live on, really.

What are your ideas about the health of jazz in the UK? If you were a marketeer?

Well, when you go to other countries, it's quite a pleasant surprise because people really do go out to gigs and that's lovely. There is a certain lethargy here at times. I think, that's why the vocalists do so well, because people will always like something light around the house to put on. Sometimes it's not really much to do with jazz. We are all very affected by what serves a corporate need and quite often the real musical food won't be interesting to the corporations. Despite this, we do have some great festivals here and very discerning audiences.

But you've got to look at the up side too. Robbie Williams did all that big band stuff —he introduced a generation that knew *nothing* about those songs and they are great songs really, so it's good for us all.

And the same for the singers that are getting a lot of attention at the moment — there's one particular male singer that's currently been chosen as the next star — and good for him. But when you put him next to some of the young players who can play at several levels at once, like Gwilym, there's no contest in my view — they deserve to hit the world stage, not instead of, but as well as the singers.

There are two music disciplines now — one which is making recorded music and another which is putting on great live performances. You learn to do both as an instrumentalist, but the digi-recording culture is eclipsing the organic *here and now* tradition that was once closer to our community.

So I'd like to say that it's healthier - but I do have doubts! Fortunately there will always be true creative musicians. The music will always be healthy underneath, it's just the amount of time that the media choose to give to it.

There's a lot of good young players coming through, maybe there'll be a wave resulting from that?

Yes, there's always been good players — but it's whether they'll ever get any attention. The way to get really good is if they get a chance to keep playing, building rapport with musicians. To get alongside people far better than them, so they can really get whipped into shape and taught.

But when you play at festivals and you get these really great audiences, you do feel as if they've understood the music — they are *blessed* times because you feel that humanity is listen-

ing, one to the other. Not to you in any 'ego' style way, but that these people are all *open*. You feel as if you could sit any one of them down and have a fascinating conversation with them - there's hope for the world. Even when I'm part of the audience, you feel there's communion going on and I live for that!

Selected CDs	
Rising Tide	Storms/Nocturnes [2003, Sirocco Music]
Soho Story	Dean Street Underground Orchestra [2002, Dean Street Records]
Change of Season	Tim Garland [2004, Sirocco Music]
Website: www.timgarland.com	

Geoff Gascoyne

Geoff Gascoyne, born in Nottingham in November 1963, is a much sought-after jazz bass and arranger whose experience covers the spectrum from pop music and crossover to modern jazz mainstream. His interests are migrating increasingly towards arranging and composing. He tackles composition and arranging challenges across a wide range of music styles in an imaginative and original manner and is valued by bandleaders, especially currently the singer Jamie Cullum.

Geoff has worked in a variety of bands from Everything but the girl (1989) to best selling rap, jazz sampling band US3 in 1994. Then, switching to acoustic bass and jazz, he gained experience playing in the bands of Jim Mullen and Georgie Fame. He is currently the bass player and principal arranging force behind the remarkably successful Jamie Cullum, as principal arranger of his albums, including the platinum-selling *Twenty Something* [2003, Universal] for which he also wrote the piano music score and book. Since this interview, he has come to work exclusively with Jamie Cullum.

Geoff has played with a wide range of other leading jazz players including Gerard Presencer, Tim Garland, Ben Castle, Jim Watson, Andy Panayi and singers Claire Martin, Trudy Kerr and Ian Shaw.

Under his own leadership, Geoff has issued three acclaimed albums of original compositions; *Voices of Spring*, *Autumn* and *Songs of the Summer*.

He is married to the Australian jazz singer Trudy Kerr, for whom he arranges.

What music can you first remember listening to?

At home I can remember listening to Nat King Cole – my parents used to listen to him a lot, my Mum liked the Stylistics, that soul stuff, while my Dad liked the big bands. I wasn't actually particularly fond of it at the time.

When did you first pick up a musical instrument?

I started playing piano when I was six, so by the time I was ten I was very into classical music. I was playing Beethoven, Chopin and Mozart - that kind of stuff. I remember being taken out to hear orchestral music, and I was quite into that. Though I was not then particularly into the music they listened to, I've come back to it in the last few years and I love it now.

They didn't play any instruments so the only influence I had was my granddad, and he played piano in a pub. The family's from the East End, my Mum's family are from Bethnal Green and her Dad was really into that honky-tonk piano, which I was fond of when I was 13 or 14. I was a bit bored by that time with just classical music, so I discovered Scott Joplin and piano rags, and that was my first introduction to jazz.

When were your first gigs?

By the age of fifteen, classical music had dropped out of it a bit. I'd rebelled a bit, I'd started messing around with other instruments and had started playing electric bass.

I tried clarinet, electric guitar and some others, but finally I got to play in a school group. They needed a bass player so I decided to buy a bass and that's how it all started. We were playing rock and punk music really – so those were my first proper gigs when I was around sixteen.

Was there any other music?

I took my piano lessons outside school. I was very good very early and I actually did my Grade 8 [exam], the highest piano [Board] exam when I was thirteen. The stuff that went on in school was mainly singing and there wasn't much piano. I did a few concerts in school assembly, playing piano and a few talent shows.

I was more into art to be honest and was good at painting, so that's what I was concentrating on. When I left school I wasn't totally sure what I was going to do, so I decided to go to art college.

I had grown up in Hertfordshire and came up to London to go to art school. I got into St. Martins, a very good school, to do a painting degree and stayed there for three years, but during that time I was still playing music and there was a kind of conflict between the two.

When was your decision to be a musician?

It was a bit awkward, especially in my last year at college - I was signed with a pop band - not well known - but it had a publishing deal and we were on a retainer, so we got money every month for just being with the band. Then the demands of that became a bit too great. So finally in my last year I decided to leave college - I didn't actually finish my degree course, there was such conflict and it was a difficult decision.

But when I made it, it was a big relief. I realised that was what I was going to do with my life.

I love painting but I love music as well and they are so similar but it takes up too much of your time and too much of your creative energy to keep them both going to the same intensity. I remember the day I left college - it was such a relief, it meant turning into an adult if you like, deciding where you're going to go and what you're going to do. So it was a big turning point in my life.

You've played in a number of jazz-influenced bands.

I hadn't discovered jazz at this stage, I was just an electric bass player – I'd stopped playing the piano at the age of 15, didn't touch it for maybe 10 years, which I kind of regret now in some ways. I learnt the electric bass, got lots of experience with pop bands and this led on to getting the gig with Everything but the Girl, a big turning point for me in 1989-90. So I went on my first world tour with the band and we went round the States, Japan, and Europe. It was amazing - proper tour buses, proper hotels, proper treatment. It was fantastic music and it had a bit of jazz influence, in that they had recorded the music initially in America with a producer called Tommy Lapuma. He'd got in a lot of jazz musicians to play their pop music, so it was kind of jazzy and played with a jazz attitude. And all the other musicians in the band were kind of jazz musicians anyway and I was just starting to get into jazz by then, it was influencing me more and I was starting to study it. Plus while we were on tour we had an American saxophone player called Kurt Whalum, a well-respected guest jazz player, who would take us round to the jazz clubs – a great experience.

Then there was US3, in 1994-95, they were a rap, kind of crossover group I played with for a while. They were well known for taking Blue Note samples – then a producer and a DJ made them into loops and put back-beats behind them and got guys to rap over the top. They went on tour with a rhythm section and horns and I did a world tour with them as well in 1995. Not quite as enjoyable as 'Everything but the Girl;' but just another thing I did.

And now jazz in the form of Jim Mullen.

Jim Mullen is one of the musicians I credit as being one of my influences on the British jazz scene. When I was learning, I used to go and hang out down the 606 Club in Chelsea, like a lot of musicians. At the time it was - and probably still is - a good place for meeting other musicians and a good place for jamming very late.

You jam with the guys you're inspired by. So I remember sitting in with Jim Mullen's band. He was very supportive and then I got some gigs. I used to get some gigs deputising for Lawrence Cottle on electric bass and finally I got some gigs with Jim Mullen's band and I just remember him being so supportive as a musician as well as a human being.

Then in 1995, I recorded my first album [*Voices of Spring*] as a leader and I asked him to guest on it, which he did willingly and supported with some ideas for arranging. He's a very well respected musician - a backbone if you like, of the British jazz scene.

I used to go down to the Half Moon in Putney where Morrissey-Mullen used to play. This was another hangout for musicians and a big influence on me. At this time I have to say I wasn't playing acoustic bass - I was only playing electric bass, so it was about then that I started learning acoustic, probably in 1993/94, and started taking it seriously. My reasons were I

was getting more and more into jazz and that's the traditional sound everyone wants.

I was quite a well-established electric bass player by this time, so people found out I was starting to play acoustic bass and I started getting gigs for it – I'll admit I wasn't very good at acoustic bass but it's like the old joke – the guy comes for an acoustic bass lesson, and the teacher says 'the first lesson is the E string'; he comes back next week and 'it's the A string'. He phones up the third week and says 'I can't make it; I've got a gig!' It was almost like that, people book you because they like the sound, you know?

Since then I've obviously put a lot of time and practice into it while I was working with Ian Shaw in his band on electric bass and with Jim Mullen.

You've been playing regularly with Georgie Fame.

I was doing a festival with Jim in Germany - in Inglestadt I think - and that's when I first met Georgie Fame who was guesting with the quartet. I remember talking to Georgie and getting on quite well and he remembered me because a year later he called me. I met some other guys who were in his band, Alan Skidmore and Guy Barker and I was recommended to join his group. I've been in Georgie's band ever since.

I have also been working with the opera singer, Sally Burgess for a long time. We met through her husband, Neil Thornton, a piano player and she started cabaret, crossover opera work, so I started with her. I've worked with her and the English National Opera and various stuff with orchestras, which has been fantastic. It involves a jazz trio - we did a crossover thing of Rogers and Hart with the ENO last year as a tribute for the centenary of Rogers and Hart. I thought it was amazing.

In 1997 when I was quite well established and started getting a lot of acoustic bass work, I worked with the piano player, Peter Churchill. He is one of the main piano teachers in London and teaches at the Guildhall School of Music. We used to play a lot. I was teaching at the Royal Academy part-time, and I had some studio time at the Academy. So me and Pete were on a gig together and decided to play some Christmas carols and it sounded so good, we thought 'Let's make an album.'

So May or June the following year we put this album out, *Winter Wonderland*, mainly duets and good fun to do. And every year now we play a concert at the Royal Festival Hall, just playing that same music.

You were involved in producing the RockSchool syllabus?

This was a venture run by Adrian and Norton York. Norton is a piano player I met – you realise how incestuous the whole jazz scene is – you can follow everything back to people I've met! And it's interesting how all these things follow through the ages, one thing links to something else!

Anyway I met Adrian York in Ian Shaw's band initially and I've been working on and off with him through the years. He was involved with this RockSchool, which was a Trinity-validated course for guitar, bass and drums. They set up a syllabus, have exams, like the graded piano exams but they wanted to have grades for rock, pop and jazz guitar, bass and drums. So Adrian decided to put this syllabus together and I was the bass expert. It took weeks of work and came up with a whole list of books, which I believe are very popular. There's a play-along CD with each one - so we spent 3 or 4 weeks just recording all these exams, for grades 0,1,2,3,4,5, 6 and 8. There's no number 7! And each had about 5 or 6 pieces which we had to record, mixing each track without the bass and

each one without the guitar, so each instrument could play along with it as well.

It's been really successful – I know a lot of people who use these in schools. I use it in my teaching as well now, for sight-reading and things to play along to. It's a very good teaching tool. It's a bit more specific than the James Aebersold series – that's really for jazz musicians to blow solos over. This is written, all the parts are written and specific. There are small snippets of improvisation but most of it is grooves and the types of tunes that we've written. We couldn't use copyrighted material so we were all commissioned to write specific music. I wrote a tune that was a bit like Spice Girls, something a bit like Oasis – they all sounded like something else, something the kids could relate to – and the tune would be called the *Spice of something*. I still get small royalty cheques for the compositions, so the books must be selling!

What did you have to learn when switching to jazz?

Firstly, *nobody* tells you what to learn when you start. What I did was *listen*; it's a listening art form. I used to transcribe things; I still do, but not as much any more. The way I look at it, it's like learning a language and you learn a set vocabulary that other people have established - you know we call it 'licks' – where you recreate a lick or phrase. I remember when I started transcribing – I used to love Charlie Parker, still do – transcribing a couple of his solos, writing them out note for note and then to play them - it's not as easy on the bass but you're still learning the *vocabulary*. I think that's the crux, if you like of, how to learn jazz. You have to learn the vocabulary and use the licks to find your way through the chord changes you are playing over.

How do you teach jazz?

It's very difficult *teaching* jazz, I've found all you can do is just say to my students – 'this is how I did it, listen to this – what do you think?' For instance, on this C chord I could play this chord or this other – but that's not the end of it, your

options are infinite, you know? But in jazz, you can play anything you like with any tone, any style, and any speed you want.

That's the beauty of it and I think that's why it's such a great art form and why I'll never stop learning – you're always creating something and learning as you go on. That's why I finally came to jazz, because I want to keep learning - I'm very inquisitive.

I think maybe, in some ways, jazz education is a bit of a contradiction really. But I remember going on the Wavenden Jazz Course Summer School and I think that was quite a good environment where people are all thrown together for a week. You get to play a lot with no distractions and I'd recommend that to anyone.

How do you explain what distinguishes a competent bass player from a first class bass player? For instance, getting different character from each note?

That's not really so much about jazz, it's about getting a good sound out of your instrument, that's something completely different. Getting to be one with your instrument and getting a good sound and knowing your vocabulary takes a lot of years too. There's no shortcut to being a good musician or learning jazz, you have to know the vocabulary, the idiom.

I don't talk about my own sound too much because it's hard for me to judge, I still consider myself a beginner in a lot of ways, I've got so far to go.

Who are your main musical influences?

The pop industry gave me my grounding - it gave me a good discipline for the way I am now. The way that pop musicians view music is eight bars, then another eight bars, so it's very sectional, and you'll get very aware of that when you play with discipline on a tour, the same music every night. You can be almost playing the same notes every night. You get aware of very subtle things like the length of the notes or how short they are, where you're going to play a fill or something a bit out, so that has maybe given me some more discipline than some jazz musicians have.

This discipline is probably why I play with a lot of singers - that together with having a good feeling for a song. But it's hard for me to judge.

Within jazz, the bass players influencing me are the obvious - Ray Brown, Charlie Haden are my two inspirations, I think. There are electric bass players like Jaco Pastorius. But I tend to be more inspired by composers and players, you know piano and sax players – John Coltrane, Charlie Parker, Duke Ellington - all the obvious people I listen to.

And I'm always buying different kinds of CDs - the last I bought a couple of days ago was the Oscar Peterson Trio, Count Basie's *April in Paris*, Blossom Dearie – I quite like a lot of singers actually – I love Harry Connick Jnr, he's fantastic, Frank Sinatra - I listen to him a lot. Also a lot of the newer guys, Kurt Elling, mainly the male singers probably because I'd like to be a singer. Probably frustrated!

What about technique and speed on the instrument?

Again, that's a personal thing – when I teach, it's funny, I never talk about technique and when I've thought about technique for myself, it's just kind of evolved. I was always interested in playing standards, so I used to play at home as many different standards as I could in as many different keys and this is what you need out on a gig. If a singer calls for *All the Things you are* in C instead of Ab you must be able to switch and know the changes so well you just use your ears.

Now you have the opportunity to do your own CDs as bandleader and your own compositions seem very well critically received.

For the last few years, as I'm working more and more I tend to practice less at home, because I'm playing all the time in the evening. So what's happening is I am taking up with the piano again, which is why I'm composing and arranging more. So when I get time at home, I tend to compose.

I do a lot of arranging for people – mainly singers and people are always asking me to do arrangements for them – so for Claire Martin's last album, Ian Shaw's albums I've done some stuff, some for Georgie Fame's last album, Trudy Kerr's albums – of course we arrange together – Jamie Cullum's album and we'll be doing a new album for him soon.

It's ongoing so I'm getting better and faster at it. And I'm arranging for other people you wouldn't know. Of my own compositions, I throw out a lot but sift out all the good stuff.

What future developments are you looking at?

I'm in the process of putting a new band together. My quartet on *Songs of Summer*, which is Ben Castle, Gareth Williams and Sebastiaan de Krom, I've had that group for three years and I've decided now that I'll get back to playing electric bass again, as it's getting a bit neglected. Currently everyone just wants acoustic bass. So this year I've got another week at Ronnie Scott's in April and I thought I'll put a new group together and play electric bass maybe.

Also get back to my roots and play some Charlie Parker music – I'm trying to arrange some Charlie Parker music for electric bass, electric guitar, alto saxophone, and drums with a completely new group. That's what I will do this

year, I'm just working on it at the moment. So we'll see what happens.

In the future, I want to arrange for big bands, get commissions – all that because I love composition more than anything at the moment.

How do you view the current state of jazz in the UK?

Since I started in the last fifteen years, I think there's been so many new great musicians coming in and more jazz courses opening up. Trinity College has just moved premises and that will open out their course. The Royal Academy's course is expanding, so this is creating a lot more young jazz musicians – it's great, not so great when you haven't got as much work because the young guys are coming up to replace you but – I don't seem to be losing any work, there is always enough work – probably just good healthy competition. So it's all in a good state and there's a lot going on.

Are we comparable with the US?

Oh, they're a few generations ahead of us, aren't they? Give us another fifty years, maybe just twenty years, it's difficult to say...

Selected CDs		
Songs of the Summer	Geoff Gascoyne	[2002, Jazzizit]
Autumn	Geoff Gascoyne	[2000, Jazzizit]
Twenty Something	Jamie Cullum	[2003, Universal]
Website: www.geoffgascoyne.com		

Nigel Hitchcock

Nigel Hitchcock, born in Rustington in 1971, is one of the leading virtuoso jazz alto sax players in the UK, with a career spanning jazz and a wide variety of leading session work. This has included playing or recording with Ray Charles, Carleen Anderson, Robbie Williams, Pink Floyd, James Brown, the Spice Girls and music for a documentary on Uzbekistan. He also plays tenor sax.

Nigel first picked up the alto at age eight, joining the National Youth Jazz Orchestra at the still tender age of eleven. He turned professional before leaving school at sixteen. Nigel's jazz playing career has included membership of the contemporary jazz saxophone quartet, Itchy Feet, with whom he toured Europe and Asia.

He has played with leading players including Don Weller, Guy Barker , Lawrence Cottle and the singer Claire Martin. He has gigged and recorded with groups lead by Stan and Clark Tracey, Colin Towns' Mask Orchestra and many others.

As leader Nigel recorded *Snake Ranch Sessions* in 1997 with Robin Aspland (piano), Lawrence Cottle (bass), and Ian Thomas (drums).

He was a member of the award-winning *Celebrating the Jazz Couriers* whose music commemorates the music of the legendary 1960s band led by Tubby Hayes and Ronnie Scott.

Among awards he has gained are the Schlitz Prize for Rising Star, the Cleo Lane Personal Award and the Pat Smythe Award.

What was the first kind of music you can remember listening to?

There was lots of classical music in the house, because my eldest sisters play violin, piano and flute and my brother was learning the clarinet. But then after a short period of playing the clarinet, my brother moved to saxophone, and he started bringing home Count Basie, including a version of *C Jam Blues*, plus things like the Syd Lawrence Orchestra and Glen Miller, Bennie Goodman, Artie Shaw. So there was quite a mix.

When did you first pick up an instrument?

I started on the recorder when I was six, and started playing the alto when I was eight. Then flute and clarinet came shortly after, more out of necessity than want. I wanted to be like my big brother, so they said go off and see this saxophone teacher and after one lesson, he put me on alto in the local big band. Then it was playing everything from *In the Mood* to *Edelweiss*.

That seems a terrifically early start.

Yes, well when you're a kid, you soak up things like a sponge, totally open to everything. Also you don't realise how difficult it's supposed to be. It's a great advantage – my brother is five years older than me and that gap was just enough for him to realise how difficult some things were. I heard Michael Brecker when I was eleven. 'Ah, so this is how you're supposed to play the saxophone then.'

Did you do other things as a boy? Go out and kick a football?

Did a bit, but wasn't that interested. I would come home from school and started playing, from age eight to eleven. I just didn't put the saxophone down at all.

Then when I joined the National Youth Jazz Orchestra [at age 11], I realised some things about playing, that it's not the be-all and end-all' of it. It's more important to have a life-enhancing experience, be it going to the pub, it's more beneficial to your playing than sitting in and playing by yourself. Because it makes you the person you are and the character you are — *that's* my philosophy.

You joined the NYJO and within a year you had been given the main alto chair. When do they play?

Every Saturday morning there's a rehearsal in central London and then there were gigs at all sorts of times. Generally there'd be gigs at odd times throughout the year, and once a year there'd be a tour with a singer. In the first few years, we played with Vic Damone, Peggy Lee, Buddy Greco and Al Martino.

That's an impressive collection.

Absolutely! Yes, they'd say to them, come and play with this youth big band, because though this orchestra is for young players, the standard of musician is as good as you can possibly get *without* booking a professional band at full rate!

Did you go through the music exam system?

I took Grades on the clarinet – grade 3 and grade 5, I think I got distinctions. I took Grade 5 theory which you need in order to take Grade 8, and then I never bothered to take Grade 8 because by that time, I'd already done numerous TV shows [laughter] on clarinet, sax etc. It's kind of irrelevant to have a piece of paper that says Grade 8! I'm glad that I had the experience of the examination board though, because that's one of the hardest things that I think a

musician can ever do. It's terrifying auditioning and taking exams.

So at the tender age of sixteen, you said goodbye to school and on with session work in Central London.

Well, funnily enough, in my last year at school, when I was 16, I'd been working so much I had about an eight percent attendance record and the only exams I got were English Language, Maths and Music. I'd already decided to be a musician and I'd already been on the road for three to four years and touring. My last day at school, I was there for a couple of hours, then moved straight to a flat in Marble Arch and didn't stop working for about five months – I was doing TV adverts, pop records, - I was playing with the Pasadenas, a pop band at the time – a black soul outfit. I worked in the background – I like to go into the studio, do my thing, generally first take and then I go.

However, after a few months, the work dried up. There was a general consensus among musicians that somebody sixteen years old didn't need to be earning £1,000 a week when there were people of forty and fifty who had four kids and a big house. So though I went in and did things, there was still a pecking order, which when I was that age was *unbelievably* infuriating - but now I do understand it.

There are also relationships, who works with who?

Yes, well there are relationships, but I've had some lean times you know. I've moved away from home and moved back about half a dozen times. The last time was two years ago when I was back with my parents again for ten months. So it's not easy.

What types of session work do you do?

Absolutely everything! Every style of music conceivable I have played! There are straightforward things like pop solos, I've done lots of movies – there was a shot of Kim Basinger in a film, made up as a cartoon called 'Cool World' and Mark Isham did the music. For cartoons, the stuff is always off the wall, instantly changing. We did 'A Hundred and Two Dalmatians', in fact they got me to play some really fast bebop, and then they animated one of the spots on a dog's back to the time of the bebop – interesting effect!

Another time I turned up at eight o' clock on a Sunday morning to find a harpist, a cello player, a sitar player and a guru tabla player with ten disciples – mad, but it was to do a documentary on Uzbekistan!

The staple diet has been pop singles for a long time – the scene now is nothing like it used to be – but still some of that, some film music, a few TV commercials – again nothing like there used to be – there was time when I did at least five a week - now I do about one every 4 months!

Because a lot of library music is used, the Musicians Union have changed the rules, made it cheaper for television stations to use music.

The business is going to die if we're not careful. Anyway, so I do any and all kinds of music from Ravel's Bolero to Madness.

Tony Coe's memorable sax recording was of the Pink Panther theme, what would you say yours was?

Oh, that's tough! What about EastEnders – for a short spell of time there were two different saxophone players – which was Dave O'Higgins and me. But so many people wrote in and complained about it they put the old theme back on!

On the Fast Show, *Please release me* is me. Also there's a bit at the front of Blue Peter now 'dubben-dubba, dubben-dubba, dubben-dubba, dubben dubba, da'. Two saxes in unison. A few things like that. So the big thing I'm famous for has yet to happen, something to look forward to!

You were doing session work and then you joined the band *Itchy Fingers* – what age was that?

I was seventeen – 1988 – no, not very old. One of the saxophone players, John Graham, had been away in South America and had seen this crystal blue water, and had decided to dive in and it turned out to be about six inches deep – so he managed to break three of his fingers! And two days later they were going to Berlin for ten days for a Saxophone Quartet Festival.

They'd heard that I'd got a photographic memory and I could do this and that, so I got called to his place in Clapham where we did all the rehearsing – and that's how I got that gig.

What sort of a band was Itchy Fingers?

Just four saxophone players, I played alto, John Graham played alto, soprano and tenor, Mike Mower played tenor and flute and Howard Turner played baritone. And because you can all carry your saxophones, it means you can do gigs in strange places, go to the middle of a forest in Bavaria and not have to worry about having to plug an amp in. Also we went to Indonesia and played for the Sultan of Brunei – one of his grand-children was in this school and had all his minders around him, but the school only had a roof and a few fans to it, and was open all around, no walls, and there we were, playing to these children who had never seen saxophones and at the same time, here was this kid with about a million pounds worth of gold hanging round his neck, really bizarre!

We also toured around Europe a lot and I enjoyed that. The music was mostly written down and we played with clip on microphones so everybody had to learn it. I was with them for 18 months and during it there were a number of tours, around three weeks in each place. We would go to Hong Kong for a week, come back, then three to four weeks in Germany, come home have another week in Holland.

It was Stravinsky-esk, mad, off-the-wall a lot of it. He's a fantastic arranger, Mike Mower! Really contemporary saxophone music. You know, lots of variety – madness!

You've received 3 jazz awards – firstly the Schlitz Award for Rising Star.

I'm always baffled about the jazz awards, all of them. I don't know who votes for them or who decides. I guess being in Itchy Fingers must have given me enough profile to be noted. And I have to say from the musician's point of view, it's the kiss of death to take them seriously. For instance, I don't remember if it was the Schlitz or another award, but they can't hand it out to the same person every year. If they could, Pete King will still be winning it in eighty years time – everybody loves him, everybody knows him, right generation, so most people vote for him, so it's only out of default that we have a lucky dip of one of the other ones this year.

How about the Cleo Lane Personal Award?

It did mean more as I do know John and Cleo quite well. And she was lovely as well, because she invited me to a lunch with Princess Margaret

to collect my award, and I did have to say 'I'll join you for desert, because I've got a session', so the least I could do was join them after. So I did the session, and forgot to get dressed up so I'm sitting on a table with Cleo Lane and Princess Margaret and I'm wearing gear like this! So I said Hi, I nicked a piece of roast beef and a sweet, got my award and went off to do a gig somewhere. And she loved it – she was completely impressed...possibly...

The Pat Smythe Trust Award?

That one means a lot to me – because that was voted for by musicians, and Pat Smythe though I never met him, has obviously influenced an awful lot of people on the scene here. Jason Rebello's got it, and probably Gerard [Presencer]. And also I think I was only about the second person to win it. But it was very helpful because I bought a car with it so I could get to some of these gigs!

What have you been working at since then?

It's been a truly *bizarre* mix over the last few years. From doing the Jazz Couriers at the Bulls Head one night, to doing Robbie Williams at the BRIT Awards the next. It's been up and down the whole time.

Is one more rewarding than the other?

Yes, well, let's say I don't do Robbie Williams

for fun, or lots of things with Tom Jones and TV Specials and so on. I much prefer doing the jazz gigs. If only they paid as much as the pop thing. Actually as time goes on, the pop gigs are getting worse and worse paid, even the guys in the band become more like extras, staff, and the 'turn' [end of line] is all they feel they need. – it doesn't interest me any more.

Because the recording industry is getting squeezed these days?

Oh, unbelievably. With all the downloads of MP3s across the Net, that kind of thing. It's changing the way the record business works. And as a jazz musician I support it really because for me the best thing I could do is make an album, sell it off of a website, you know? Make ALL of the money back on it.

As it is, the best jazz deal I've been offered is £1,500 up front and 5% of the takings. Just 5%. Now the word jazz covers many sins. When you say you're going to make a jazz album, most people consider the album I made – that's who I am - I'm *that* alto player. They'd probably be horrified to hear me play like Pharaoh Saunders on the tenor. As a session musician and as a passionate lover of music, I'd like to play in *hundreds* of different styles – I like to play like Stan Getz or John Coltrane or whoever, I like the variety. I hate this trying endlessly to prove you are this one thing, this one identity, because I'm not at all.

I notice that in the *SnakeRanch Sessions* album – a pretty virtuoso session - no matter how fast the music, your tone still remains good.

Yeah! I try not to throw the tone out the window just because you trying to do something flash. It's all about control, with the alto. It's *such* a woman, you've got to get it by both hips!

Tell me about your revival of the Jazz Couriers? Mornington Lockett had a chat with Martin Drew to start it off?

Yes, well Mornington and Martin had both played with Ronnie Scott a lot before he passed away, and the music of Tubby Hayes and Ronnie Scott from the Fifties are still *burning* modern contemporary tunes. Basically the energy that they put out at that time is what a lot of British people were missing on the British jazz scene. So Mornington thought it would be a good idea to transcribe some of the tunes.

And actually right from the word go there's been a real vibe from some of the gigs, you almost feel like Tubby and Ronnie are having a laugh up in the stalls. You know, occasionally we play little pastiches of Ronnie and Tubby and the way they played, but we're not trying to emulate the way they played it, it's just paying homage to them in this time, you know? So it's not really the Jazz Couriers but we call it 'Celebrating the Jazz Couriers' and it's great fun! Mornington Lockett's such a fine player to have; we spark each other off so it's quite inspiring. And both me and Mornington have a vast vocabulary and sometimes you can't retain that on a gig all the time and it takes one person to play something to remind you of a whole load of other stuff - you then play that and have a really good night!

When you were first picking up the alto, how do you reckon you learned how to improvise?

Well, the first time that I came across this, my jazz teacher said, 'There's something that says 2 bars '*extemporisation ad libertum*' and I said, 'What's that?' and he said, 'Well, it's basically in the A major chord, here are the notes in that scale, so that's what you play – but I'm not a jazz musician so don't ask me! Go away and listen to Charlie Parker or whoever.'

And I was just put in the right direction of listening to people and picked it up naturally really, from the people around me, from records. I was lucky because my brother was five years older, he had older friends, so someone said, 'Oh, listen to this' and they gave me a National Youth Jazz Orchestra record with Chris Hunter, an astounding saxophone player. I thought ok, that's what the saxophone is supposed to do, and just learnt all that kind of stuff.

A lot of it is also being around people and having things played to you that you love and you genuinely have to want to know what it is they are doing. It's one thing to listen to something and say, 'That's amazing' and be a punter, but if you listen to it and say, 'I'm going to listen to that two seconds a million times now because I don't know what it is!' That's the sort of brain I've got.

Have you ever had any of these recording devices for slower playback at the same frequency?

What I did have was my mother's linguists record player that plays at half speed so I recorded it at half speed and then transcribed it at the soprano – did that with a Michael Brecker solo, just did it on the one solo, now I can hear Michael Brecker at full speed…just write it out, which is great – but I spent about one month transcribing one solo three octaves away from where it was. That is, about five to six hours a day and going over it to make sure I got every note right, making sure I could play along with it.

Do you do anything like that now?

I love to play so much that it's a sacred event to me and I feel I'm watering it down listening to music at home. When I'm at home I'd rather cook fresh food, watch movies and play games, so it's great when I go out and play jazz with that enthusiasm again!

We did two gigs about two weeks ago, and then I went away on holiday and I didn't touch my tenor all week. Got back, got to the gig, said to Mornington, 'I'd better have a look at the sax, you know, haven't played since the last gig.' Got it out and played the best I've played in months. It's about being fresh and being a child!

Who are your main musical influences?

Michael Brecker, he's god number 1, has been since I first heard him, aged eleven. Obviously Charlie Parker, Cannonball Adderley – Chris Hunter I have to mention, an English alto player who was in the NYJO. He moved to New York and started doing a lot of work with David Sanborn – that kind of player but more technical.

As far as music generally, I'm a big fan of Chick Corea and I was weaned on Johnny Hodges. When I first started playing – I'd been playing a couple of weeks, my teacher said, 'Look, this is the sound, what you do to make the instrument sing, really put a voice through it.'

If I listen to music at home now, I'd rather listen to Stravinsky, and I find I'm more and more into the heavy classical things. Because there's a very fine line between classical music and jazz in the sense that I feel that when I'm playing the saxophone it should be more *instant composition*, as opposed to reeling out things you know all the time. And what Stravinsky did I now think is astounding, I'd be very happy to incorporate some of that into my playing.

Was your Quartet playing regularly?

At the time I made the Snake Ranch CD, we were doing a few odd gigs here and there, and we'd all been playing together for years - so no problem, we just went and made the CD. But just the same I never really got it together to go and do gigs – the sad story is I sat down and spent two months calling fifty venues to get a gig with my quartet – I got a gig at the 606 [Club] and one at the Bulls Head. And even though I'd got the Cleo Lane Personal Award at Wavenden, they didn't know who I was. And I couldn't play there because my name wasn't on the list. Things like that. So you know, it was so impossible to get gigs, I gave up really. I love jazz, but I don't need to suffer and starve for it. Rather do something else.

What about working on the continent?

I have been doing a few jazz gigs in Europe in the last few months, and there are some fantastic players over there. Unfortunately they seem to have the attitude, that if you're not from America, then you're not the real deal! I was playing with a rhythm section in this club in Holland, and they'd been there with Rick

Margitza, and Bob Malak, and Tim Armocost as well – three amazing New York tenor players.

But when I played there they said the musicians had the best fun they'd ever had. I didn't give them any bullshit – I'm not American, not big-time, I'm out for the good of people out to have a nice time, don't need to ensure I got such-and-such a quota of vodka in my room. But basically the club wouldn't have me back again because I'm not American and didn't pull in enough people! And that's so sad. It makes me just think well, I'm not that interested in it. But if there's a gig, I'm quite happy to go to places, I love to travel and do these things.

How's the future looking?

More and more what's coming up is I'm writing library music – the music that gets put on a shelf and then when somebody wants twenty seconds of music to go behind the sports results they call up a library company and ask, and they say – have this! And they licence them the music. Most of what I've done is a minute or thirty seconds long and aimed at TV.

It's like a lottery ticket, mostly it's sitting around waiting. One of my pieces was on a Head n Shoulders advert - they use just 3 seconds of sexy saxophone at the beginning and I make quite a bit of money out of it and that's a nice surprise. But there are people who make a very good living – you could make two hundred grand a year if you do nothing but write library music. And with the Internet, there seems to be less and less need to be in the city - I'd much rather have

a nice home life, an organic vegetable garden and a dog, and send files across to where its needed.

These days I write files and send it to a drummer who sends me the drums back and sends it to the bass player and he sends me the bass back. There's no need to use studios any more. So the only need to get together is to play jazz, which is great!

More and more, my ambition is to have a reclusive life. I love the countryside, I love nature, and I much prefer animals to people on the whole!

Whatever the state of health of jazz in the UK, it's generally agreed that there are a lot of graduate students coming up, have you any words for them?

Er, yes... good luck! I've had a couple of students from the Royal Academy whom I've given lessons to. They're fantastic players, full of enthusiasm, dying to do everything. Now I'm 32 years old and I'm still looking up to the generation above me in their forties who are doing all the TV things and stuff and they're still waiting for the generation above them to move out. Now these kids are 19 years old or so, they are going to be 50, before they get a sniff of my work. So I don't know what they are going to do, where they are going to play, or who they will play with. What I notice is that they seem to be a bit cocky about the fact that they know this, or know that, how that works, and 'I don't want to learn to become a great reader, I just want to be a great jazz player and have my own voice.'

Well, if you want to be shouting at yourself in your own home, OK, but if you want to have a voice to get out to the public, you need a different medium because jazz *isn't* going to get you heard, you know? Jazz is a fairly small world.

Really I hope they can get it together, I hope there's enough of them. But it seems to be that jazz is only for musicians. There's a few people above 50 years old at these gigs and anybody younger than that is a *player*. Now musicians don't pay to see other musicians, they get in for free. But the only people left who are interested, are musicians.

There are different brackets to jazz, the Bulls Head [at Barnes] is more realistic in that it's Stan Tracey and straightahead bebop, whereas if you go to the Jazz Café, it's to see the YellowJackets and Kenny G or maybe Diana Krall. So is it jazz or is it commercial?

Last question – do you have perfect pitch and can it cause problems?

Yes, I do. It winds me up if things are out of tune. It's not too bad on a piano, the things that drive me nuts are records just playing slightly fast, or slightly slow – drives me absolutely *crackers*!

And when you play in England, the tuning frequency is A440 and when you play in Germany it's A444 and in America it's A442. So England is the flattest of them all, but to me that is the *true* note, don't know if that's something you become attuned to or born with. It's a really subtle amount; you can make up the difference by different lipping! But you go into some bands here, you think, 'Ah, *German* tuning!'

A true 'A' is actually A448. An A is 7 and for each octave it's multiplied and it comes out at 448. I know about frequencies. The relation of maths to frequencies I find absolutely fascinating – and things like a seashell. That's a Fibonachi Sequence – the growth rate of each section is the same as the Fibonachi Sequence, which is adding the previous numbers together. – 1,2,3,5,8, 13 and if you do that all round you get a seashell. Its also related to the maths of music, all tied in together.

The way a tree grows is pretty much the way that music grows, that notes are formed, say in overtones. Heard of the *Mandelbrot Set*? It's a mathematical number where the answer to the equation gets put back through the equation, a sort of feed back loop. It throws off patterns. There are examples in nature like beetles, sea-horses, the paisley pattern on a tie. God's thumbprint, if you like. You can look on a computer screen to see it all happening. They put one number in and it forms a sycamore tree, another number in and it builds an oak tree. So if there's a God, he's a mathematician!

In jazz, there can be an argument about whether something is mathematician driven, playing a particular pattern, or playing with heart and soul. To me, the heart and soul is seeing the beauty of the maths. But the perfection of it – when you're playing Cherokee, the maths of the chord sequence is *really* difficult, but the form when you get into it is just beautiful maths. So there's no division between maths and music, to my eyes at any rate!

Selected CDs

Snake Ranch Sessions Nigel Hitchcock
        Quartet   [1997, Black Box]

5 Live   Laurence Cottle
                          [1996, Jazzizit]

Stability   Clark Tracey
                          [Linn, 2000]

Website: www.nigelhitchcock.f9.co.uk

Nikki Iles

Nikki Iles, born in Dunstable in 1963, is a highly accomplished jazz pianist, combining the roles of player, composer and educator. She played clarinet and alto before settling on her earliest favourite, the piano. At eleven, Nikki gained an Exhibitioner's Scholarship to the Royal Academy of Music and later joined the Bedfordshire Youth Jazz Orchestra. She then studied jazz at the Leeds College of Music, afterwards becoming a member of the contemporary jazz group, Emanon. As a founder member of the Creative Jazz Orchestra, she worked alonside composers such as Anthony Braxton and Mike Gibbs, and has herself fulfilled a number of composing commissions including 'The Printmaker's Suite,'(1994) while teaching at Leeds College of Music. As Nikki played increasingly in London, she moved south and is now a Senior Lecturer teaching jazz at Middlesex University.

Nikki has played with most of the UK leading jazz players including Kenny Wheeler, Peter King, Iain Ballamy and Julian Arguelles, Alan Barnes, Tony Coe, Dick Morrissey and Jim Mullen. Her ongoing musical relationships include working with Stan Sulzmann, Tina May, Norma Winstone, Martin Speake and Canadians Anthony Michelli and Duncan Hopkins.

Among her numerous CDs, her recent album *Veils*, released in 2003, included a selection of her favourite compositions.

In 1996, Nikki won the John Dankworth Special Award for Outstanding Individual at the British Jazz Awards.

Deeply involved in jazz education, Nikki was part of the team developing the Associated Boards new exams for jazz horns, launched in 2003. She is married to Peter Churchill, a highly respected jazz educator at the Guildhall School of Music.

What kind of music can you first remember listening to?

Well, my father was a semi-pro drummer and loved jazz, so I heard a lot of Nat King Cole, especially his piano playing and I listened to Oscar Peterson, Billy Holiday, Sinatra and some Motown classics. My mother played the piano for pleasure so classical music was also heard a lot about the house. But it was the jazz that caught my ear. It was rhythmic - as a kid, I found it great to dance to!

What were the first musical instruments you played?

There was always a piano in the house and my parents consistently encouraged me to play. The compositional side was there from the start and I was continuously experimenting with sounds and devising my own music.

But actually, one of my first instruments was the mouth organ. Our teacher at primary school, Douglas Tate, was a well known international player, so rather than learning the recorder, we were all taught to play the mouth organ – a great instrument for expressive, bluesy inflections. Later, as a piano player, even though I knew I couldn't physically bend notes, it didn't stop me from searching for those sounds. Then after that, the clarinet was really my first serious instrument.

You then became a Junior Exhibitioner at the Royal Academy of Music.

I really enjoyed playing the clarinet and took Grade Eight by the age of 14 . Around this time I was beginning to be involved with the Bedfordshire County Wind Band and orchestra and one of the teachers suggested I have more tuition at a higher level.

I auditioned successfully for all of the London colleges and decided on the Royal Academy of Music where I was taught for seven years by a wonderful professor, Christopher Ball. I did a lot of accompanying at that time and already knew in my heart of hearts that I wasn't interested in a solo career. But chamber music or essentially any group music-making really interested me – I just needed to find some like minds.

You were developing within classical music, but your thoughts were working towards jazz?

It's amazing how a teacher can affect your direction. At my school a new teacher Brian Willoughby arrived with a load of saxophones in tow. He started an incredible swing band playing all sorts of exciting music. Then as a band, we had the experience of touring Europe, which was great. Then having changed to the alto sax, I joined the Bedfordshire Youth Dance Orchestra and that was where I finally met up with like-minded jazz musicians. I was so excited about that whole scene! Then somebody was ill, so I went onto piano and that was it! The chords and being in the rhythm section - I just stayed there!

Thinking about my future, I came to realise that there wasn't anybody at the Academy who really understood about jazz. Towards the end of my time there, my clarinet teacher hoped I would continue onto a full time performer's course. But once, when I was asked to find a version of Mozart's Clarinet Concerto and turned up with a version by Benny Goodman, I could see by his reaction there were no sympathies in the jazz direction!

But funnily enough, my piano teacher, who'd always said my strengths were in listening and accompanying, encouraged me to, 'Go, go and do your jazz course.' Well at the time, I think that Leeds was the only place in *Europe* that offered a full time jazz course – then called 'Jazz and Contemporary Music'!

What did you like about the Leeds set-up?

Oh, it was the whole community, the playing. The staff were all out there gigging so that was the first priority and we'd play from dawn to dusk really. It was an amazing time for me!

Though I transcribed a lot, I wasn't really sure where I was going, how to improvise. I knew the sound, but it was all a bit cobbled together, bits from here and there. I was lacking in confidence, so I would transcribe and then play those transcriptions on gigs.

But as soon as I left, that all started to develop much more. I had done a lot of groundwork. I'd transcribed a lot of solos by Bill Evans, Dexter Gordon and Chet Baker, so hopefully things were beginning to seep in.

Learning through transcriptions is a process you have to go through, a really essential part of the understanding. The more time I've spent in teaching, the more I recognise there is importance in self-expression, though there are not many one-offs like Evan Parker who speak completely their own language! So you have to learn how to form sentences in the music, put things together and be able to speak to people through music, learning the language that's in there. You start to make your own sentences out of those basic structures.

Had you decided to become a professional jazz musician as you left Leeds?

Yes, well that was my ultimate ambition.

You stayed up in Yorkshire?

Yes, I married and settled in Horsforth, Leeds. My first job was full time for about eight years in an FE College in Ashton under Lyme - tough and incredibly character-building!

Being over that side of the Pennines, near Manchester, I met Mike Walker the guitarist and Iain Dixon [sax]. This was a really formative time for me and my husband, Richard Iles – we had a band, Emanon, which all five of us wrote for. That's when I really started writing in earnest.

We were all like-minded musicians and loved American jazz but also wanted to do our own thing. We were together for quite a few years and all moved on together. It was a great time, a really challenging but supportive group, talked about music a lot - about what was working and what wasn't.

It was contemporary jazz?

Yes, I suppose at the time we were influenced by Kenny Wheeler and John Taylor, more the ECM side of things but with roots in American jazz.

Then an appointment came up at Wakefield College and Leeds to teach part-time and I thought it was time to concentrate more on my playing, so I moved back to Yorkshire.

Around this time, Nick Purnell formed the Creative Jazz Orchestra, dedicated to commissioning new music, together with Mike Walker and Iain. This gave us the opportunity of working with the likes of Vince Mendoza, Anthony Braxton, Kenny Wheeler and Mike Gibbs. This was a fantastic time - the experience was invaluable and a CD called *By the Way* for Mike Gibbs with Steve Swallow and Bob Moses followed.

The Orchestra worked with Mark Anthony Turnage, the modern classical composer.

That's right. He loves jazz and the CJO commissioned Mike Gibbs to arrange his music. The harmonies adapt themselves well to jazz, though clearly the lines can get a bit blurred between contemporary jazz and contemporary classical.

It worked brilliantly, especially with Mike arranging it. I learned a hell of a lot about being daring with arranging because Mike Gibbs can write the most outrageous orchestrations! Soprano saxes up in the Gods, the things you're not supposed to do - but they work!

Your northern links very much include the Wakefield Jazz Club.

Yes, thanks to Alec Sykes. Having a place to play and try out new music is such a bonus and it gives you the opportunity to get new bands and musical relationships off the ground. We probably played some pretty awful gigs in the early days! The music could be rather dark ECM type music! He'd say 'Stop playing the bloody dirges' but he *would* give you the gig again!

I was also given the opportunity at this club

to accompany several visiting Americans such as Scott Hamilton, Art Farmer and Teddy Edwards as well as Peter King, Don Weller, Jim Mullen and Dick Morrissey - amongst others.

I had a great evening celebrating my fortieth birthday gig there recently - it felt good to be back. That club is a whole social scene revolving around the personalities that run it. Alec and Faith get good audiences for everything.

You've played a lot with Stan Sulzmann [saxes] for instance in the CD *Treasure Trove* in 1996. What is it about Stan that you like?

Well, his sound is so personal, it's just him. Whether hushed or really big, it's very warm. And his time, he's so easy to play with. There's a deep swing in him, but it's loose as well. Plus he's very generous with his music, so you don't feel like you're battling.

I know for *me*, when I think about my favourite players, it's the sound gets me first. You can hear Stan and you know who it is in a couple of notes. He has such a beautiful sound - often people think the hushed way he can sometimes play is the *only* way he plays - but he can *certainly* roar when he wants to. He is also very good at not telling you how to play but letting you find your own way, which is great.

In 1996, you recorded the CD, *Tan T'ien* with Martin Speake [saxes].

I like Martin. He's very different from Stan, but again, very individual and quite uncompromising, he really knows what he wants - which I admire. He's amazing playing changes and playing standards, because he loves that side too. But I find his tunes interesting. They make me think in a different way, not about harmony, more about rhythm. For example, one of his tunes, 'JT's Symmetrical Scale,' is based on only one scale, which forces you to think in another way, about rhythmical variation.

For me, harmony is an easy starting point for a composition. I love chords! However writing constantly from this viewpoint can be limiting. There's a piece on my CD *Veils* called *Fly's*

Dilemma where there's no element of harmony in the piece. It's just essentially written in two parts. This development for me has come out of playing with people like Martin.

Can we touch on your own larger compositions? How *the Printmaker's Suite* came about in 1994?

Well it was a suite to celebrate the role of women in jazz at that time, because there are some heroes of mine, I suppose - Norma Winstone,

Geri Allen and Carla Bley. It was coming up to International Women's Week, so I thought I'd write a piece celebrating them. Nick Purnell from Jazz Northwest got behind it and it became a commission for The Creative Jazz Orchestra - we did a couple of tours. It felt very good, the first time to be up and out there. And I used cello, bass clarinet and French horn, so there were a few classical musicians in there too.

It allowed me to find out what worked, what didn't.

In 1999, you composed the suite, *In All Your Holy Mountain* for the New Perspectives Group.

Yes, the poet Roger Garfitt had written the words about the life of the writer Mary Webb. It's about her life, set in her birthplace in rural Shropshire. Sometimes you get commissioned and you get only one performance which is a shame, but this has been ongoing which is lovely. New Perspectives is John William's group with Dick Pearce, Trevor Tomkins, Jeff Cline, Pete Hurt, Phil Lee and Jim Tomlinson.

Then came *A Gentle Prayer* [1999] with the London Sinfonietta.

Yes, that was quite challenging! This was for the Ellington Centenary celebrations at the South Bank and I wrote it for big band plus French horns. I was in the company of Carla Bley, Richard Rodney Bennett and Gavin Briars - so it was some pretty heavy company. You had to have your own angle on Ellington, on why you were writing the piece. He was writing for the individuals [in *his* band]. So I wrote something for Stan and he played it beautifully.

It meant working with a conductor. That was the scariest thing in some ways because jazz musicians are so quick at finding what you want or taking it on themselves to play things.

Maybe don't really want to be told either?

Yes, occasionally things were a tiny bit stressful! But a great experience!

From your many playing partners, can you talk about Kenny Wheeler and Norma Winstone?

I first met a lot of these people as a teenage student at Wavenden [John Dankworth's Jazz School in Bedfordshire] in the early eighties. I was taught by Bob Cornford. I played for him a bit and he said, 'You obviously like Bill Evans - similar harmonies'. I hadn't even heard Bill Evans then, so he sent me some albums to listen to and was really kind. For a time he was quite a influence while I was developing.

Kenny Wheeler is one of the veteran greats of British Jazz.

Yes, he's nearly seventy-five but he still plays like a young man. His writing is a big part of the whole with him and he's a big influence on a lot of us I think. I've always loved his music and worked with him in various different situations - John Taylor is normally there. But it was fantastic for me when I played with his big band at the Appleby Jazz Festival. His sound and music are just so passionate.

He appears to be, along with John Taylor [piano] and Norma Winstone [vocalist], possibly a high point of British Jazz: is that how you see it?

In terms of influence, certainly. John Taylor's one of my heroes. Norma, I think of her as a musician's singer really. She's as flexible and inventive as an instrumentalist. She demonstrates the same kind of daring on the gig as a horn player.

How did your long association with vocalist Tina May begin?

I met Tina in Halifax as part of a few gigs with my northern trio in 1995. We got on very well so she asked me to join her band. We've been through lots of different enjoyable projects including a CD with Alan Barnes, a duo CD, a tour and a CD with Scott Hamilton. I love how, for most of the gigs, she gets *very* good grand pianos!

We also did a few trio gigs with Alan Barnes [alto] and realised how much we enjoyed it. So we decided to carry on with that, and then Tony Coe took over from Alan – Tony's one of my heroes, so it's marvellous to be playing with him and we're now planning a trio record with Tony Coe.

Tina's very good, she such as amazing singer, particularly in duo without drums or bass. She's like Norma, she improvises, so every night it's different. Also she's a good friend, as we've both been through divorces and hard times and we're really a good team. It comes out, hopefully, in the music! She's so hard working, out on the road all the time. She does get awards, but I'm not sure it's recognised enough just how good she is.

Have the vocalists also gone through colleges like Leeds?

Several studied at the Guildhall - Christine Tobin, Anita Wardell and Stacey Kent – the course equips singers to feel more independent and in control of their music. Anita can play the piano well, write her own charts – so you don't have to rely on anybody to sort the arrangements out, which is good.

There will always be people who can sing, haven't done the formal training and need an accompanist, but it's good to see a crop of singers coming out now who can control their own music.

On singer/pianists, you've noted Jamie Cullum's arrival?

Of course! He was a student on the Mediterranean Summer School a few years ago and we all knew he had star quality! He'd been busking in Paris for a year and he's not green – so the best of luck to him.

You played on the Ingrid Laubrock album, *Some Times*, where you combine on a beautiful duet called *Hands*

Yes, I was taken by how she had a poise about her playing. I met her while she was at the Guildhall and we'd meet up a few times during the year and have a play. I like her – she's very direct and her playing has this focus. On the course she was starting to write more and some of the jazz things that she was not so much into before the course were seeping in.

Who were the main influences as you were learning how to play jazz?

Well I listened to a number of people – Nat Cole for technique and touch and the swing feel

and also Oscar, Herbie Hancock, Lennie Tristano, Geri Allen and John Taylor. However, my greatest love has to be Bill Evans - the sound he creates – the beauty in his music. He sometimes reminds me of Kenny Wheeler - he's got that feel too, though he and Bill can be sparkling like all the rest.

Bill Evans generally springs some harmonic surprises that are maybe echoed in your playing.

Oh...are they?

The critic John Fordham has referred to your 'obliquely resolving harmonies!'

Oh yeah! I think it's the [harmonic] lines. I love to play on harmony and one of my goals is to be able to play a tune that is pretty complicated harmonically and feel as free as I would on a piece with three chords. So I've been really working at trying to find my own ways through lots of different harmonic situations.

Paul Bley also is someone who at times plays the weirdest stuff but somehow it is always connected to the roots - the blues and that American tradition. He's moved on from Bill Evans, he sometimes has unresolved lines, but I love the cleanness of his line.

And I also like Geri Allen, that *dark* harmony again. When she appeared on the scene with Paul Motion and Charlie Haden, the music sounded very fresh. I've continued to listen to her.

An important revelation for me was seeing John Taylor perform live. I'm told he used to play like Oscar Peterson! Probably a similar root – he loves Bill Evans, Herbie Hancock, but has his own sound completely. I loved the Azimuth albums he did with Norma and Kenny on ECM records - wonderful examples of his sense of space and hearing - his sound and beautiful touch in the foreground of the recording are great.

But it's when you go and see him live – that's what I say to my students - John shows this spirit and total commitment! And you can sense he's not worried about things going wrong. You really get a sense of going on a journey with him.

How did you learn to improvise?

Well I did a lot of playing along with records and trying to imitate people like Oscar Peterson, Bud Powell, Bill, John Taylor and all sorts of people, to find the notes and the touch.

Not formally transcribing them?

Not really, learning them by ear. Tran-scribing is another way, but by ear, the music is in your *head!* Then you can sing it. It's crucial to use the records and learn every nuance of the notes and feel what it feels like to pull a phrase back or play some notes in the phrase short. It goes in more by osmosis in this way, rather than formally try-ing to analyse a swing feel.

Also transcribing helps you to recognise

blocks of sounds - the building blocks of har-mony and if you're not doing this kind of lis-tening, especially as a non pianist, you don't stand a chance !

Through my experience, I believe that al-though you may have a teacher to steer you in the right direction, the more listening and try-ing to figure things out yourself always leads to a deeper understanding ultimately. It may just take a bit longer to get there!

Also it's been about learning sounds. In a way, with most of my age group -when there weren't so many jazz colleges around – it can be a bit of a mish-mash where you've got things from! Even when *I* started there were big band scores, with piano parts written out in full. And I liked the sounds but didn't know why they fit-ted together or anything like that.

So I'd take a couple of voicings away with me - I didn't try it in all twelve keys! Then later, the penny drops and you start to put things to-gether. But in the end, although I'm a teacher, enjoy it and really believe in it, in a way when you learn it *yourself,* it's much deeper. You may have doors opened, or people help you in a way, but if you've had to go away and slog at it, it's definitely in there!

Certainly the course you run appears based a lot on practice and performance, but you still have to teach while allowing for personal creativity to come through?

Oh, yes. It's difficult. Obviously there's basic skills, and understandings are important for say a first year student – they've got to be able to play in time and understand about chords. For me, I try to teach them the *processes* of getting there so they can learn how to learn themselves – like the modes of a major scale. If they can do that and understand that and why it works, they can do it on the harmonic major or harmonic minor, then they can do it on their own! So I teach from that premiss really. If they understand *why* and *how* then they can do the rest and they are on their own. And will come up with all sorts of things!

Rhythm and time are the fundamental elements of jazz. Often we concentrate on scales and more scales – and the importance of a good time feel or groove are overlooked.

Then afterwards, is finding venues where the new people can play an issue?

That's the most difficult thing now. In a way, the most ideal thing would be to have a course with its own night club because that's where people learn! It's difficult, because people learn all the techniques and the knowledge but have nowhere to put it into practice. Or to hear people play.

I want to be in teaching, but a lot of us are worried that there's too much jazz education. People arrive and want a quick fix, often wanting to be spoon-fed the information - and attempting to learn an aural tradition without bothering to listen to any of the music seems mad. But if people come with the right attitude, it's fine.

It's a different relationship that people have with music nowadays. I was talking to Scott Hamilton recently about this. Jazz musicians played for dancing in the thirties and forties and your average person was out there dancing to some fantastic musicians at times. Scott asked 'What do people do now?' because the environment isn't there for the musicians or the people. However, despite this, there's still a lot of great music coming from some very committed people.

Alan Barnes' *Sherlock Holmes Suite*

uses jazz to characterise his ideas of the great detective, those heroes and villains. In your own composing work, your starting inspiration is through the arts or literature?

Yes, I did my *Nine Swallows – no Summer* piece for Barbara Hepworth. And my *Fire and Ice Suite* was based on the short stories of AS Byatt. I've always loved art and reading, so those things are an obvious source of inspiration for me.

I was reading a book by Gil Goldstein called *The Composer's Companion* and it's very interesting where it looks at the different motivations for composing. Horace Silver just says, 'Well I get up in the morning, and if it happens, it happens.' And Mike Gibbs, says, 'If the commission's there, *that* gets me going.'

But for me, if I've got a story or a painting or a poem, I'm away... same for groups. We've just been away in Canada, with The Secret Band in Toronto for ten days. Martin [Speake] had said, 'OK, we'll need a whole new load of music.' We're going to record another album, so that got me going too.

The Secret Band?

It resulted from Martin Speake visiting the Banff Jazz School around ten to fifteen years ago, where he played with Duncan Hopkins [bass].

Duncan was coming to Britain for a visit recently and he gave Martin a ring to see if there was a chance of getting together for a play. Martin also around that time heard Anthony [Michelli, drums] playing at the Jersey Jazz Festival and decided to form the new band. So we've been out to Toronto twice.

Could you describe the making of your new album *Veils*, your quintet's 2003 opus?

Well it's taken me forty years to get there! There is a horrendous pressure these days to record a debut album before you've had a chance to develop. I haven't felt the need to do this, although I've obviously been involved in other peoples' recording projects. It just seemed the right time to gather the people I'd played with over the years and who I felt would do the music justice. It's all my originals except for one tune by Stan Sulzmann and is a good example of the different sides of my musical character, the reflection of a varied personality!

And in 2004?

I've recently done a piano trio album in Toronto, again with Duncan and Anthony, called *Everything I love* on Basho Records. There's a couple of standards on there, a couple of Bill Evans, a couple of John Taylor tunes and my things, so it's a combination of the things I love to play We've been a great little team, all get on very well and we're doing a tour to release my new trio CD in England.

I know a lot of people find standards dead now, but I still find there's lots to do in them. For me, to be able to be as free on a standard or something with chords as I would be when playing free, that's the ultimate thing.

Modern composers are not generally writing songs with the harmonies that Cole Porter and others in that period did, are they?

Not as much, though the tradition of writing a tune on an existing head, that is, on old [chord] sequences is still alive and kicking. Martin and Stan do it, like Lee Konitz did. Those sequences are classic, aren't they, so you've got to find another way, and that's the challenge.

Your husband Peter is also a jazz educator. Do you compare notes on how jazz should be taught?

We're really both quite different in how we've come to jazz. He's a pianist as well and a lovely singer. His parents were quite well known classical musicians, but he didn't want to go along that path. He's got incredible ears and started out learning most of his jazz by ear, whereas my relationship with music began with the written page. So, as you can imagine, we bring different approaches to teaching and are probably quite complementary in our styles. I've introduced him to different music and different things he could use and him similarly with me. It's great, actually.

How do you see your future, combining playing and composition?

For me, composition and playing – they're not really separate. If there's a major side to me, it's really the playing because I would always feel I was able to spontaneously compose through improvisation. All the things I work on start from improvising. So to me, composition is just improvision with hindsight!!

Selected CDs	
The Tan T'ien	Martin Speake/Nikki Iles [1997, FMR Records]
Secret	Secret Band [2001, Basho Records]
Veils	The Nikki Iles Quintet [2003, Symbol Records]
Everything I love	The Nikki Iles Trio [JAZZCDs 2004]
Website: www.nikkiiles.co.uk	

Julian Joseph

Julian Joseph, born in Hammersmith, London in 1966, is an internationally respected jazz pianist, composer, bandleader and broadcaster. He started piano studies at the age of six and in 1983 attended London's Weekend Arts College where he and an array of highly talented young musicians developed jazz skills, later forming a rehearsal band that included Courtney Pine and the drummer Mark Mondesir. In 1985 he gained a scholarship to Berklee School of Music, Boston, where he met Delfeayo Marsalis and toured with his brother Branford Marsalis in 1986, playing in the company of Wynton Marsalis and Bobby McFerrin.

Returning to London in 1990, Julian formed a quartet and in 1991 recorded the album *The Language of Truth* for the East-West [Warner Group] label with Jean Toussaint, Alec Dankworth and Mark Mondesir. There followed many appearances by his quartet and trio in London and abroad, also involving artists such as Johnny Griffin and George Coleman.

In 1993, Julian released his second album, *Reality*, followed by tours of America and Australia in 1994. He also performed Gershwin's Piano Concerto with the BBC Scottish Symphony Orchestra and in 1995 released his album *In Concert at Wigmore Hall*, featuring duets with Johnny Griffin and Eddie Daniels.

In 1995, he became the first jazz musician to put on his own late night Promenade Concert at the Royal Albert Hall. Among his many arrangements and original compositions, his main work to date is *The Great Sage* for big band. He has played a large number of the major jazz festivals across the world and tours nationally and internationally. His fourth album, *Universal Traveller*, was released in 1996. Julian has made two jazz series for Meridian TV, one for Sky's Artsworld and on BBC Radio 3 presents the weekly program *Jazz Legends*.

What kinds of music do you first remember listening to in your youth?

The thing that really sticks out is my Dad rehearsing in our basement with his band. My father was, is and continues to be a soul and a blues singer. I particularly remember him doing a jazz version of 'A Spoonful of Sugar' from the Sound of Music. I was also listening to James Brown, because my Dad liked that; while my Mum liked classical music - a bit of Beethoven, Liszt and music from the operas.

Then when I was coming into my real consciousness about music, in the early Seventies, you could hear jazz festivals on TV, Duke Ellington, a lot of Oscar Peterson, which we were very lucky to grow up listening to.

Around ten years old, I was listening to Stevie Wonder, Earth Wind and Fire. Herbie Hancock was really the discovery of my brother John, who's a year older than me. He said, 'This is the guy you should listen to if you really want to play piano; his improvising is fantastic.' That was a big trigger for me. A friend, actor Errol Shaker, bought us a Ramsey Lewis record, playing not just *Wade in the Water* but *Maiden Voyage*. What an incredible version! Herbie Hancock composed that, so I thought that this guy must be important!

When did you first start with a musical instrument?

My early thing was singing, but I remember when I was about six, me and my two brothers came back from school - John one year older, and James, a year younger, who's my manager. We all came back from primary school one day and we walked into the front room and there was a *piano*. Mum said, 'And you're all going to learn!'

Was it a classical programme put in front of you?

Yes, it was totally classical but that's the way you learn. There's a method there and I started studying straight away.

So you were working hard at this when in 1983, you joined the jazz workshops at the Weekend Arts College in London.

An English teacher, Mrs Peterson, told me that there was this great workshop at the weekends in Kentish Town. Another pupil Robert Forjour was already attending, so I asked Robert, ' Do you think I'll be good enough?' and he laughed, 'Of course, you'll be good enough, Julian.' I had a bit of a reputation at school for being a good musician but that didn't mean *I* thought I was a good musician or that things were easy. I certainly felt there was a lot of ground to cover and I hadn't covered nearly a fraction of it.

Jazz intrigued me. The thing that I grasped early was that for music you make up, improvise, you have to understand the landscape of what's going on and invent something to go on top of it. And I thought, 'How does anybody do that?'

So I went there, was very nervous, and I played things I did on the piano at that time. I did pretty well and ended up being one of the better players there and one of those who had something to say. But it still didn't make me think that I'd got it all sorted out.

How did they teach you at the Weekend Arts Centre?

Ian Carr [trumpet, composer, bandleader] was

there and he was really good. Courtney Pine's current drummer, Robert Forjour and I were very close friends back then. We also had the same drum teacher, the very wonderful Mr Trevor Tomkins, who taught me a lot about music.

Ian was great for teaching us about music through repertoire that we wouldn't normally play. He would introduce us to *Stella by Starlight*, *Blue Bossa* and those kinds of tunes - simple tunes but still things you had to get your head round if you weren't familiar with that kind of harmony or harmonic movement. Ian would write out things for a piano player or a horn player to do and see how well we'd tackle playing the changes. He was always very supportive and strict without being like a school teacher. He expected a lot because this was a talented bunch of guys.

I met people like Mark Mondesir and Michael Mondesir there. I met a bass player, Paul Hunt, who said he knew the best saxophone player in the world. Of course, everything at that age is not exactly exaggerated but the best in town if not the *best in the world* – it was Courtney Pine. I met Cleveland Watkiss, Steve Williamson. Philip Bent was there right from the beginning and you know, all these guys could really play!

They weren't all necessarily participants in the workshop but we all were getting familiar with themes that Ian was giving us. He would give us things to do with the United Jazz and Rock Ensemble and things he would do with Nucleus [his own jazz-rock group]. We had all these challenges playing pieces in different time signatures. We also had the benefit of people from his band coming and taking us, Jeff Cline, Nic France, an incredible drummer, Geoff Castle on keyboards would come and inspire us.

Afterwards we all started meeting up and I started this band, the Ivo Quintet because we had a guy called Ivor, now one of the big Managing Editors or Directors at KISS FM. Philip Bent the flautist used to tease him by not calling him Ivor but *Ivo*. We would be playing compositions by Courtney and me. The band was me, Courtney Pine, Philip Bent, Paul Hunt and Mark Mondesir. So that was our rehearsal band that would get together every week and play.

You did weekend gigs and then it broadened out?

Yes, then Courtney started to become a star. He was a little bit older than us, twenty and he was starting to make his mark. So from there, everything else grew and we started to play gigs and people started to notice me - and at *that point*, I went to America!

You got a scholarship to go to the Berklee School of Music in Boston.

Trevor Tomkins said, 'Julian, it would be really good if, when you finish your studies, you went to America, a place like Berklee, because that's for you.' Then my teacher and Mum liaised with the Inner London Education Authority and that was instrumental in getting me the award.

I got all the prospectuses for the universities and colleges that did jazz or anything related to jazz. I wanted to be somewhere where there was jazz, so I chose Berklee!

I had also sent in tapes. I was encouraged to send a tape to Berklee through Donald Harrison the alto player, who was playing with Art Blakey and the Jazz Messengers, and he and Mulgrew Millar and Terence Blanchard and Jean Toussaint (playing with them at the time) helped me.

You went there to study composition. Classical or jazz?

When I got there, I thought I knew how I wanted to play jazz - quite different from my attitude when I was sixteen - I knew the direction I wanted to go in with my playing and my big hero at the time was Herbie Hancock who studied *composition*. So I thought, let me go and study composition - albeit formal and classical composition, because I can get material from that and bring it into jazz, like he does.

During your time at Berklee, you met up with the Marsalises; later Branford asked you to join his band.

I'd met Branford and Wynton when I heard them play at the Royal Festival Hall in 1983 be-

fore I left to go to America, talking to them as I would to every jazz musician. I didn't really know them, but those guys were so great, so open, they gave me their number, I could call them up.

When I was at Berklee, I was good friends with Delfeayo Marsalis, their little brother who plays trombone. Delfeayo was very encouraging and a big supporter of mine – we were all in this together! – saying, 'My brother's got to hear you!' So when Branford came into town, he'd just come over for a couple of days, he just got surrounded by musicians. Then Delfeayo said, 'I'm going to have a jam session for Branford, so come along!' So

I went and he played all these tunes, and he would say, 'You don't know that?' 'No, I don't know that,' and he's like, 'But you play with Courtney Pine!'

And that's a risk for the upcoming jazzman, that he's expected to know a couple of hundred tunes?

Branford has an incredible capacity to re-member things. Also he doesn't really need to know a tune to understand one. Other than Mark Mondesir he's one of the closest people I know to genius. So he'd call a tune, and I'd ask, 'What are the changes?' He'd say, 'I don't know, man.' Then he'd just pro-ceed to go into his head and visualise it, then write it out on the blackboard.

Later Kenny Kirkland couldn't make some gigs and Delfeayo said to Branford, 'Why don't you use J,' as they used to call me. So he called me and said, 'Do you want to do a gig tomorrow?' I said 'What?' He said, 'You're on a plane tomorrow to Jacksonville!' So I did this gig with him. I'm not going to go into the details because I was just *in awe*, couldn't say anything to anyone! Jeff 'Tain' Watts was on the gig and a bass player called Delbert Felix.

Branford called all sorts of tunes on me, stuff I didn't know, but I got through it. We did a Herbie Hancock original, called *Number Sev-enty-Two* and my playing was an absolute disas-ter! But after the gig, Branford asked, 'What would your Mum say about me asking you to come on the road?' So I said, 'I don't think she'd mind!' And that's how I got the gig with Branford! We toured the States, Canada, we went all over for about twelve months.

After Berklee , you toured with Courtney Pine.

Yes, I was then still based in America and Courtney was doing a tour of America, Aus-tralia and Japan. In 1988, after the European tour, they came to America and met up with me and we continued the tour. Courtney was tour-ing all the time because he was very popular. I was in college, so I couldn't do many of the gigs but it suited us for him to call me when he came to the States. We went all round, West Coast, East Coast, then we toured Australia and then we went to Japan.

How would you describe the style of music?

It was acoustic, high energy, high octane music! It was just the most exuberant, fiery kind of music ever! Incredibly undisciplined but just the most wonderful type of music to play. I was playing as loud as possible, Courtney was play-ing as fast as possible, as humanly possible! And Delbert Felix on bass was just looking at us like he was wondering what on earth he had got him-self into! Just brilliant! We played to some of the biggest audiences I've ever played to, espe-cially in Australia where Courtney broke all records for audience capacities.

Then at the end of Berklee, you came back to the UK.

Yes, back in the UK James, my brother, had al-ready started fielding calls from many record companies asking when I was coming home. Does he want a record deal? James had more than three contracts waiting for me. I signed in 1990 with East-West Records, part of the

Warner Group and in 1991 I did my first album, *The Language of Truth*.

Two players you use a lot were there, Jean Toussaint on tenor, and Mark Mondesir on drums.

Well, when everyone met Mark, nobody could believe that such a young guy could play the way he could play. He is my definition of genius. He truly can perceive things in many dimensions.

You're talking about polyrhythms?

I think it's an oversimplification to call it polyrhythms. Yes, polyrhythms means playing one rhythm against another rhythm that is differing and they have a resolution somewhere. But what Mark does, he can perceive different times at the same time. So he understands the resolution of one in collusion with another. He knows how that resolves and he can add other elements and he can improvise in the kind of timeframe that it creates, the double time frame that it creates or in the single timeframe of either one. So it's way beyond a polyrhythmic concept.

If you spend time with him, you'll understand what's going on. I've never got any other drummer to work with me except maybe Gary Husband, who's another remarkable musician.

Jean Toussaint I knew from when he was working with Art Blakey and the Jazz Messengers. He's somebody I've always looked up to – not because he's a giant but because he's a massive musician. And he's one of the hardest swinging musicians that's ever lived.

Swing is a important factor for you

I find it irresistible - if you can swing, you can have the world, I'm happy.

So those two guys are integral. I also had Alec Dankworth on bass. I've always found him a really good musician, fantastic reader, knew loads of tunes and very down-to-earth about everything. Also he came from what I would call the royal family of jazz with John Dankworth and Cleo, so you can't go wrong there.

I had Sharon Musgrave, a great singer from Canada, who brought a real beauty to the songs. One by Curtis Mayfield became a single, called The Other Side of Town, and she would also sing live a tune that I wrote, called the Magical One.

In the early Nineties, you were playing in Ronnie Scott's with Johnny Griffin and George Coleman. Can you tell me about them?

I didn't know Ronnie Scott well, but he was really kind and very encouraging to any musician who was up and coming. So when George was in town, I have a feeling that Ronnie was instrumental in saying, 'You should try Julian Joseph.' So he did and we did two weeks in London at Ronnie's and a week up in Birmingham at the Ronnie's there. With George you *always* have to be prepared because I had seen him in England putting pianists through their paces, also in America! Now George can call any key on you with a tune or change at any time and the tempos could get furiously fast or in something unusual like 5/4. So I would practice playing *every* tune that I knew George would play in *every* key.

When I played with him, it was just a real joy. It was me, Mark Taylor on drums and Dave Green on bass. Dave is great to have because he really plays by ear. He can read well, but he really has the jazz musician's ear that we're all striving to have. I'd say, 'Do you know this tune?' We'd all be panicking, and he'd said, 'No, but I'll pick it up, I'll be all right.' And so, half the time I'd just be listening for him to open up a tune that *I* wasn't aware of.

Through George I really got to understanding what playing jazz is all about, on a technical level, just in terms of preparation. I had a lot of fun listening to his sound, his history. All those records he'd done with Miles [Davis], Max Roach and stuff, just came flying into my mind while I was playing with him. Thinking I can't believe I'm doing this. We've been friends ever since and when he comes to London, I play with him – and on recent Wigmore Hall and Festival Hall gigs, I called him over.

The same goes for Johnny Griffin. He's been someone I admired for so many years as one of the giants of jazz music – gorgeous tone, amazing technique, played with Thelonius Monk, and every major artist you can think of. I called Johnny over to do my first Wigmore Hall series in 1994 and had such a good time playing with him. Two calls for visiting artists coming into town were myself or Jason Rebello, and I knew that Jason had played with Johnny as well, so it could be either of us. The other great thing about Johnny is he writes very well, really beautiful and also playful music that still has the fun of jazz, like his great piece *The Cat*.

Both George and Johnny were on at my last concert at the Festival Hall, at the 2002 Radio 3 London Jazz Festival. It was a privilege, tapping into that great history. That's what I love, really learning from the guys that were there when the music was being created and developed.

Around that time, you also went to the Montreux Jazz Festival which has always seemed special. Was it special for you?

I'd been there before with Courtney Pine, in 1988 or 1989, and it was a serious ambition to play Montreux. When I went there with my own group a few years later – I did Montreux several times – the first time, I really loved it. We played in a club called the Q Club, put together by Quincy Jones. I was touring for my first album at the time. It was wild, people were coming in to see us and loving what we were doing, playing off each other and I realised maybe we had something to say on a world scale.

Then I went back again as a trio and I was thinking, I don't think I'm at a *jazz* festival. We played, the audience was great. Joan Armatrading was there and lots of pop, and it was a great festival of music – but it had lost the *jazzness*. Maybe this was the end of an era.

Montreux is a beautiful setting, and its jazz

has had this spark with Wynton Marsalis and all those guys from New Orleans, but it seemed to be taking a bit of a dip that year. Maybe the position of jazz has changed because its popular heyday exists far back in time now. Rock music and the big pop acts of the seventies are taking the place of those jazzers from the Fifties and the Sixties. So the landscape of music is changing.

One of the things going for British jazz is maybe that it's being fed by different cultural influences. Maybe therefore it's stronger?

You know, I think jazz blows hot and cold in

Britain, to tell you the truth. There was a really buoyant and prosperous time for jazz in the Eighties, with a lot of black musicians coming up. But it had never happened before – there had never been such a strong contingent of young second generation West Indian or African musicians taking on this jazz mantle. It wasn't a black music in this country. Obviously its roots were black, but it was the first time blacks took ownership. That was something unique and special.

In this buoyant time, you could become popular as a jazz musician and I'm talking about popular musicians like Courtney Pine, Andy Sheppard and Steve Williamson, all saxophone players. The *image* of a jazz saxophonist was a very positive force for selling the music in this country.

As well as that, it did encourage a lot of young people to get into the music and think that there was somewhere to go with it. But after that boom, a lot of the major jazz artists of that early Eighties creative explosion folded. Steve Williamson disappeared, Cleveland Watkiss went into drum 'n bass, a lot of guys diversified. Jason Rebello retired.

So there was a disillusionment among people who'd been very successful up to that time and jazz needed to look at itself in a new way. So new musicians like Nikki Yeoh, Andrew MacCormack and the NU Troop guys, Jazz Jamaica, were coming on to be flourishing again. There was a whole new movement of people saying, 'You know what? It may not be like it was, but we can still enjoy the music and we can still be the masters of our own destiny.' It was turning into an independent label time and then a lot of other young talent in jazz like Orlando la Fleming, Denys Baptiste and now Soweto Kinch have started coming out and flourishing – in a new scene, in a new and differently pitched way, with its own underground, if you like.

Some new players like Soweto are really strong and have something to say and there's no trickery to what he's saying, it's really honest. He adds a rap element, that's aside from the jazz but in a sense, part of his own continuum. It reflects what he listens to and the fact that he comes from a literary family with that background.

You've performed with a number of classical orchestras including Gershwin's Piano concerto with the BBC Scottish Symphony Orchestra, but your direction seems more jazz than

classical - and maybe more player than composer?

No, composer, because that's what I did in college. What the guys will tell you, is at that time, all I did was *write,* mainly concentrating on *jazz* music.

I appreciate the stylistic differences but choose to combine everything I've experienced. Writing and playing is still a work in progress.

Your Big Band - you first introduced it in 1994, then you used it in presenting a jazz Late Night Promenade Concert at the Albert Hall in 1995. It's a vehicle for your jazz arrangements and original compositions, the largest of which is *The Great Sage*.

The Great Sage was composed for my big band and the strings of the BBC Philharmonic, a commission for the BBC. Compositions that I've written specifically for the big band, the latest was the rearrangement of *Rhapsody in Blue*. I also adapted *The Great Sage* for just big band as well. So tunes like *Guardian Angel* and *Jean - EE - T* and things from some of my other albums, an arrangement of Thelonius Monk's *Ruby my Dear*, there's lots of material I wrote for the big band. I love the big band, I surprised myself with how cohesive the writing sounds because I didn't expect it to come up to my expectations.

Who is the Great Sage?

It is dedicated to two people; Wayne Shorter and Patrick Gowers.

Wayne Shorter is an enigmatic character in jazz with a unique personality and cosmic take on the world, the universe. As a player he's a pioneer and as a composer he's equally pioneering. He's seventy now and continues to surprise audiences and push boundaries. He's an inspiration just to behold as a musician, composer and thinker.

Patrick Gowers is an amazing British composer who has composed lots of film and choral works. He is just one of the most remarkable arrangers and composers I've ever met, with a jazz sensibility along with true classical technique. I just find his music very soulful and very inspiring. I don't think we look at our own composers enough in this country because we're always looking away at what's most popular. I feel grateful that I've had the wherewithal to realise the greatness of Patrick Gowers. He's become a good friend of mine over the last ten or so years and I see him as a kind of guru. An unsung hero but a master willing to share his great knowledge.

Can I take you back to how you reckon you learnt jazz?

From listening, intense listening. Everything that came into the house that had a jazz purpose, I could sing every single nuance, from the drums to the bass, piano, and the other things I liked in it.

You could hear the intervals?

It wasn't a technical thing for me, I have to be honest. It was an emotional thing. It's like recording music into your brain. Then when I would apply that to playing, maybe playing in an approximate way when I was trying to decipher things, but the purpose of it was the same. Eventually when you become more familiar with the harmonic area, and the melodic application to those harmonic areas, then you've already got the emotional and logical impetus that you picked up from the masters. So that's how I learnt.

On a technical level, I was transcribing things. I was writing my own tunes as approximations of things that I'd heard. I also had a lot of encouragement, not least my elder brother saying, 'That was good! Why don't you try playing along with the records, just to get the feeling of what it is to play with those guys?' And it would have an immediate effect on the way I played.

I was always searching for something to help me get better. I always knew what I had to do, a lot of transcribing. It wasn't till later on that I realised that through *repertoire* my brain would actually learn to decipher the language of jazz

and recreate it in different ways to tackle different tunes – that's the *purpose* of repertoire. That's what my teacher at Berklee, Donald Brown, was trying to impart, as I realised afterwards!

Now I've read who your influences are reckoned to be - Fats Waller, Duke Ellington, Thelonius Monk and Keith Jarrett. But I hear maybe McCoy Tyner?

The *true* influences are McCoy Tyner, Ramsey Lewis, Herbie Hancock in particular, Duke Ellington and Thelonius Monk. Those are the major, major influences that *I* can hear in my

playing. And also Kenny Kirkland, he made a big impact on my playing, along with Mulgrew Miller as well as Donald Brown. I studied Bud Powell in some detail. But what I grasped from those guys is - material vocabulary.

Influences affect you in differing ways. I might use those influences to play in a way similar to Keith Jarrett *but* – it won't sound like Keith

Jarrett because it's not the same material. But *conceptually* I'll try and emulate what I'm hearing from him.

Regarding your piano style when playing with saxophone players, your style is not passive, it's interacting...

Having grown up listening to Herbie Hancock, or Kenny Kirkland or Chick Corea, their playing is highly interactive. The music is about conversing, but conversing with empathy. A number of sax players give you the freedom to do that. Some players don't like you to be like that, they like you to be more passive, more supportive in an obvious way.

Teaching and coaching in jazz: you were involved in putting together the new Associated Boards Jazz Syllabus.

I was involved in writing some music for them and also in being one of the champions for that course, because I do encourage any broadening or greater acceptance of jazz. And I've been on television, playing and presenting for Artsworld. I did a Masterclass for Meridien network where I took a student, Zoe Rahman, the young British pianist, coaching somebody who can already play.

And finally what do you think of the health of the UK jazz scene?

I'd like to see it get more healthy. I'd like to see real jazz stars being created. I think it's starting in a way, you've got Jamie Cullum coming up but I think they're really going for more popular elements there.. But I'd like to see him successful and still acknowledging jazz when he is successful.

Soweto Kinch is getting a lot of attention, but I fear for him because it may be he is being sold an empty dream. In this country, where do you go after you've won a Mercury prize or a MOBO? And you know, give the guy some gigs that earn him a lot of money. And the same for Denys Baptiste, because I think a lot of musicians had to change their way completely, like Courtney Pine and do things that appeal to a broader audience and actually take away the impression of the greatness of the musicianship.

So I live in hope that we will support our jazz artists. I'm not saying that jazz artists should just be staunchly jazzers and ignore everything else. No, because most jazz musicians you talk to love all other kinds of music. I'd just like to see that kind of *acceptance* come back to jazz, to the people who are actually *doing* the music - not just people who they are selling to the mass market - who the public may find really unhip.

There's a lot of *hip* stuff going on!

Selected CDs		
Language of Truth	Julian Joseph	[1991, East West Records]
In Concert at Wigmore Hall	Julian Joseph	[1994, Eastwest]
Universal Traveller	Julian Joseph	[1996, East West Records]

Ingrid Laubrock

Ingrid Laubrock, born in 1970 in Stadtlohn in northern Germany, plays soprano, alto and tenor saxes, but now mainly the soprano. Originally a classical piano student, she arrived in London in 1989 and immediately began learning the alto saxophone, three years later adding the soprano and then the tenor in 1994. She has studied with Jean Toussaint and US sax player, David Liebman.

She joined singer Monica Vasconcelos' band Nois, a Brazilian jazz group exploring Brazilian musical cultures and performed in As Meninas with Monica and Ife Tolentino and Chris Wells. In 1999 she took the Guildhall Post-Graduate Jazz Course, which has developed both her playing capabilities and her confidence and directions as a respected composer.

Her first album on Candid in 1997 *Who is it?* demonstrated both her playing and singing talents and her thorough absorption of Brazilian musical influence. Her post-Guildhall album, *Some Times*, [Candid, 2001] in contrast, was largely own compositions of a contemporary jazz feel.

Besides continuing her Brazilian connection, Ingrid leads a quartet and is a member of rising trumpeter Tom Arthur's band Centripede and a jazz musicians' collective, F-ire, that has the objective of gaining more performing opportunities for young jazz musicians. F-ire won the 2004 BBC Jazz Award for Innovation.

What kind of music can you first remember listening to in the home?

Both my parents love classical music and a lot of music was being played at home. My father played the piano late at night after finishing work or whenever he had time to, especially Beethoven, Mozart and also Bach, whom I particularly love. He used to teach music at a grammar school.

In your teens, did you listen to more than classical music?

My home town was very small, so there wasn't much besides classical and mainstream popular music. It's a traditional kind of place, so jazz hadn't even arrived there. (It still hasn't, it just sort of bypassed that area, apart from a few very curious people.) It was mainly classical and church music, so I played and sang a lot in choirs.

But when I was ten, I was given a massive old valve radio and started to check out different programmes. I found quite a few strange free jazz late night programmes. And that got me started listening to other music — way out kind of music but it really interested me at that time.

I wasn't into pop music at that age. I was even given some grief by people in my class at school. I did like heavier funk and some rock, but not the 80's pop at all.

It was pretty terrible in Britain.

It was mainly British!

Er, yes. I understand that there were German oompah bands at large in your area?

You didn't hear much of it, but when you did, the 'folk music' was awful. I grew up in a tiny place, in a little village outside Stadtlohn -we didn't even have a shop! It's a farming community and the music they listen to at their summer festivals - like the Octoberfests - is really terrible and very loud, there's no escape.

May it have influenced your music more than you think?

Don't say that! It's only once a year - two or three days of suffering.

So in your teens, you were progressing well as a piano student playing classical music. Then in 1989, when you were nineteen, you came to London.

I had a lot of friends in Germany between fifteen and eighteen who played jazz. We were listening very intensely mainly to Miles, the Seventies Miles Davis. Afterwards, Sixties Miles, almost three years of listening to that music.

I went to my friends' jams, to their rehearsals, to gigs and then I met someone and moved to Berlin to live with him. He wanted to come to England. I didn't really know what I wanted to do, I'd just finished school and was a kind of free spirit, or maybe just lost... So I followed him to England and I did love it – I came for a holiday to see what it was like and we just stayed! And here I am now, fourteen years later!

But suddenly you wanted not just to listen, but to play jazz?

That's right. I guess when I lived in Germany I was just very shy about trying it out, coming from a classical background and the safety net of having scores in front of you, even though I have been performing in front of people since I was seven.

In Germany I had been surrounded by these musicians who were learning but was too shy myself to ask for help with it. So I needed a

change of scene where nobody knew me and I didn't have anything to prove.

I picked up the alto saxophone and suddenly changed into the complete opposite – went busking without being able to play and probably made a complete fool of myself! My boyfriend, a guitarist, had some knowledge of jazz and we lived for about eight months just busking. We 'worked' in tube stations and places like Notting Hill Market and were constantly running away from the police but I had a great time learning and for the first time knowing what I wanted to do. I would play all the time, tried to learn more standards and got really interested in improvisation. I played during the day and practiced when I came back.

Then I started having lessons with Jean Toussaint [tenor/soprano sax, ex-Jazz Warriors] on harmony. These were private lessons – I rang him up and he said he doesn't usually teach beginners but somehow he made an exception. Must have been the desperation in my voice! It was fantastic, he took so much time and helped me a lot .

When did you make your decision to be a professional jazz musician?

It wasn't really a conscious decision, like saying I'm going to college, it just happened. I just got really interested, so from busking I started doing gigs, restaurant gigs with other musicians and the path slowly appeared, so to speak.

In 1993 you teamed up with Monica Vasconcelos [singer, bandleader of Nois] from Sao Paulo. How did your Brazilian connection came about?

I met Monica through some German friends that I had over from Berlin. She had just arrived from Brazil and came over to our house to record something in my partner's studio. She heard me practicing and asked if I didn't want to try a few things with her. Then she would come over and we worked out songs, got a repertoire together and started playing some gigs. Then she got Ife [Tolentino] involved on guitar. She's been living over here since then and we've been working together for ten years now.

In some of your vocals you sing in Portuguese and you capture those beautiful nuances in the language.

I learned Portuguese because I've always wanted to know what I was playing and of course singing about –I think it helps if you understand the lyrics of songs to reflect on them in your improvisation - I think it adds a separate dimension to your playing. In the case of a song, the words are half of it, so why ignore them?

I discovered that Brazil has composers and songwriters with an amazing knack of doing beautifully poetic things. One of my favourite ones, Chico Buarque, writes the most touching lyrics - you could make a book out of just those poems! Though somehow a lot of these lyrics lose their poetry in translation.

One of your teachers was David Liebman; how did that start?

At the time I found his books, *Self-Portrait of an Artist* and *How to develop a Personal Saxophone Sound* really helpful. I felt the need for some guidance especially as I had been mainly self-taught and had never been to any college. So I wrote a letter to David and he invited me to his masterclasses in Pennsylvania. I went and it was great – extremely full-on and very honest.

You mean pretty candid assessments?

Well, he really shreds people you know, he takes people to pieces, but then he also builds you up. He's very experienced and he doesn't pussyfoot around. He sees your weaknesses and strengths and then he points you in the right direction (or what he thinks is the right direction…).

What did you find you were weak on at that time?

My knowledge about a number of quite basic things, that stemmed really from being self-taught. Firstly getting a better understanding of the tradition, what other people have done.

Plus I've always transcribed [recorded music] but I hadn't always done it in a thorough way. I came back from that course and I took almost a whole year out just to practice, going back to Germany for six months and just practicing. I've been to his masterclasses twice - in 1998 and 1999. In between I sometimes meet and chauffeur him around and hang out, because it's part friendship but always educational.

What kind of things were you practicing?

Bebop. Practicing bebop and not much else. As incredible as it seems, because I'm not sure how much of that you can hear in my playing! But that's all I was practicing – bebop tunes, standards, language, I did many transcriptions and also worked a lot on sound. Oh, and I made a point of writing at least one tune a week.

It's part of making yourself 'secure' as a player?

That's right. It was so helpful for understanding the music. I'm not a bebop player and have no aspirations to be one but it is the root of things and everybody borrows from it – even pop players steal bits. In those six months I mainly transcribed Sonny Rollins, Dexter

Gordon, Sonny Stitt and Charlie Parker and it was great! It makes me appreciate it all so much more now.

In 1997, you recorded your first album. How did that come about?

It was mostly chance really that I was able to do that album. I had been doing a gig with Monica when Astrud Gilberto's band came and sat in and we played all night, till about five o' clock. The next day they invited us to their gig at the Jazz Café. The trombonist, a guy from NY called Luis Bonilla, was signed to Candid. He introduced me to Alan [Bates, MD Candid], saying, 'You have to listen to her.' Alan came to a few gigs of Monica's band Nois and after a bit he said, 'Why don't you do your own thing?' Well I was completely shell-shocked, trying to run away from it really, because I'd never written any music, hadn't thought of having a band, or didn't think I was able to direct a band.

You were co-leader of Al Meninas but you'd never written for it?

No, never. So suddenly I was having to write music and it was a real challenge. I feel grateful to Alan for believing in me at that time. Without that I don't think I would have gone ahead with it.

You said once it is quite revealing composing yourself?

Yes, well you have all the time in the world to do it so the finished result is a really personal statement. It says: this is my taste, this is what I hear and this puts you in a position where you can be – well – trashed! So you feel really vulnerable and it took some getting used to.

Yes, Denys Baptiste was saying you feel you have just one chance with your first album, you need it to be good.

That's right, but I've always felt that you grow with every album you do as you learn so much every time. I have felt so far that each album I did was better than the one before, but that is natural I suppose.

Every recording can only go as far as you (and the other musicians) are at that point in time. It's obvious but this also means that recording is a long term process that documents your development. It's like a photo album. I'm much less nervous about recording since making that clear for myself.

Many have commented glowingly on your compositions though you'd fought shy of it.

Yes, I was shy of it but again it was David Liebman who encouraged me. He said, 'You really have a thing for composition, so you should do it.' I've been writing much more prolifically in the last few years. It's all practice really. I would love to study composition with someone, but so far that is a plan for the future.

Were you pleased with the reception to your first album?

Yes I was. It was a way in for me. Before that, nobody knew me so it was a better way of getting gigs, getting promoters to hire the band, a kind of business card really.

Then in 1999 you took the Guildhall Post-graduate Jazz Course.

Yes – it was a bit late – I was kind of the old one! But I enjoyed a lot of the course. I was pleased because it cleared up a lot of things that I had sort of pieced together. It was good to have someone demonstrating in an analytical way how things work.

The course gives you the chance to try new things, even if they didn't end up sounding good. You could allow yourself to take all the risks…

But the biggest benefit of a course like that must be meeting people and having a chance to play together all the time. Having rehearsal rooms was great, no neighbours to worry about, no audiences. It's just so hard in London, you have neighbours everywhere and rehearsal studios are a luxury.

Then it was time for your second album?

For that I tried to convince Candid that I didn't only want to do music influenced by Brazil. I said it's one side of me but not really what I want to do.

Was that anything to do with the Guildhall course?

It was through going to David Liebman, listening to music far more than before, checking out things that are closer to me and also things that I had listened to as a teenager. So revisiting a lot of Miles, a lot of Coltrane and these things made me think that was the most you can get out of a saxophone – music where you can stretch and really express yourself.

The Brazilian thing is playing songs, something I really love doing, but the saxophone has a different place in it and it is not what I ultimately want to do. I said to Alan that I'm spending so much time trying to improve, to become a better saxophonist, I don't want to play just one style of music. I really would like to do a jazz album. They said to be sure you include guests, use your arranging skills, get more horns on it and make it varied. So I used many of the tunes and arrangements that I wrote while at college.

It seems both contemporary and very clearly arranged and played across a range of styles. For instance, Hands, a duet, seems very poetic.

Yes, with me and Nikki [Iles, piano], I love that. She is someone I immediately felt comfortable playing with and would like to work with more. It just hasn't happened so far.

You've also played with some remarkable players like Django Bates and Kenny Wheeler; did you enjoy playing with them?

I just always find it amazing how different people work; especially those people like Kenny Wheeler or Django Bates who really are special.

Every bandleader does things in his very own way and it's great to watch. There's no rule as to how to do it - that's a fantastic thing to learn. And of course it's inspiring being involved with people who have produced so much amazing music.

Can we talk about some of the tracks on your last album?

There are a number of them from the second album we still play in live gigs, *Some Times, Hannah's Song, Lennie's Pennies, Friends* and *Hands*. These are the tracks that have survived and have really grown and moved into different directions now.

Others, like *Access all Areas*, were written for a larger ensemble and we haven't played it very often since the recording.

You say that you don't compose down to a great level of detail. Instead you like to see the tune develop...

Sometimes I might compose down to great detail, but I really want people to give of themselves to the music, or it can become a bit like a dictatorship. I don't assume that I write a better line than the bass player, or a nicer voicing than the piano player — basically because I won't! If I let people play what they hear, within the frame of the tune, they will make it sound a lot better than I myself could have imagined. The choice of musicians is more important than the written material....

The interplay between the horns is a feature of the album — using Julian Siegel.

Julian has a very special voice and approach. The tenor and soprano conversation between him and me on *Nuff Said* is a moment on the album I really enjoyed. I also love the way his bass clarinet compliments my singing on *Beatrice*.

What about your future now? Perhaps you could tell me about the last album you've recorded?

I have recorded a new album called *Forensic*. My quartet has been playing live now for two years and the music has moved on quite a lot. It's become a lot freer — we're playing the tunes and the harmony, but take many more risks now. We might play a tune one day and then completely differently the next day, vary the speed, the form, the way we start, whatever. After our last tour, I thought I needed to document this band now.

I've always loved working with groups — with the same people whom you know. I think that most classic albums are actually bands, not super-groups, or bands stuck together for one occasion.

And I'm really determined to keep working with the musicians whom I've got to know so well. Basically record companies always want a hook which usually means high profile guests — of course they want to sell the CDs, which is fair enough. But I believe in bands, so I kind of decided to go for it myself — pay for it myself. I did get one guest, Ben Davis on cello, a fantastic improviser and he plays on seven out of the eleven tracks. The rest is the quartet, all original material.

You still continue with your Brazilian music?

The other side of me is still working with Brazilian music, which I love. Our band, As Meninas has just been to Brazil to record a new album, *Coisa Musical* for Candid Records. We recorded with musicians from Brazil like Swami Jr on 7-string guitar and bass, Toninho Ferraguti on accordion, Guilherme Kastrup on percussion, Webster on cavaquinho and Guinga, one of the most exciting songwriter/guitarists around at the moment. We have plans to bring at least him over to the UK and do some gigs together later this year.

We also played a few gigs in Brazil which was great fun, so we hope to go back soon.

Now about the general health of jazz in the UK, what are your views on how it's doing?

I think the London scene has a lot of talent, a lot of creativity. It's the kind of scene not everyone knows about, because the exposure isn't wide enough and the media unfortunately concentrates on the most commercial stuff! There are definitely a lot of musicians here who deserve wider recognition than they are getting...while the record industry and press focus on a few...

I am bored with the fact that the same few people are getting the exposure – good luck to them obviously. But I know of a number who don't get the recognition they deserve, but who are writing and playing amazing music - but promoters, producers, the media are scared to touch them.

So I question whether the media is fulfilling its function as an impartial means of providing information to the public. I don't think so…

Many musicians are concerned that their music isn't getting enough exposure and about people being very conservative musically. So a few of us have now joined forces and formed this collective called F-ire. We have an administrator and we're starting to put together our own festival. We have a website, [www.f-ire.com] and we have a compilation CD, trying to take things into our own hands. Because we know how much good music there is that people don't know enough about.

Someone has mentioned that jazz club audiences have been known to prefer standards to original pieces?

I like standards, but I think the real nature of jazz is shown by people who've moved it on – like Louis Armstrong, Charlie Parker, Miles Davis, Coltrane, Keith Jarrett or Wayne Shorter….the list is long. They have not held back and have always incorporated new ideas and emotions, so I don't really understand why people think that needs to stop! It's positive that people try to explore and stretch themselves (and the audience for that matter). I understand that there's a place for music that is played more or less exactly as it was in another era, and why not, it's great music and it can take a lifetime to play it well.

But there should be room and tolerance for musicians who don't want to do that…I think listeners should have a right to be able to choose what they're going to listen to, and a variety of music should be on offer to them - and not just in London or the big cities.

It's possible to modernise standards with new harmonies and styles..

If the song is good, the possibilities are infinite. Most jazz musicians play and practice the standards, though it is a challenge to come up with anything different from what's already been done. But I've done a lot of gigs with almost all original music, played all over England and the audience does usually get into the music.

The better players demonstrate a clarity whatever they're playing, whichever styles?

I can listen to music from all eras, ranging from Sidney Bechet, for example, to avant-garde music. I can always see the thread of what makes somebody good and the conviction about what they're doing – as well as their knowledge and personality.

So I feel that if you have real clarity about what you are doing, you can ignore any rejection better…and after all, it is what *you* hear that will be your own guiding light!

Selected CDs		
Some Times	Ingrid Laubrock	[2001, Candid]
Gente	Nois4	[2003, Candid]
Centripede	Tom Arthurs	[2004, Babel]
Forensic	Ingrid Laubrock	[2004, F-ire]
Website: www.ingridlaubrock.com		

Steve Melling

Steve Melling, born 1959 in Accrington, Lancashire, cut his teeth as a jazz pianist in pubs in Northern England as a teenager then came south to take a classical music degree at Goldsmiths' College, University of London. He then joined the National Youth Jazz Orchestra and played there for three years. On leaving Goldsmiths', Steve joined the band of Harry Beckett and Elton Dean. His next move was to the exciting but tough New York jazz scene and after a year of much gigging, returned to England where he worked with bands including Barbara Thompson's band Paraphernalia. Steve was a long-term member of the successful Clark Tracey Quintet in the 1980's and 1990's. He has since evolved long term relationships in the bands of Peter King and Alan Skidmore.

He has also played with many visiting players including Phil Woods, Elvin Jones, James Moody, Charles McPherson and Perico Sambeat.

Steve has played and recorded with the singers Claire Martin and Trudy Kerr. He is a gifted composer and a number of his tunes are on his 1996 album, *Trio, Duo, Solo*. His latest CD, *Solar* [2003] features his quartet live at the Appleby Festival.

His current main gigs are the Peter King Quartet and Quintet, Alan Skidmore's Quartet and Ubizo and Celebrating the Jazz Couriers, a band that resurrects the legendary 1960s' music of the Tubby Hayes and Ronnie Scott band.

Steve was awarded the Pat Smythe Award as Most Promising UK Pianist in 1986.

What kind of music can you first remember listening to?

The first music I remember as a small child was rock and roll and seeing my Mum and Dad jiving to it. That was my first of any kind of music – Bill Haley's 'Rock around the clock' and Elvis.

When did you first start a musical instrument?

I started on piano when I was about nine years old. One day in school, we were inside because of the rain and there was a piano in the classroom. I knew this girl the same age. The teacher asked 'Would you play the piano?' So she played for us and I thought, 'This is fantastic!' I turned to my friend next to me and said 'This is great;

wish I could do that.' And he said, ' I can play.' And I thought, 'Can everybody play?' and 'Why can't I?'

Well the next day it wasn't raining, so people were out, but I said to him 'Let's go in and play!' So we snuck in and he showed me his little tune. So I learnt the little tune, went home to my Dad and said, 'I can play the piano!' So I kept saying it to him and he said eventually, 'Would you *really* like to be able to play and take lessons?' So he found me some lessons from a classical teacher. He got me a piano from down the road, someone gave it to us, quite a heap of a piano. I had it for about five or six years until I changed it for something that I had for a good twenty years or more, and then I got the piano I've got now.

Your Dad sounds really supportive.

He and Mum didn't play anything themselves but they loved music to dance to. My parents were divorced when I was around six, but my Dad continued - we lived with my Dad - to support me. When I was in gigs with the youth bands he would drive me all around Lancashire to different schools – he was always there.

Were you learning classical?

I learnt classical music from age nine with a classical teacher, Miss Jessie Lawson. A brass plaque announced 'Teacher of Pianoforte' outside her house – serious stuff, you know – she was recommended by a guy who played jazz, a jazz pianist who played in the local pubs and clubs. So my Dad took me there.

I had learnt classical music from her and then tried to learn jazz on my own, because I was being influenced by my Dad's record collection, which had Dizzy Gillespie, Stan Kenton and the Ted Heath orchestra. And I started to try to play it by ear when I was about eleven, and then got together with a couple of guys at school and tried to play some traditional jazz from the music - the chord symbols were written out there as sevenths. It was seeing the two together- that's how I worked out what the chord symbols meant. By the time I was sixteen, we had an eleven-piece band at school playing Glen Miller and Count Basie.

By the time I was sixteen, I was sitting in with bands. My Dad would take me to hear jazz at local clubs and pubs, normally mainstream bands. After a while I would sit in, not knowing what I was doing, but got through it somehow. Good experience.

Your decision to become a musician?

Well I did my A level music, then it came time for university. But I didn't know where to go, my father had never been to university, so I just went to the music teacher.

He said that while [London's] Kings College was good, Goldsmiths was the one because it was more actively musical than the others. So I went for an interview and got in, to do classical. One reason I went to Goldsmiths was that in their prospectus they had a picture of Stan Tracey, saying that he taught jazz there at the college. By the time I got there, he didn't teach there anymore! And there was no jazz.

Obviously I know Stan, spoken to him since and he couldn't face turning up there every week and to have people turn up every week having not practiced anything, or knowing anything really, they weren't into it. So he stopped.

There was no jazz there, *except* an evening course run by Don Rendell. It was an Adult Ed thing and I was just passing and heard it, and ended up doing one gig with them. That was it, I wasn't really part of the band, and it wasn't very good. But there I met somebody who played with the National Youth Jazz Orchestra. He said 'Why don't you come and sit in, see how it goes?' So I did and within a few months I was in the band and played there for about three years.

What age range did the band use?

Well the youngest person that I know who's been in the band is Nigel (Hitchcock) and I think he was thirteen to fourteen and playing lead alto for Christ's sake! Bill Ashton, who runs it, lets people go eventually. I joined up at nineteen, toured Australia with them for a couple of weeks and did a tour of Turkey.

Then after that, I got my *first* freelance jazz gig! But my first actual *paid* gig was after I had left college, made the decision to do it. I was getting commercial work then, and a few jazz gigs. But my first *proper* jazz gig was with Harry Beckett and Elton Dean — we did a Jazz Services tour. That's when I considered myself to be starting properly as a jazz musician - at about twenty-one or two.

Did you stay to the end of the Goldsmith's course?

I left after about a year and a half. It was because I was doing a lot of NYJO gigs, and other commercial work which made a bit of money, and my college work had gone down and I thought I might not get to the end of the year! And I'm starting to do what I want; this is really what I'm interested in.

What style of jazz did Harry Beckett [trumpet, flugelhorn] and Elton Dean [alto sax] play?

Well it was a surprise to me because I went there to play a few tunes, but they *played free*! There were tunes, but they were played in a very free style. Harry would write a tune that he would say was a ballad, would probably be about eight bars long, but it would take him about two minutes to play the melody, because he would play a little bit of it and then improvise then play the next part and then improvise… so the tune was very stretched and the chord sequence would just say E^b. But you could play within E^b wherever you wanted – it was really a *modal* kind of piece based around E^b major. So I remember you were very much required to do your thing and put your ideas into the music rather than play a set of chord changes.

This was following the time when Americans like Bill Evans and Miles Davis were doing modal jazz.

Miles had been experimenting with modal music since the 1950s and this was 1980 when he was much more free, more of a fusion. But yes, Harry is influenced by Miles, very much.

After that band, I lived in America for a year in Brooklyn, New York, and I had met my first wife then, got married out there, did a few gigs, played at the Blue Note – one night – to a lot of people talking. But I played a lot – didn't make much money but I

played a lot, met a lot of musicians and learnt a lot.

Then my first wife (American) and I decided we would come to England, again as neither of us were seeming to get where we wanted to go, we were struggling. I knew I could get work reasonably swiftly and I did, working in a West End show to make some money. While I was doing that, I think one or two people heard me but obviously playing that sort of show music, you're not going to get people giving you jazz gigs. So

then I did about a three month stint with The Three Degrees and toured round with them. The saxophone player in that band lived in Sutton - and as he was going round the local

Sainsbury's, he met Barbara Thompson [leader of Paraphernelia, saxes]. She said we're getting some music together, doing a tour, we need a keyboard player. He said, 'I know a good one,' so I auditioned, got the gig and we did a tour of Germany for a month.

That was a jazz-fusion style of music?

Very much so, it was a fusion of many kinds of music, all original material, as all Barbara's is. Also she had her husband Jon Hiseman [drums], formerly with Coliseum.

Were you pleased with the piano material you were playing there?

No, it was in the right area in that it was jazz with improvisation, but it still wasn't the kind of style that I wanted to play in. *And* I wanted to play the *piano*! *Not* electric. I had two synthesisers and an electric piano and that was it! And it was loud and I didn't really know what I was doing, faffing around with these sounds, not really enjoying myself. It wasn't as much modern jazz as I wanted it to be, it was fusion which is different. Swing – I wanted to swing and they didn't. Even when they were swinging, they weren't swinging!

Then I met Clark Tracey around 1989 through a little rehearsal band at somebody's house. We did one or two gigs over a period of about a year. Nothing much happened with it, we just played. Then Clark said, 'I'm getting a band together – we need a couple of horn players' – he had the rhythm section - he got Guy Barker and Jamie Talbot and we rehearsed one or two times then started doing gigs. That band lasted for *quite* some years, three CDs, two tours of the Far East, a tour of Yugoslavia – short one, just before they blew it to pieces – and that was hard bop really. You may know that Clark is very influenced by Art Blakey so that's the kind of vein it was in – 'The Tribute to Art Blakey' band, which I play in.

Looking back on it, and after listening to a recording that has recently appeared, we did play a few different kinds of music. We did an album called *Stiperstones*. West Midlands Arts and Shropshire County Council sponsored it and I co-wrote a suite called *Stiperstones* with Clark. We did a vinyl album; mine was the first side and his was the second. That was my first real venture into writing jazz tunes.

A lot of the bands these days are pickup bands. How much does a regular relationship like this help you to play better?

A lot! When you are asked to do a new gig, you always ask who's on bass, who's on drums, what style it will be and you know if you're going to have a good time.

You've worked with Tim Whitehead?

Yes, I don't work with Tim now, he has his own thing going, but I worked with him for a few years and we made an album, *Decision*, with John Parricelli, Dudley Phillips and Nic France. And that was all Tim's original compositions, one of mine, and a standard. And *that's* the one they play on the radio, or they did!

It was a good recording experience that album, because we worked on things in the studio, we didn't prepare something and then trot it out in the studio and say, 'There, that sounds fine.' We actually went in, recorded, listened to it and then said, 'No, let's do things in different ways, change things radically.' It was a luxury really, to have that time – lot of money spent on that item! But good studio experience.

Tell me about working with Alan Skidmore [saxes].

Well, Skid asked, 'Can you do a gig down the Bull?' so I did these gigs with Skid. He's extremely influenced by John Coltrane. He says he's dedicated his life to try to emulate that kind of spirit and he's been doing it for about 40 years now. He turned sixty last year. His background is full of great names that he's worked with - he was involved with the European Jazz Quintet and he toured Europe playing *free* jazz. He also had bands, a three-saxophone group - SOS, Skidmore, Osborne [alto sax] and Surman [baritone and soprano saxes] and SOH, with Tony Oxley on drums and Ali Haurand on bass.

Skid was very important in the free jazz area in the Sixties and Seventies, and like me, he has also played with Elvin Jones and his 'Jazz Machine'. There are *four* British musicians who have played with Elvin – Skid, myself, Pete King and John Surman. That was something fantastic for me.

But playing with Skid, when I first joined that band, I didn't know I'd joined it. He still hasn't said, 'Will you join my band?' or anything. I was sort of booked to play in this band and I thought, 'This is music that I really love; I can't play it, but I'm doing it anyway.' And it wasn't right and Skid would go, 'OK' and then he'd book me again and he'd say, 'OK,' - not much really, but when is he going to say, 'That's great'? Again he says, 'OK.' And we carry on for many years till *eventually* he starts saying, 'This is starting to come together now.' And it took *years* to come together in the right style, in the Coltrane vein – modal, elements of free jazz, swing, the right kind of drummer, right kind of comping, with the right feeling or *spirit*. McCoy Tyner has always influenced my playing and that has been

my *Tyner* 'outlet', where I could *really* play in that style.

There's early and later Tyner styles?

Yes, there's a difference and with Skid's band we do play quite a way across the board. And there's a lot of more popular kind of standards that we play, as well as the more free, groundbreaking style. It's not all free.

Another band that I work in with Alan Skidmore, called *Ubizo*, is an amalgamation of European musicians and South African percussionists and that *certainly* does have wide appeal right across the board, to kids too.

You also play with Pete King [alto] - that's a regular gig?

Yes, it is. Well, the first time I ever played at Ronnie Scott's, it was with Pete King. And that was when I was twenty-one. He just phoned up and said, 'Can you play just one set?' So I did it and he said it was ok, but he didn't call me or anything. Then I happened to do a gig with Colin Town's Mask Orchestra, some years back, I was deputising in that band at a festival - not an easy gig, because Colin is a fully–fledged composer, he doesn't hold back. Pete came and asked for my number after the gig, and started to call me.

He was going through a transition, wanting to get away from the bebop tag, because of course he can play in the Charlie Parker, Phil Woods sort of style but that's not what he wanted to do. So he started to book me more and more and I've made about three or four CDs with him now.

I see there are a couple of your compositions on his album, Lush Life.

Yes, *Brazilian Thoroughfare* and one called *In a Monochrome*. One of those I did on my Trio CD.

You've played with Elvin Jones?

I did two gigs in Germany with Elvin with his band - Ravi Coltrane [saxes], Delfaeyo Marsalis on trombone, Greg Williams on bass. It was quite an experience. Elvin's not only a big, powerful guy, he's *forceful* in the way he speaks and the way he wants his music. Very driving and it's all centred around him, he doesn't cut anybody any slack. If you're not with him, you're wrong, whatever he's doing! If he's playing something that's off the time, or away from the time, that's where the music is. You have to listen hard, can't just comp [accompany] away in four — no chugging along with Elvin, work around him, and stay out of the way, basically! It's quite an oil painting he comes up with, instead of music coming out like toothpaste out of a tube.

And now you're in the Jazz Couriers. They've had great reviews.

Yes, it's great; such a fun band to play with. The music is so alive, it's happy music. Other things are more serious but it's not a *serious* band really in that we're not playing 'serious' type music. It's music to be enjoyed by the audience and by the players — it's got wide appeal.

Tell me about the making of your own album, *Trio, Duo, Solo*.

I'd been playing with lots of different bands at Ronnie Scott's and its Managing Director, Pete King, said I'd like you to play with *your* trio. So I got a trio together, we rehearsed, did some gigs, and the next news, he's put me on at Ronnie's opposite the Brecker Brothers, which then was a *plum* gig, it was wall-to-wall listening people every night. Well, the week went fine, the Brecker Brothers were very nice. After the week, he said 'I want you to make a CD, I'll talk to Derek Everett about it' — he runs the Jazz House label.

At that time I was flavour of the year at Ronnie's, working with my own thing, with other bands, backing an American artist, so there for several weeks. These days you're lucky to get a couple of weeks a year, but I was there then for about 13-14 weeks.

Are you pleased with the CD?

It was certainly the best job I could have done at the time and there are some good things on it. They used to play a couple of tracks on JazzFM, Humphrey Lyttelton and programmes like that.

I try to do a bit of everything and I'm pleased with it on that score, because a lot of the great jazz composers are represented. There's Duke Ellington, John Coltrane, Bud Powell, Thelonius Monk, and I kind of play in those sorts of styles. And there's me, as well, doing *my* thing!

There's a recording being done at the Appleby Festival later this year of my quartet featuring Nigel Hitchcock on alto. We'll call the album *Solar*.

It seems it's tricky, with the sax-led bands, to have a pianist-led band these days?
Sometimes Dave Newton leads his trio but... do you see that as changing?

Well, it's difficult to see that changing — it's just the nature of the instruments — people just *do like* a saxophone, and it can just go anywhere and get gigs. With the piano it's different. Some places don't have a piano, or they have a pile of —— and I just don't want to go there. Other places will supply an electric and I don't really want to play that either. So it's difficult. Some of the places are getting better, but there's still places that just don't have it or they've got a piano and nobody's complained about it – or they just don't have the money - when a couple of thousand quid - which is not really a lot of money these days - would buy you something that's getting there at least.

How did you approach the challenge of learning jazz as opposed to classical music?

Well, I tried to play things by ear from records, playing them over and over again and trying to play it. I just listen to the record. And as I discussed earlier, I was lucky enough to have the chord symbols for big band parts, which often have them written out on the music so you can actually see the voicings that are given, and work out for yourself what they mean. I've never had a jazz teacher, only a classical one.

Have you used transcription machines for slower playback?

No, I've never used those.

Who are your main musical influences?

Well, pianistically – McCoy Tyner, Art Tatum and Chick Corea. Otherwise, Coltrane has to be the main influence.

And classically, Messiaen and Ravel I love – they're great to listen to.

What do you think are the best techniques for learning jazz?

I can recommend people to learn their own way like I did. I was very lucky to have the opportunity to make music, play music with others, even if it was down the pub on a Tuesday night – that's ideal, anything like that. Opportunities like that. *Live music* inspires you, whether you're just listening to it or taking part. If you're taking part, it does inspire you to practice, to get better, to listen to other people, recordings. So listening to whatever music you can, though mainly of the type you want to learn.

But I think you have to have a good teacher as well. The way I did it was I had a classical teacher – it might seem that it doesn't quite work but it does. I believe that having a classical grounding with lots of theory in it too, which I had, was invaluable in making sense of jazz - because that's what you've got to do. You never exactly learn it, you *keep on* learning it, and you just make sense of it as you go along. That to me is the way that it ought to be done.

Is your style still changing now?

Mmm, yes it is, only little by little, because I don't put the hours in that I used to. I used to play all the time! But now, I do so many gigs, that my practice goes out of the window a little bit, [so] I keep my chops in order by playing gigs. Occasionally I feel I've lost it and have to put some hours in at the piano.

How was your time as Professor of Jazz Piano at the Royal College of Music?

Well, that's a very lofty title, isn't it? I taught piano at the Royal College of Music. I was called a Professor, they're all called that, and I didn't fulfil any prescribed criteria! Jazz was an option within a classical degree course. No department under you, although it needed one. Now there *is* one, that was formed by my successor, Charlie Beale, together the Associated Board Jazz Piano exams. He's there now with, I believe, a department.

I taught a few students. But I thought the College was surprisingly ill equipped. One or two people were reasonably accepting of jazz and jazz musicians but there was also a lot of decadence about. Their resources were very small, too. I went and asked for any jazz recordings and they came up with late nineteenth-cen-

tury American marches – it had to be under American music! I managed to get some jazz books into the library for them but that was the only little bit of money they could spare.

Any current involvement with Goldsmiths'?

Well, I occasionally provide piano accompaniment for singers' classes run by Louise Gibbs. It's good practice for a pianist with singers singing in all different keys all over the place – they'll have their music but it won't be in the right key and must be transposed at sight. That's hairy at

first but then you get into it and it becomes second nature, a good workout. As for gigs with singers, I worked with Claire Martin for quite a few years ago now and I'm now working with Trudy Kerr, and naturally her husband Geoff Gascoyne.

So what kind of activities do you see for yourself in the future?

What I'm wishing for is that my writing opens out. My eleven-piece band got off the ground last year, thanks to the Friends of Appleby Jazz Festival who commissioned me to write an hour of music for them, so I'm hoping that the band and all kinds of writing will flourish.

I'm writing some other stuff, for example, for the Jazz Couriers. Because the original Couriers only made three recordings we've almost exhausted those now, so I wrote an original in that style.

And I'm always writing for Peter King, that's something I love to do. I write the music down using my computer's Sibelius program. I love to sit there and twiddle and fiddle around, especially with a bigger score, playing it back – it's wonderful.

But that is something I have made progress with since I've really started, two or three years ago and I hope to be more known as a writer, composer and arranger. It's only small scale at the moment, because not a lot of people know that I can actually do that. People who've heard can be surprised and said, 'I didn't know you could do that!'

Is jazz on the up in the UK?

Well, I think we need money. It's the old tale that we always need more money in order to put little gigs on but also to do some of the *larger* scale things that are in people's heads at the moment. Because there just are. If I think of myself, I've sat playing the piano for years and come to the stage where I've been working on something and thought that I can't play it anymore because it's too big. So I need to write it for a band. Then how do you get it played, you need money! And when you think of the amount of money that goes into classical music – people have been banging on about this for years and it's still true, that the amount of money that goes into jazz is a pittance compared to what gets put into opera, supporting orchestras etc. So that is *still* what we need.

We do get some Arts Council money going into Jazz Services – there is a limit to it – but we will get some money to do a tour, but you do have to organise the tour yourself. Then some money goes in, but they don't organise it for you. You get the gigs first and then say, there's a shortfall. Then you get money if you qualify. It's not a lot of money – I remember a tour eighteen months ago or so, and the money covered our expenses, that was it. We got paid what we got paid from the gigs. We did ok, but it wasn't fabulous.

So what do you think of the jazz pianist's life? Better than working in an office?

Yes, it is. Sometimes when I haven't got any work, I think I could have been a train driver or something, but no, it's much better than *working* for a living!

Selected CDs

Trio, Duo, Solo	Steve Melling Trio [1996, Ronnie Scott's Jazz House]
Footprints	Peter King Quartet [2003, Miles Music]
Solar	Steve Melling Quartet [2003, Jazz on Line]

Website for albums: jazzstoreonline.com

Jim Mullen

Jim Mullen, born in 1945 in Glasgow, is a wonderfully gifted jazz guitarist whose music has migrated from jazz to rock to jazz fusion and back to straightahead jazz. He was leading jazz groups in Scotland until tempted down to London to bands at the jazzy end of the rock spectrum, joining Pete Brown's Piblokto and later Brian Augur's Oblivion Express. Later, just as he was deciding to leave the rock scene in 1975, he and saxophonist Dick Morrissey received invitations to record with the Average White Band in New York. Jim and Dick discovered their identical musical aims of developing their kind of jazz fusion. On their return from the States, the Morrissey-Mullen band became hugely popular and influential in promoting jazz fusion for fifteen years till it broke up in 1990. Jim then formed his own jazz quartet which has since produced four albums. His Organ Trio featuring Jim Watson and Matt Skelton has brought out two albums.

In 2000 Jim's quartet issued the album *Burns* based on the songs of the Scottish bard, which attracted wide critical acclaim. His quartet is made up of Gareth Williams (piano), Mick Hutton (bass) and Gary Husband (drums).This was followed by *Animations*, based on early cartoons. His latest Quartet album was in 2002, *Somewhere in the Hills*.

Jim has played with many leading American and British players including Gene Harris, Mose Allison, Jimmy Smith, Jimmy Witherspoon, Percy Sledge, Tim Garland, Mornington Lockett, Laurence Cottle, Geoff Gascoyne and Claire Martin

He is a three times winner of the award for Best Jazz Guitar in the British Jazz Awards and also won the BT Jazz Award for 2000.

What kind of music do you first remember listening to in the home?

I was born just a few months after World War II ended, so the radio was the way computers are today. It gave you all the great singers of the time and the great songwriters – the Cole Porters, the Gershwins, you heard these because they were the hit songs of the day.

School also opened things up in terms of folk music and the pop songs of the day. Elvis was such a shock when he started. Then we found out that it was all a corruption of Southern States black rhythm 'n blues music.

Your first musical instrument?

The Lonnie Donegan thing was happening and I was in the neighbourhood skiffle group - the tea-chest bass player. I think there was just something about being involved in music, like how democratic it was. I'm not a big political animal but I liked the sharing and I thought it was a real opportunity to make a statement.

Was there any classical music? Any musicians in the family?

No, there were no musicians in the family, nor any classical, though you would hear it on the radio. My particular passion in classical music has always been Italian opera, because I just love those great big *fat* tunes! Beautiful melodies and I've been fooling around with some Puccini recently. [Short, enticing demonstration followed.]

What age were you when you picked up your skiffle group bass?

I was seven, then I got my first guitar when I was eight. I kept pestering my Dad who was a carpenter to make me a guitar. In the end I said to Dad, 'Look can I get a guitar and pay for it on the hire- purchase?' Now working class families were not very keen on the 'never-never' and I remember my Dad giving me very stern lectures. 'If you miss one payment it goes straight back to the shop!' So I bought this guitar for just £10 or so and paid it back over a year, but it was piece of rubbish!

The next thing was trying to figure out something about music. I met this older guy about fifteen or sixteen - he became a life-long friend - who was into jazz. He had a really nice, *proper* arch top electric — a jazz guitar! And I used to go up to his door and ask to just *see* his guitar!

But he knew about jazz and he started to explain. When I went away something had connected and over time I would go up and ask him to play me the records again. He had all the West Coast guitar players - Barney Kessel, Tad Farlow, Mundel Lowe. From that point on, it was just a matter of trying to figure out how to become part of this and that way was through the bass. When I was eleven or twelve, I moved on to bass guitar. At that time there were no bass guitarists playing jazz.

Then the double bass - when I was thirteen or fourteen — it was the only part of jazz I could figure out in the beginning! Then I realised that wouldn't work, my fingers were a mess. This was in the days before bass amplifiers so you really had to have tough hands and pull those bass strings, so I would come home with blisters and the strings would be red!

It also very difficult to play double bass and *then* go and play the guitar, because you've got these big fat bass strings and then you've got

these cheese wires just waiting to slice up all your callouses! I decided to go back to guitar after a few years on bass. Also I wanted to get more into the guitar, to learn harmony, more about chord construction.

I was seventeen or eighteen when I got my first band together in Glasgow.

There was a shop in Glasgow where you could get Blue Note records. I'd grown up listening to all the West Coast stuff but Blue Note was essentially East Coast which meant black - New York, Philadelphia, Washington. So it was a change from all this cool, smooth stuff to this really raw, exciting stuff. A lot of the state of the art players were brought in by Blue Note - people like Herbie Hancock, Wayne Shorter, Freddie Hubbard. That was an important time in my life.

But I think with jazz, it's a process of *absorption*, so that if you're being honest, you need to find some *personal* way to express what you want to do within all the influences and things that have happened to you.

Are you self-taught?

Yes, I'm totally self-taught - never had a lesson. Well there was only one guitar teacher in Glasgow. I didn't go to him because I play with my thumb and he would have said to me, 'Don't do that!' and made me learn correctly. Now the thing is I'm actually left handed but I play right handed because when I first picked up the guitar at eight years old, I wasn't smart enough to figure to turn it over and reverse the strings. All I remember is that my hand-writing fell apart - something to do with the left side of the brain trying to deal with the right side of the body.

Also because I was playing right-handed, it felt weird to hold a pick, they used to go flying out of my hands. In the end, I reckoned I had as much technique with my thumb and this is a bad habit that didn't get corrected.

It can seem to listeners you play so fast that that thumb must be doing better work than a pick?

Well, I don't strike every note. I think that Wes Montgomery also did this - hammer-ons and pull offs - I might strike it once but hammer-on two extra notes and you do the same pulling off, strike one and then pull-off. And you just try to work out a system where you can get rhythmic continuity doing that. It's a little hit and miss, whereas a pick player – you know you play down-strokes with the thumb, with a pick you can play up and down, so I've got 50% of a pick player.

But that raises other questions because everyone has technical limitations anyway. I think it's a matter of maximising what you can do with your technique, rather than trying to have blistering technique without a reason to use it.

Maybe using the thumb enables you to be more expressive than with a pick?

It's the difference between flesh on steel and plastic on steel. Flesh is softer and that created problems for me, simply because I couldn't get enough attack. For a pick player, he can beat those strings, and really make them jump out but for me, I was struggling to get that because the flesh doesn't have such a hard effect on the note. So just learning how to project the sound and get a dynamic was a painstaking learning experience for me, learning by myself. It pushes you to think out what you should really be doing in the music.

I was also learning how to play – I was one of those guys who was allowed to learn how to

play on the bandstand. That really doesn't happen any more, but because I was a bass player and there was always a shortage of bass players, I was getting gigs way above things that I knew how to play.

Meanwhile how was your work in journalism developing?

Well to start with, I worked for a daily paper in Scotland which meant you worked nights. That meant, with only two nights off a week, I wasn't doing a lot of gigs.. Then I moved to an evening paper which meant working office hours with every night *free*.

Also the paper that I moved to was so far inferior to the daily paper. I was a sub-editor and I was having to re-write almost everything I got because it was all written in archaic language that nobody spoke. The City reporter actually looked like something out of Dickens time, he walked around with a pinstripe suit and a monocle! I'd hear a loud, 'Who's rewriting my copy?' So I had to justify myself – the Editor came out and gave me a hard time! So my days may already have been numbered.

But because I had all this time free, I started getting more involved and having all these bands and I could play music seven nights a week if I wanted to. So I started to get my musical life together. Then I got a call when I was twenty-three to go and play in this band in London run by a guy called Pete Brown who was involved with Jack Bruce and Cream, in fact he wrote a lot of their big hits. He's made a fortune, this guy. But he wanted me to be part of his band and although it wasn't really what I wanted to do – it was a rock band – he was into jazz and he said to me, 'The sky's the limit' - no limitations on what we can do here. So I'm thinking this is a gig that gets me into London, with a much bigger scene. I already knew about the London jazz musicians and stuff, been to Ronnie Scott's and things.

I decided to take my courage in my hands and give it a go. I grew my hair and all this stuff. But it was a *loud* band. I mean – Jesus, you'd finish a gig and your ears would be ringing for the next two days! So many people I know from that time have serious hearing problems, tinnitus at the least or complete deafness in one ear. So I got out just in time, I think.

There was a demarcation line between musical styles. The jazz guys had no interest in the rock guys and vice versa. I would go along and try to sit in with people. I'd have the long hair and they'd look at you, like, can you play jazz? Yes, I know the song and I'd call out song titles but they'd be suspicious, they wouldn't let me, you know? People I've played with many times since. I liked the idea of playing in different areas, of maybe bringing the styles together.

Then I joined Brian Augur, the great British Hammond organ player. I was in his band for a couple of years and that was great, touring Europe most of the time. Brian was a great musician, he was everything that most rock guys aren't. He started out playing real music and he gave me a lot of space, more space than I was able to fill really, because Brian's band was a blowing band, you know? A lot of fast, very exciting rock grooves and you could play as long as you

wanted. Well I didn't have enough to say then. I felt overextended and I left Brian's band – which was a big mistake and played in other nondescript sorts of bands. I got to the point in about 1974 when I'd left the last band I'd been in and I thought it was over for me,. I'd had a bellyful of the loud stuff; the sonic battering ram.

About that time, I got a call from some friends of mine in Scotland who were having a big success in the States as the Average White Band. The tenor player, Malcolm Duncan, whom I'd known since we were quite young said, 'Do you want to come over and play on an album we're doing with Dick Morrissey?' So I said 'Yeah, I'd love to' and they said 'Here's Dick's number, call him up and see what he wants to do about this.'

I was living in Wimbledon and I found he was living in Tooting, like next door! So we met in a pub, chatting away over a pint of Guinness and it was just so weird, like serendipity. He had gone through exactly the same experience as I had. He said, 'I'll never play another rock band again, I've had enough of it. I just want to play some nice, happy, swinging music.' I thought, 'Great, me too!' So he had some tunes and I had some tunes, adapted a few other things and then we went over to do this record in New York. And the Average White Band played on it and something just clicked and we felt really good.

We did the album for Atlantic records just as their transition was happening from jazz, soul and R'n B label to being a white rock and roll label. We got lost in the shuffle with this record – but *not* before it got rave reviews in Billboard!

We played at this club in New York called

Mikels, it was like the 606 of NY, where they tried things out. We ended up doing six weeks in this club and the whole thing used to come alive. That's when Dick and I knew that maybe we had something here.

But eventually, after a year and a half, I wanted to come back. First because at that time New York was a pretty dangerous place, I mean everybody had *guns*. I was living in a street with a pharmacy on the corner and there was always somebody getting shot dead for the takings of the till, some junkie would be around.

But I came back really just to get away. I mean New York is a tremendously exciting place, inspiring and I heard great music there. I got to do the loft jam sessions and the whole thing. But I needed something that was a little slower - it's to do with the quality of life issue - moving from New York to London was like moving to a village in the Cotswolds. Also when I moved back, my girlfriend, later my wife, was here..

When we came back from New York, nobody knew anything about this type of music, that sort of jazz-funk or fusion. Jazz Soul but with a funky rhythm section.

Slowly people were starting getting into it and after about six months, it really grew... Then it became a very successful club band and that went on for almost fifteen years. It was just great to hear Dick Morrissey in full flight, wonderful player that he was.

Fusion often involves repetition, but I was less aware of it with Morrissey-Mullen.

Well, it was a jazz group – they were all good players – you're right in a sense that as soon as you have a band with the drummer playing a backbeat, you have a certain amount of repetition. But that was the thing that connected us with the non-jazz people, if you like, brought them in and for the first time actually enjoying what live music could be.

Until in 1990 we finally ended on a high, I think, with the best band we'd ever had.

It was Dick who left first because, I think,

by then he had had enough and wanted to do other things. Not be on this treadmill, because it was a *very* busy band with five or six nights a week. Dick just wanted to go back to playing a more loose, open kind of jazz. And I eventually did the same because however good a band is, if it's kind of formulaic in a sense, in a rhythmic way, then that's limiting ultimately.

I've changed guitars. For Morrissey-Mullen, I had been playing a much more blues based style using a Fender Telecaster which is a much more biting electric sound if you like. Now I'm playing these big fat guys, it's a mellower sound, but as I get fatter, the guitars get fatter! Now I prefer something that has more weight to it rather than something thin and biting. Also because I'm playing more-or-less straightahead jazz most of the time, the fat sound works better.

In the early Nineties, you formed the Jim Mullen Quartet.

I was doing other things during the early Nineties, getting little quartets together, getting more involved with some of the younger guys who were coming up at that time around the 606 Club which was quite a catalyst in this town. I had a band with some of those talented guys – Mornington Lockett on saxophone, Laurence Cottle on bass, there's several albums of them with Ian Thomas on drums, Mornington or Dave O'Higgins on tenor. This was another period of growth for me as a player.

I think of jazz as *impressionist* music. Whatever it is you're playing, you try to make jazz out of it – not in a cheesy, cutesy way, but to try to make it *valuable* as a jazz piece as well. And I think that's one thing that jazz musicians have contributed to various styles of music over the decades. When you hear Miles Davis play *Bye, Bye Blackbird*, it's suddenly not this novelty song it started out as. He made it into some kind of anthem.

For over ten years, you've been working with the singer, Claire Martin.

Yes, I got involved with some things in Claire Martin's band and I did three albums with her.

And I still work with Claire. She works in many different situations as I do, and we occasionally come together and do the duet, which I always enjoy. She has wonderful repertoire sense and then really personalises her songs in interesting ways too. I love the way she sings. She makes people feel comfortable - the great performers have that.

You've toured with the pianist Gene Harris, who'd been part of the Ray Brown Trio.

What a gentleman, what a sweet man! We had done all these tours, but he *never* ever called a tune. Normally guys come up and give you some music and say 'Here's what I'd like to do.' But he would just play these big, rubato introductions that would give you no clue as to what was coming up, then he would start playing. Fortunately I knew 99% of the tunes that he played.

But could he *swing*! He swung so hard, it was a life-fulfilling experience to be around this guy! Everything he touched swung like mad. Really intense groove! The fact that I'm talking about it now with so much enthusiasm - he's been dead these past three years - tells you what it meant to me. You see I grew up listening to black music. All my heroes were black, not only blues and jazz but I loved gospel music.

I also got to work with Mose Allison, who I had loved since I was a kid. I remember all those records, *Parchment Farm* and the *Seventh Son*, and I got to play those things with him. He's seventy-five now but he's still going great, he's a very fit man, and he's a very interesting guy.

Mose is great for writing those cool, humorous, ironic songs. He does a song called *Getting There* – 'Ever since the world ended, I don't get

out so much, all the people I befriended, don't bother to keep in touch, But I'm not disillusioned, I'm not down-hearted, I'm not disappointed, but I'm gettin' there!' A really wonderful man, full of imagination and he has a quirky piano style I enjoy.

How did you decide to set up the Organ Trio?

It was Jim and Matt's idea to get this band together . They called me up one day and I thought we were just going to do a session. But they had booked a rehearsal room and we played all these tunes and it just felt great.

You have Jim Watson on organ?

Yes, he's fabulous, just a fabulous young musician. Versatile, he's got ears for everything, can play in so many different styles - like Matt Skelton, our drummer, who's only about 30 years old! But they're veterans already, they both went to college.

I've always loved the organ trio concept. Rather than do a *Homage to Jimmy Smith* style, we took it along a more contemporary route, new tunes and not stuck in a blues groove. So originals, reworkings of other songs. People like that sound, so the last year and a half, I've really been working pretty solidly with that band.

Your *Burns* album in 2000 attracted praise across a wide range of listeners.

Yes, that quartet's got Gareth Williams on piano, Mick Hutton on bass and Gary Husband on drums - really wonderful musicians. Gareth never knew any of those songs and I hadn't written out scores, just sketches, a few chords and suggestions. With musicians of that calibre, you don't have to instruct them, just count them in. Gareth's quite a radical player, full of input. Unlike most jazz musicians, he doesn't work out of a vocabulary, he is a true improviser, goes for broke every time. When it goes wrong, it's a train wreck! When it goes right, it's absolutely staggering, like on the album.

But for some reason that band didn't really take off. I didn't understand, but basically we couldn't get arrested! So like Alan Barnes, he does what I do, guest spots up and down the country, because they can't afford to bring a band. I do a lot of that. So you go up and play with the local guys and you find out what tunes you've got in common. There's a network of little clubs up and down the country run by enthusiasts on a knife edge. And they keep the club by having a guest once a month or so. I'm not speaking from any lofty position here but every musician is obliged to help these people out. They are providing work, with no funding or support, so bums on seats is what pays for everything.

This situation is in a way related to learning jazz and jazz education. I have to say I have a problem with jazz education as it exists right now. The main reason is that when you *methodise* teaching of an art form, the danger is that people learn the methods and not what the method is supposed to unlock. For instance, looking at the Berklee School in Boston, which is generally regarded as the number one academy, if you like, if you are a saxophone player, you get your degree by learning Michael Brecker transcriptions. If you're a guitar player, you get it by learning Pat Metheny transcriptions. I think, what they *should* be doing is helping people to unlock their *own way* of doing something. I was never interested in playing people's solos when I was growing up.

Never done transcriptions?

Never done transcriptions. I mean, I was listening to everybody but it never interested me to try to play their solos. I'd be trying to hear what was happening and trying to learn what good effect was created by what, but I didn't want to *copy*. The other big change is, *nobody* taught all the great players to do what they did. They figured it out for themselves, there was *initiative* involved here.

So they should be encouraged to find their own identity. I know they're young, but everyone has an individual character or personality fingerprints. So they should be encouraged to put all the things they like together in a personal way - encourage them to find their *own voices* much sooner.

Also jazz needs to get more exposure. Jazz FM is a disaster! Only one show with jazz on it. So I think they should have their license taken away because they do not fulfil their remit. The term 'smooth jazz' which they invented, there's no such thing!

There seem to be differences between those who want to swing and those who don't see this as an essential jazz ingredient. What's your view?

I don't think there's enough swinging happens these days. I think that's something that you can never bypass in jazz – the intense swing groove if you like. I think that's the common denominator that links all great jazz. I think there's a lots of esoteric, cerebral things happening these days. While everybody wants to be a composer and write their own tunes, there's already a great body of work out there and if you can't write something as good or better than that, then personalise and play the repertoire in some way.

There's also that all the great legendary players have gone now. . There are still great players but the legendary players like Miles have all gone. So I think they should be casting around in a more equal way to who's around, instead of looking for some new American to take over.

You hear people playing jazz everywhere, it really has become an international language. And so it should. I remember an article written by Dave Liebman saying he can't wait to hear Azerbaijani jazz and Tai jazz.

What do you want to do in the future?

I think it is possible to be part of the tradition and also part of the transition. Although I grew up listening to Django Reinhart and Coleman Hawkins, I still have a feeling for how the music is moving and evolving. Playing with the young guys and hearing their approach to things, I think you can both combine the strengths of what went before with what might be developing. I'm not just looking to be contemporary for the sake of it, the 'squeeky-bonk' part of it – I'm not interested in that at all. There must always be form, always be groove.

I remember once reading an interview with Betty Carter about what one of the young guys called 'burning pet shop' music. He asked, 'What do you think about people like Cecil Taylor?' And she said, 'Cecil Taylor? Let me tell you, only white people listen to Cecil Taylor, black people never listen to that s..t!' Absolutely scathing and I thought it was wonderful!

You've produced a number of albums in recent years.

When we did the *Burns* album, it was probably the best reception *ever* for one of my records. High brow and low brow, we got fantastic press. Now I had had the idea for these for years and I went ahead with them myself and then managed to get a deal with Black Box. Six months after *Burns*, the *Animations* follow up.

Animations covers the earlier cartoons, visually stunning and musically stunning. Peter Pan, the music was written by Sammy Khan. So we do pieces like the Second Star to the Right, and also, We can Fly. The naivety of it attracts me.

I've since done a quartet album, came out last year on Hep Records called *Somewhere in the Hills*. That's the latest thing with the quartet and the fourth album we've done. That was a mixture of things we'd done on gigs, a Scottish folk song, various ballads.

What's next, I'm open, don't have any projects planned. In this country the jazz record industry is a cottage industry, nobody is looking at massive sales, lucky to sell a couple of thousand, mostly on gigs.

So distribution via the Internet is the way to go. It's cheaper and faster than through the store. Some musicians are putting their records there rather than seeking distribution because the big companies are putting pressure on the big stores not to stock independent labels - big guys are squeezing out the little guys. So Amazon looks like the future because you're not competing with massive promotional budgets, everybody's equal. That's great. Maybe record companies will end up being things of the past, just release the album onto the net and that's it!

Selected CDs

Somewhere in the Hills Jim Mullen Quartet
                                      [2002, Hep Jazz]
Burns   Jim Mullen Quartet
                                      [2000, Black Box]
Everything Must Change Morrissey Mullen
                              [2003, Sulphuric Records]

David Newton

David Newton, born in 1958 in Glasgow, is an internationally recognised jazz pianist who manages to balance a range of demands - accompanying major jazz singers, his trio and performing in various larger groups.

He studied piano at the Leeds College of Music and then worked at various musical roles in Scotland and at Scarborough Theatre for Alan Ayckbourne. He then came south and now both manages his own trio and collaborates frequently with Alan Barnes with whom he has recorded many albums. These include, for the American Concord label, *Below Zero*, *Summertime* and *Mathattan*.

Major artists he has worked with include visiting Americans Benny Carter, Buddy de Franco and Herb Ellis and among British players Martin Taylor, Don Weller, Dave Green, Alec Dankworth and Clark Tracey.

He currently accompanies the award-winning singer Stacey Kent who is very active both sides of the Atlantic. David has also worked with many other leading singers including Claire Martin and Carol Kidd.

In 1995 Dave gained the award of Outstanding Solo Performer of the Year. He has won the UK Award for Best British Jazz Piano six times, most recently in 2002. While now resident in England, he holds on with Scottish resoluteness to his fondness for swing and some forthright musical opinions.

In your earliest memories, what music did you first listen to in the home?

The very first thing was probably solo piano on 'Listen with Mother' and I think it was Sinding, 20th century Scandinavian-type writing. I thought at the time it was gorgeous and it still is, amazingly for me. But the first *jazz* I heard was Brubeck, when I was about four or five. A record player had appeared, then my Dad picked up some EPs of Garner, Tatum and Peterson, but I'd have been in my teens before I started to listen to them properly.

Did your Dad play piano?

Yes, he played by ear. The song 'I'm getting sentimental over you' was about the extent of it and he would rework it in different keys and doing different voicings and harmonies and so forth. So I learnt fairly early on that there was

not just *one* way of playing something – you could do it in *lots* of different ways.

What about your musical education?

I started taking piano lessons at the age of eight, then clarinet lessons.

I had some very interesting music teachers at school. There was Bobbie Wishart, one of my first clarinet teachers – I was about nine then – I was dabbling, according to him - on the school pianos, much to the chagrin of the headmaster. He learnt to turn a blind eye eventually. But the teacher that followed him was a bassoonist and some deal was struck that the school got a couple of bassoons. After one year of high speed training, I was duly dispatched to play in the county orchestra, the leader of which was the guy that had supplied the bassoons.

He'd obviously wanted a bassoonist for his orchestra.

Anyway I'd always had a fascination for the bottom end of things, the deep notes, so I did that for three or four years – still carried on with the clarinet, did all the exams on the clarinet. The piano thing had fizzled out after four years – my very patient piano teacher had just had enough of me – this was about age twelve and I just dabbled after that, carried on with the clarinet. The bassoon thing vanished eventually, understandably, because it was just not affordable, too expensive for my parents. But I continued with my nice clarinet, up to Grade eight, and that got me into music college.

And you decided to go to Leeds?

Yes, I found out about it when I was seventeen. I had kind of decided that I was going to do architecture and was geared up for that. But we had formed a band at school. So the five of us went in for the Melody Maker competition during the holidays.

A pop band?

I dread to think what kind of music it was really – fusion, jazz-rock stuff that we were writing ourselves – because we all thought we were geniuses. I was one of two keyboard players. Much to our amazement we came third equal in that event. But that was my first gigging experience in front of a live audience, other than the school.

And I liked the life, I thought, 'This is great fun,' so I went back and did my last year but instead of concentrating on architecture, I took up music.

And then you heard about the Leeds College?

Yes, my music teacher at school hated me – absolutely loathed me with a vengeance, because of the times I had been thrown out of practice rooms for not playing classical music - and I had long hair. So he gave me a copy of the Musical Times which had loads of ads and said

'Here's what you want, Newton, you want to join the RAF and do the music courses there'.

I said 'ok' and took away this thing and flicking through it, the word 'jazz' leapt out, and Leeds was the only college then doing jazz courses, so as it turns out the RAF was not for me, I'm pleased to say!

The Leeds jazz degree was fairly young at that point, in fact it was *so* young it was at that strange crossover point, it was called a degree in 'jazz and light music'. The term 'light music' isn't used much these days, I suppose they were still getting over the recent demise of the Light Programme. But I had no idea what lay ahead, really. I just took one day at a time. Still do.

When you joined it was to do clarinet, but you then changed to piano?

That's right. Well there was a piano player at the college, a guy called Mike Todd in his third year when I arrived. When I heard him play solo piano in a practice room I just thought '*that's* what I want to do.' It was incredible and still is for all I know. And so I'd spend hours out in the corridor, just listening to this guy through the door, until eventually I plucked up courage and got to know him. And he was still a student but he was light years ahead of anybody at the college. Teachers, or *anybody*!

I listened the other day to a tape of him, recorded in 1977 I think, and he's *still* light years ahead of everybody.

Is he a full time commercial artist then?

I have no idea. He got out of music because – I got the impression – that nobody could keep up with him and he just became disenchanted with playing with sub-standard musicians. A rather sad situation. But there are one or two people who have those difficulties, you know.

Yes, it must take various strengths to be a professional musician.

Yes, you just have to accept, to a certain extent, the limitations of where you are and who you are. I would never actually have the nerve to complain - plus I actually enjoyed it – it didn't matter then – about the fact that the bass player couldn't make the changes or whatever.

So when at Leeds did you definitely decide you wanted to be a jazz musician?

It was a moment when I came back after the Xmas Holidays in the second year at college –

I'd switched to piano in September and this was the beginning of January. Up to that point I had been really struggling with this improvision thing, I didn't know what was going on and then I came back and had a major rethink and turned everything on its head, the way I thought about it. Suddenly I could actually *predict* what I was going to play. Up to then, it was a bit random, hit and miss. So something had happened over the two-week holiday and it all sank in. A major breakthrough.

And then I suddenly thought, 'Oh hang on,

I can do this! And this is going to go somewhere at last!'

What happened when you left Leeds College?

Ah, yes! Somebody got me a gig in a dance/cabaret band in a club called Aphrodite's on Piccadilly and that gig lasted four months. It was seven nights a week, and quite a long night - from nine pm till two in the morning. After four months the club closed down as the place was collapsing. I'd felt out of my depth in London, I really was floundering, I didn't know anybody...

However, it was useful because I spent those four months getting a pretty good *geography* lesson, so that when I came back down to London four or five years later I knew my way around. But from a musical point of view I wasn't ready.

So I went back to Leeds, ended up working in a dance band in Sheffield for a couple of years – not the greatest scene in the world but I was prepared to take from it whatever I could – and *eat*, always a strong driving force - and then one of the lecturers at college offered me this gig at Scarborough Theatre – they needed somebody for a show for just six weeks.

It was called *Suburban Strains* by Alan Ayckbourne, with music by Paul Todd. So I did that for six weeks, then Alan had written another that required more music, so I ended up there for two and a half years! With the occasional jazz gig in between.

Was the theatre music modern classical music or jazz - did it swing?

Not by any means, because we're talking theatre music here. And the guy who was writing the music came from a completely different angle from me.

It wasn't a happy time musically – I really didn't like the music because I thought it was *unschooled*. At any point when I started using harmony that the guy couldn't fathom, the guy would accuse me of using jazz – 'don't want any of that jazz stuff – keep it simple.'

When did Scarborough end?

Well, actually I broke my leg! We were doing this show called *Making Tracks* in London, I broke my leg and at that point Marjorie, my wife, had just got a job taking her out of teaching and going into educational administration in Edinburgh. So I found myself in Edinburgh and inveigled my way into the scene there using my theatre connections. I did a big show written by the late Bennie Green called 'Give my Regards to Broadway' and I MD'd [Musical Director] that. And all the guys in the pit were actually the local jazz scene! So I got to know everybody in that one experience really.

While I was doing all that I was having to do miners clubs and working men's clubs with kind of cabaret bands to earn a living which was truly the most horrendous thing, really!

In Edinburgh you met Martin Taylor [guitar]?

Yes, there was an agency wanted to do music every night at one of the big hotels, turn it into the Ronnie Scott's of the North. Martin came in, we liked playing the same things, and bless him, he liked my writing. So we did a tour and then the next year, Buddy deFranco [clarinet] came across. The tour was Buddy, Martin, Alec Dankworth, Clark Tracey and me. My recording *debut* was with that band down in London! Suddenly things took a quantum leap qualitywise and meeting Clark and Alec was my first introduction to the much larger London scene.

Also at that time Alan Barnes had been down since 1982 and had carved out quite a successful niche. Alan was really instrumental in my moving down because he wanted me to make a record with him. After that on the drive home Marjorie said, 'you ought to go down to London' and I said 'but its a horrible, *tawdry* place, filthy, huge - and I don't know if I'm ready.' And she said, 'You're ready.' So we upped sticks and moved.

My daughter Katy was only 6 months old at the time so it was a hell of a sacrifice for Marjorie to make, so bless her too.

Then things started coming. Martin had recommended me to Terry Jenkins who was looking for a new piano player at the Bulls Head, because Tony Lee had moved on. So I was drafted in to do that. Within three months I got to meet everybody! They *all* go through the Bulls Head! And at that time it had a lot of visiting American artists as well. I'd be there six to eight times a month. Just for door money, but from an educational point of view, it was *priceless*!

And you've now had a long association playing with Alan Barnes?

Yes, we'd started doing the duet thing around 1977–8, and it's cropped up periodically since, with more and more frequency. The first time we recorded it was 1993, I think, with *Like Minds* then another called *Summertime* in 2000.

Do you feel you'd gone through a similar learning process together?

No, we were in different years and to be honest, we'd always liked different music. I have to give him credit for introducing me to Cannonball Adderley. He'll tell you that I was very dismissive of his record collection but it was actually a matter of opening up some doors to me that I had not known existed. I didn't have a record collection to speak of! And still don't. It's a kind of living-above-the-shop feeling that stops me really. Hear enough already.

But with Alan, despite our differences, it's always adding up to new things. So earlier on this year, for the first time, we decided to write something together – a commission! And, much to our amazement, that was an incredibly efficient process! Up to now it's always been an entirely separate process, I write a tune with my harmonies and the same for him.

It's a swapping of manuscripts, no electronic mail. It was all very hands-on as Alan is not so

keen on the electronic side of things. Checks his email about every six months or so!

But sometimes, maybe you want to get out in a piano trio format to show what you can do?

Well, it all depends on what you want to do. My first and foremost thing has always been to make music – I don't do a tap dance every time I open the fridge door when the light comes on. My idols are really the unsung heroes – the Nelson Riddles who quietly put their private melodies in the background behind whatever is going on and they're the people I really admire… the craftsmen.

There is a development in the media these days – that you only get magazine article coverage if you're coming up with something new; for instance, merging rap and jazz. However, a contrary view is that the most stifling thing in the artistic life is to have to come up with something new every week…where do you stand?

It's a funny old business but I don't think there *is* anything new – I haven't heard anything new for twenty-five years or so, especially the avant-garde, God Almighty, it hasn't changed for forty years! And how on earth, they don't just get tired of having to avoid playing anything musical – it's just the *antithesis* of music. Coming up with something new, like mixing jazz and rap, don't know if that's new really, Quincy Jones started doing that as soon as rap appeared. Anyway, I don't think it works.

But we still have the same twelve notes that we had four hundred years ago with the well-tempered scale, and juggling them around is enough for anybody as far as I can see. You can still come up with some new ways of combining notes, new ways of phrasing – somebody said the other day about repetition being actually impossible to achieve. Just being human means you're not going to be the same tomorrow as you are today.

Tell me about your work with singers which you have been doing right from the start. Carol Kidd?

Carol Kidd is an amazing singer with the most natural voice you're ever likely to hear. Blessed with perfect pitch and a way with a lyric. And I was very fortunate to hear her at the guest spot at the Platform 1 Club in Edinburgh years ago. My only experience with singers up to that point was Karen Kaye –she was a cabaret act who could do Barbara Streisand and others, a very funny lady. And at Aphrodite's, that club, I did a couple of weeks with her at the end of which she said I was the worst accompanist a singer could possibly have. That discouraged me for about five years....

But when I heard Sandy Taylor accompany Carol Kidd I said, 'Oh, I see...' and began to figure it out, a few things dawned on me. Then I got a week with Carol and I learnt  a lot from that. When Carol was going to cut a new record with Linn, she'd decided to change her band, it was Dave Green and Alan Ganley and myself were to be the new trio, and we did four or five recordings for her.

After that, I went in and recorded three records for Linn, which lasted till 1993/4.

Then the Candid people appeared on the scene, and what they offered was *American* distribution, which at that time Linn did not have. But then within about a year of me going to Candid, Linn got distribution in America and Candid's fell to the ground! So I did three records for Candid, all of which I'm immensely proud of, but they didn't really do anything at all. These were a trio with Alan and Dave called *In Good Company* then I did a solo piano Sinatra tribute called *The Twelfth of the Twelfth*.

We then recorded *DNA*, with what was the new trio that is Steve Brown and Matt Miles - plus Iain Dixon, an amazing find. It was a good year for me, 1997 I think. I found the rhythm section I needed to give me a good kick up the backside, and Iain's approach to making music was great – he's such an open musician – only Don Weller is as open to your ideas and the way you play.

And then, not long after that, I met the European representative for Concord Records, Barry Hatcher. Between Barry, Alan Barnes and myself, we cooked up this thing called the Jazz Partnership and made four records for Concord – one of which was the Trio's *Halfway to Dawn. Below Zero* was the first one with Alan Barnes and my trio, *Summertime* a duo with Alan and of course *Manhattan* where the four of us joined forces with Conte Candoli.

So that was a happy time, the culmination of a period of recording to get a label like Concord - of the minor labels it's the most renowned in the jazz world apart from Blue Note.

And that leads on to the open road ahead of me now because we've decided to go our own independent ways. Alan and I have both set up labels ourselves, just because of our in-sight and Barry Hatcher, we've discovered the way these things work.

You don't want to be in with Concord for its US recognition?

It's nice to be on the label but other than its kudos…it didn't actually do anything, so all they did was take half the money. Really. We have a

very loyal following here in this country and I thought it would be a good thing - because they were forever saying to me, 'Anything new?' So I thought, why don't I just start a record com-pany and bring out new stuff all the time? That's the idea. So we've got two on the shelf now that we've recorded.

Then when we were out in San Francisco with Stacey last month – out for three weeks with little to do but the gigs, so with Dave Chamberlain on bass, Colin Oxley the guitarist,

we decided to record a trio album. We rehearsed every day and got some pieces together, and just recorded out there.

Do you have a name for your new label?

Yes, it's *Bright New Day Records*! Named after one of the tunes on the *Halfway to Dawn* album. We're a limited company. We will have a website, we just have to set it up and sell through the website as well as the existing shop based distribution, including Concord ties.

Let's turn to how, some time ago, you learned to play jazz?

Right! Osmosis I think. From early on I was listening to Shearing and Peterson and Tatum and Garner and all that. It never occurred to me that I might ever be able to make a noise anything like that.

Learning to improvise and do solos is a complex skill, as, besides speed and agility, it requires planning the improvisation structure etc.. Was getting the whole jigsaw sorted a big challenge?

Yes, a lot of the jigsaw I had absorbed I think, especially as far as the American Songbook is concerned, as I grew up. And I suppose I'd always had a reasonably good ear. It was the one and only thing that got me into college ac-tually. Certainly not my clarinet playing!

Your point about how do you make it up, I just started *simply*, I think. Those records with Carol Kidd - I do cringe slightly now when I hear them. A lot of knowledgeable musicians would say, 'I really liked what you did on that because you left so much space.' Well I was leav-ing so much space because I didn't know how to fill it! It was as simple as that. I also have a thing about guys that fill a space pointlessly. I think I'd rather hear the gap. And I suppose as my musical life goes forward, I'm tending to fill in some of the gaps now.

Am I right that you're one of the few

major UK jazz pianists that does a lot of trio work?

Yes, but you see I was brought up on the trio, always loved it as an entity. So to find myself suddenly in Stacey's [Kent] group – not suddenly, been doing it for eight years – but the guitar-bass-piano thing suddenly blossomed really with the arrival of Dave Chamberlain. It's just clicked between the three of us and jazz for me has always been a *communication* between the people on the stage, where you can delve into one another's brains if you like and when there are connections made, it's an amazing process! A complete mystery and amazing when it works. And I'm blessed now that I've had three trios that I can really click into. It's half the fun really, getting on musically with the guys you are working with.

Because not everybody is open enough to let you in as it were. But if you can somehow anticipate what they're about to play, you can shock them into going 'Oh! How did you know I was going to do that?' and all of a sudden, opening up slowly – nice!

Bill Evans and his bass players used to just discuss how they play before a performance: do you?

Yes, no obvious rehearsals for that particular outfit and it's the same with Jarrett, I don't think that lot ever rehearse either! They probably just have a talk through before any given concert.

Our trio is slightly different in that we will tour the recording as it were, so we play a lot of the material off that for quite a long time. But what I love about it is that we can deviate from the record and I'll just start up an intro of whatever and nobody will know what the hell's going on. It's three guys on a tightrope and off we go. We all manage to get across to the other side somehow and that's the most fun that jazz offers you really.

Stacey Kent is now coming across as a

singer with wonderful precision and a beautiful softer tone.

Well, she's a fast learner, Stacey. She now sounds like herself, she can get on with the job she does, with an *extraordinary* way of getting inside a song.

The *joy* of the gig is – although in some songs

there's only five bars you get to solo over - the whole song will sound different from the way we played it two nights previously. We approach it from a different angle getting new nuances, cooking with the lid on - really quite an art form and it's also one of the hardest!

It's a lot tougher than this demand for coming up with something new, of crossing this with that. You see what they're managing to avoid by doing that, in a way, they're shirking their responsibilities. I'd say, 'Come on, let's hear you play *Someone to watch over me* and get it across - I want you to make me cry! Come on!' They *can't* do it. Because of the newness thing they think that's where it's at, it's not at all.

As far as your playing style is concerned, your acknowledged influences are Oscar Peterson and Keith Jarrett. Do you admire them the most?

Certainly – for me they are the best. What's curious is the *juxtaposition* because Jarrett has a different way of swinging – a totally different style. And of playing – Jarrett is very much an improviser and it's interesting that you will *never* ever hear him play a lick, for example. Or if he does play a lick – it's his, made up there and then, so he's entitled to do what he likes with it.

Whereas Oscar has lots of different tricks that he will apply here and there, though he can apply the improvision thing too. So it's very odd. I'm between two stools if you like, because I love that open ended, 'let's just see where it takes it' kind of music and I like the highly structured, highly arranged swinging style of Oscar's.

I love both, but it's certainly in the *ballads* you'll hear the improvisation – but that's not just Jarrett you'll hear – you'll hear Satie and Ravel and Debussy, early twentieth century piano music. That's what, effectively, Jarrett's making up on the spot. Absolutely staggering. It's almost Sinding!

One of my records for Linn, *Return Journey* was solo piano and the vast majority of that was just improvised music. They have been described as compositions but I just take a motif and see where it goes. I suppose that's what Jarrett does but I wouldn't *begin* to make comparisons between Jarrett and me because he's in a different league altogether, I think.

Do you do any coaching in jazz? It's a difficult thing to teach?

It's an *enormously* difficult thing to teach. And the best way to learn is to put things on your record player and *listen*, just listen. And try to figure out what it is they do, to spend every waking hour trying to absorb what's going on.

I got going because I asked one of the lecturers at school, Fred Boaden, 'How do you actually *start* on an improvisation?' And he said, 'Try this' and he played this simple, stupid lick; but it had never occurred to me that it's the *diving board* and away you go.

But the turnaround for me was when I discovered that of the twelve notes, four of them I should *really* not hit if I could avoid them, the clangers. Up to that point I kept hitting them because I didn't know which they were. So instead of the eight notes you want to hit, think

of the four you don't want to play so as to free up the memory.

Then it dawns on you that you can use even the four you wanted to avoid – they all have a function, you can harmonise with all of them. So there are no wrong notes any more, if you have sufficient command of the language of harmony.

How do you see the future of jazz?

Well, it's pretty healthy, I think. Always has been. Every ten years somebody comes along and grabs someone new by the scruff of the neck, says let's give this person a hundred and fifty thousand pounds and all of a sudden, it's in the papers because there's a couple of publicists doing their business - but underneath all that, jazz just continues apace.

It's swings and roundabout really, sometimes everybody's working every night for nine months and then it all drops off for some bizarre reason or another, a mystery to me. But there's over one hundred and forty UK jazz festivals now, still behind France which now has seven hundred, but still impressive.

And Dave Newton's future?

I'm just doing my thing and if you do, I'm glad you like it. And churning out records of course. That is something that I want Bright New Day records to do - to become a jazz presence!

Selected CDs	
Pacific Heights	Dave NewtonTrio [2004, Bright New Day Records]
Manhattan	Dave Newton Trio and Alan Barnes [2000, Concord]
DNA	David Newton [1998, Candid]
Website: www.davidnewton.net	

Kenrick Rowe

Kenrick Rowe, born in London in 1960, is a London-based jazz drummer of Jamaican origin whose playing experience started with ska and reggae bands. As a teenager, after trying guitar he found his real appetite was for drumming. From being a much sought after ska and reggae drummer, Kenrick widened his drumming technique for mainstream jazz, learning from friends and contemporaries such as jazz guitarist Alan Weekes, vocalist Cleveland Watkiss and saxophone player Mike 'Bammie' Rose. Jazz courses, visits to Ronnie Scott's where he heard Art Blakey and demanding studies with the veteran legendary US drummer Clifford Jarvis radically increased his immersion in jazz culture and improved his technique.

He has played with the leading visiting Jamaican ska musicians including Sugar Minott; also British players including Courtney Pine, Steve Williamson, Tim Richard's Spirit Level and his piano trio and Jean Toussaint.

Visiting Americans he has worked with include David Murray and the UK Posse, Art Farmer and Charles McPherson.

For over ten years Kenrick has been a regular member of the very successful Jazz Jamaica and the Jazz Jamaica All-Stars, led by Gary Crosby. He has toured with them to jazz festivals all over the world, especially the Far East. He now works extensively in Japan and is also a producer for ska and reggae flavoured jazz music.

What music do you first remember listening to, probably in the home?

The earliest is hearing ska, which is early Jamaican style music based on rhythm and blues - I liked that then. My Dad also used to play a lot of Louis Armstrong and he still loves instrumental music now. I didn't like it that much, but you heard it. And there was some blues and I can hear the link now with ska, that upbeat rhythm. Also the musicians on ska were *improvising* after the singer. And we were tuned into the radio too, lots of Radio 1.

Some country n western played at home too, like Jim Reeves and Ace Cannon, a saxophone player with big tenor tone - a lot of Jamaicans liked it.

When you went out to school, what was happening with the music?

When I got to eight or nine, I was getting more influenced by pop music - the Beatles and the Rolling Stones, people like that - and in my head I was thinking about playing the guitar — I used to watch Top of the Pops, wanting it to be me and having a broomstick for a guitar. I listened to Tony Blackburn and Noel Edmonds a lot in the early seventies.

My interest with ska changed as it evolved into reggae eventually — which is a similar upbeat rhythm but slowed down or half time. Ska was made to reflect the mood of the people in Jamaica at the time it got independence in the mid-sixties and it was a time for joyous things, when people were out celebrating. Then the politics changed the mood of the people, with the fighting, so reggae was reflecting the hardship and the poverty, and violence started to creep into the music as well as the politics — I started to listen to that music in the Seventies.

And learning an instrument?

My mother had friends in the church, and I'd see that one of their sons was always walking by with a guitar and a case. Then one Christmas, I would have been about 15, I did get a guitar. But we didn't have anything to tell us how to use it, so I just over-tightened all the strings and they snapped! I did milk rounds and saved money, and eventually bought an electric guitar a copy of a Fender Strat and went to this friend and he showed me chords.

At this time, most of the bands that I had access to were reggae bands. I plucked up courage to go to a band at the end of the road, played with them and they showed me the method, and that was a start on recognising notes, like picking tunes off the radio. I progressed to playing a few tunes with this rehearsal band. These tunes didn't have much movement — they were based round two or three chords only.

But there was a better band in the area — they'd been on tours — and I thought I was now good enough to move up to another level, so when they were auditioning for guitarists I went along. I was about 17. I walked in, plugged in my guitar, and this guy comes up to me goes, 'Right, the first tune we're going to play goes from Gm to Am to F7'… When he said that .. if the ground could have opened and swallowed me up?… because this was my first time naming these chords, nobody had mentioned G, A - everything had been done by ear!

You didn't have formal lessons?

Not at that time. But then I got some lessons from an ex-pupil of John Williams. I had to get into reading music, to get the lessons for classical — and at the time you just want to play without putting in the work. He would put up the piece of music, something really simple, and he would play. But I would have memorised it straight away. I would go home and practice, come back and played it for him. And he said 'Ah, very good,' but as soon as he put up an-

other piece, it'd show me up! I was actually losing a bit of interest.

My younger brother was into drums, and when I was about eighteen, between us we managed to buy a drum kit. So at home we had this and a keyboard and the guitar. All this time I was studying to become an automobile engineer but music was starting to distract me - particularly the drums, where I was playing around with different tones.

Around this time in the mid-Seventies, there was a drummer from Jamaica called Sly Dunbar — he probably did for reggae what someone like Coltrane did for jazz — he took the rhythms and created so many things — I listened to him on reggae records, he brought in a lot of co-ordination between the hands creatively. My brother used to skip those bits but I said, 'Why don't you play them?' and he said, 'That's only for professionals.' But I thought it was possible, so I sat down and slowed the pattern down and then speeded it up and showed my brother.

But to make music your career at the time — well, you wouldn't even consider it. But I pushed myself and went to Goldsmiths' [College] where they had drum classes. I was there for a while, but there was still this thing about the need to learn para-diddles, mummy-daddy rolls. I had thought you could just go in and play the beats. But I learned that I needed to develop my technique.

Sometimes with reggae bands I went into recording studios and doubled on drums for some of the tracks. There was this singer called Sugar Minott, a famous Jamaican singer. About 1980, he heard me playing drums and asked me to do some sessions for him. So I recorded with this guy and some of his mates heard it and called me. So from there, I started to get known as a good solid reggae drummer.

While working on these sessions for Sugar Minott I met a lot of players - a guitarist called Alan Weekes and Cleveland Watkiss the singer who was a backing vocalist, even Django Bates. Django Bates did a lot of reggae sessions back then. I also met Jackie Mittoo, one of Jamaica's best known keyboard players and Michael 'Bammie' Rose [alto sax], who plays with Jools Holland now. .

When were you introduced to jazz?

Alan and Cleveland had studied jazz a lot, and they would mention places like Ronnie Scott's and the different jazz names and say, 'Have you heard of this guy?' At their homes they'd put on jazz, and I'd think, 'Do I want to hear this?'

But with the reggae band, on the bus they'd be constantly playing this reggae and Mike Rose would be saying, 'Put on some jazz!' So he'd put on this crackly tape – all horrible, but it'd be Charlie Parker. By this time, around 1982, they dragged me to Ronnie Scott's to see these guys, and I started to appreciate what the drummers were doing! I couldn't believe I was seeing someone's left hand going so fast. I was knocked out!

But when I saw Art Blakey and the Jazz Messengers for the first time, that was it! There were four horns - their harmonies! The dynamics! That really started to warm my heart. Not all the early stuff I heard was really appealing to me but I could relate to that fat, warm sound of Art Blakey. He was very technical but he also had a strong groove that I could relate to.

And learning jazz drumming technique?

Every drummer I talked with kept coming back to this Mummy-Daddy paradiddle thing, so I thought, I've got to do this now. I realised I was playing them but in a different way. But you develop that extra strength in the left hand, and doing things equally between the hands.

As time went on and I went to more jazz concerts, I thought it'd be nice to play that kind of stuff. So Cleveland Watkiss, Alan Weekes, myself, Mike Rose and a bass player decided to form our own jazz band.   And I started to buy drumming books. Just keeping basic rhythms

and keeping the high hat on [beats] 2 and 4. Because of the style of drumming I was used to, your left foot only just opens up *occasionally*. Now muscles that were never worked ache after just a few minutes! People don't realise the

physical demands that drummers go through, like having the right arm out here constantly – another thing to train.

No lessons in jazz drumming initially, but I worked up to a certain standard where the main thing I had was groove. I really like the way Art Blakey drove a band and wanted to have that left foot crashing down – dum-chick, dum-chick, dum-chick – really strong and I worked hard on it.

Me, Alan Weekes, Cleveland Watkiss and Mike Rose rented a room above a shop in Dalston, East London and decided that we were going to improve our musicianship and learn some jazz. Alan and some of the others had training – so I went along and had to do all the ear training, had to learn all the melodies on the drums, that was my way of doing it. We gave ourselves the challenge that we would try to learn a new jazz tune every week. Might be starting off with 'Straight no Chaser' then 'Cherokee' –

and I started to build up more jazz repertoire. So between that and going to Ronnie Scott's regularly, talking to other drummers, that's how you get the interest. I did that for two or three years, not gigging as a jazz thing, because we weren't ready yet.

By then my reggae connections were starting to dwindle. Also in the mid-Eighties more drum machines came in so the need for live drummers reduced, so it was fortunate that, in the jazz world, drummers are still live!

Then we auditioned for this Blake's Wine bar in Covent Garden and ran through a few tunes and I remember being so nervous. Anyway the guy says, 'You've got the gig.' It worked out at about a twelve pounds each. It was a new phase that time at Blake's Wine bar – with jazz being, especially at that time, not the thing for a lot of black people, so I'm learning this new music form.

Your decision to turn pro-musician?

Well, when you fall in love with something new you want to pursue it and I used to spend all night listening to records. I'd decided I would be a musician full time anyway from age twenty.

I'd done a lot of sessions with Sugar Minott – I spent hours in recording studios for a while, did a lot of reggae albums. I was very busy and in demand as a reggae drummer in the early eighties. I worked with many British bands and Jamaican bands that came to England.

What about training the ear for jazz?

I remember going past this shop and I had a fiver in my pocket, and I saw this Thelonius Monk album. And you know, sometimes you just go for the name and want to impress the other guys. So I bought this album for about £3, only two pounds left. I put this album on, I nearly cried, thought 'What a load of crap!' Anyway the bass player took the album – five years later I go to his house, he says, 'Take it back', so I put it on again and it's beautiful music to my ears!

After you move from two or three chords to lots of chords, you start to want to know what's going on; suddenly you're hearing chords moving. All the guys were going on courses and saying, 'Ken, you've *got* to do something!' So eventually I went to the City Lit [College] and did a year's music theory course. Doing the guitar thing before was an advantage for me then, knowing the Cycle of Fifths, identifying major and minor chords, diminished scales etc. and

the homework forced me to write a piece and bring it in every week and this was fantastic for me.

One thing I did was get chord charts and listen to the music while following the chords, to identify chord sounds, chord intervals – lots of that. It really trains the ear.

Then the Covent Garden gigs happened and we thought we were about the only black musicians playing jazz - really hip, you know? After a while we started to hear about Courtney Pine, who had also come up through the reggae thing. He was a reggae sax player and also Steve Williamson. Other more experienced jazzmen would come down to listen and that made us feel like we were doing something right.

Then you met the American drummer, Clifford Jarvis.

For a few years I really did go out and study more – not at school, but checking out all the concerts, visiting Americans, British players.

This is when Clifford Jarvis came in. [Born US, 1941, played with leading figures from Coleman Hawkins, John Coltrane, Charles Mingus to Archie Shepp.] Clifford and Billy Higgins and Philly Joe Jones all were close friends, used to work out together. The first time I heard Clifford Jarvis playing, it was either I *gave up* drumming or I really pushed myself. Meeting him was what I needed to cement certain things. There's only so far you can go by ear alone, you need advice from an expert and I got a lot technically from Clifford, especially that paradiddle for jazz drumming. I had wondered why certain things didn't sound a certain way, why this roll didn't sound like his roll, how you get that snap in the wrist and the flams. Clifford was like an army sergeant, I felt my arms would fall off. But you went on a gig in the evening and you were firing! This was what you needed - not to sound like the next person.

Clifford would start turning up on my gigs, I use to dread him coming down, but if I knew he was coming, I would woodshed [practice] seriously. It was a shame [when] Clifford died a couple of years back.

While we were at Covent Garden, Cleveland would get called to join Simon Purcell Jazz Train, so we thought here's some recognition. Then we got the confidence to go to other jam sessions with our quartet. So I would get asked to gigs and slowly people notice that you're around.

There's a pub in Brixton called the Atlantic. Courtney Pine and others used to play there a lot, and it opened my eyes to the other black jazz musicians. Courtney Pine was the first *name* guy I can remember getting a gig with and I was really surprised – he was always interested in trying new names to see what they were like! But I was not really ready at the time; I know that for a fact because I saw Mark Mondesir playing at the Atlantic, and the tempos he was

doing - 'ting-tica-ting, ting-tica-ting, ting-tica-ting' – just so fast! I could just barely keep up with the tempo.

I would sit down afterwards and play to the fastest records, because you have to build up an armoury, a vocabulary when you start with jazz. You've got to learn for instance how your brushes are used – which was new after reggae or funk. I bought a book by Ed Thigpen to develop brush technique. You can learn, using your fingers first to get the feel of something, how to get volume, how to use brushes on cymbals – quite different – how to place yourself within arrangements – where Art Blakey was a real master – just building up the dynamics, and people say to me now that they like the way I don't just go crashing right through the tune – even if I do *get* loud I make sure I can still hear all the other players.

Now I've been playing jazz for 15 or so years, I realise I play completely differently now, I'm more selective. When you're young and carefree and you practice something for three hours, you will want to play that on the bandstand that night. But it might not fit in, might be selfish but everybody does it because that's the only way you find out when it's going to work. You can listen to some of the sweetest players, like how Miles expresses himself, with some of them it's just one note. As they say, its what you *leave out* that matters. Sometimes I work on that.

Then Tim Richards called.

I joined the Tim Richards [piano] trio round about 1988 with Kubryk Townsend [bass]. The guys in the band would put on a record that had the most demanding drumming parts and would expect me to produce it, you know? You can feel the pressure. But Tim said, 'I really like the way you swing.' Tim was very good at hustling work and it put you out to the public, and the public like you, so it all means more work.

Then I joined Spirit Level – Tim's original band. It was one of the longest running jazz bands in Britain but eventually Tim cut the band and then we just had occasional projects.

Once I started to play with more established people like Courtney Pine and Tim Richards, promoters hear you and like you. A lot of the times you get put forward by promoters, so you get to work with visiting Americans, like Art Farmer. Also Charles McPherson – that was not *so* nice, because he wanted to play *so fast* – even the audience shouted for him to play something slow. But he's like, can the British keep up? Art Farmer started fast but then it was mellow and his tone was gorgeous.

I had some very good experiences with David Murray [US sax, 1991 winner of Danish Jazzpar Prize] – we did two tours with Alec Dankworth, myself, Jonathon Gee, David Jean-Baptiste [saxes] and Orphy Robinson [vibes]. The band was called 'David Murray and the UK Posse'. The music was fantastic with the organic way it grew.

Again when you start to get called and get work, you're starting to achieve a bit of something, we started to go abroad. Eventually you see that the work you're doing is paying off. You get critic's reviews that you 'made the drums sing.' You think, 'Wow!'

With these demanding tours, especially big band situations, I realised I had to develop my sight-reading, because these bands could have arrangements written down, not just this ear thing anymore.

What about jazz education?

There were periods I used to hang out at the Guildhall School of Music when Cleveland Watkiss was going there, where I met Jason Rebello. We even had a band with Jason when he was just seventeen. My experience suggests it's classical training for your technique and jazz for your ear. I feel all musicians should study jazz at some stage, if only to get into the form of improvisation because it opens you up.

I've done workshops and I used to teach. In some workshops you might start off with clapping exercises – you go round the class and you get everybody to play the same thing with each person doing four bars, then ask them to improvise with different forms of clapping within the four bars. You see how easily they catch on to improvising, you realise it's all within us. But if you are trained to only read [music] you could be losing out on something.

Sometimes just reading can make you lazy. For instance with Jazz Jamaica, the parts are not that difficult, I've got so used to looking at the paper that if I was to fold over the paper, I'd get a panic attack! Whereas if I'd learned it by ear, no problem! So I look at the charts only occasionally now as a safety net.

How did Jazz Jamaica begin?

Jazz Jamaica was formed in the early nineties when Gary Crosby discussed with the manager of the Jazz Café, how about putting on some Jamaican music? We fitted the bill with the jazz and the reggae background. Gary came and got me, Alan Weekes, Clifton Morrison on piano, Tony Uter, a remarkable percussionist, Eddie 'Tan Tan' Thornton – done the Beatles, the Stones - they've done everything and are pushing seventy by now. He got Rico Rodrigues [trombone] who plays in Jools Holland's band now – another trombonist from Jamaica. So he put this night together at the Jazz Cafe and it worked so well, people were dancing, we had to do this again! We started to do gigs here and there and suddenly this thing was taking off. Some of the ska tunes of the day were jazz standards redone ska-style – 'I'm in the Mood for Love,' that kind of thing, known as *skazz*. We'd also pick some old Jamaican tunes and mix them up with little jazzy arrangements.

As it picked up, we found we could go to reggae festivals and jazz festivals - *all* the festivals started to want to book the band. Often now jazz festivals put on things that are *not jazz*. It's like Jazz FM [radio], it's middle of the road to rock and over the years there's been a decline in the venues I had to play in.

Jazz Jamaica had started to get *more* popular *out* of England - our first major record deal was with a *Japanese* record label. Jazz Jamaica started in 1991 and our audiences were going up from

30 to 3,000 to 10,000 people, like when we did the New Orleans Festival. Most touring has been round Europe – Germany, France, Italy, Spain, Hungary, Czech Republic, some Eastern Europe, [also] round Africa the West Coast, to Singapore, Canada, America – but Japan was our biggest market! We stuck some money together, got an investor, did this album, and loads of companies were interested in Jazz Jamaica but they never wanted to pay…but the Japanese did back up their talk with money and we did this

album, and went out to Japan touring around some places – got some good interest. We got signed to EMI-Toshiba in 1993/94, and did an album covering the Blue Note catalogue – doing their numbers in a ska or reggae style. So we'd pick tunes from the artists that they'd signed like Herbie Hancock, or Songs for my Father by Horace Silver. We did two albums of that kind of stuff, and it made the Americans interested as well – in the end we signed to Ricoh Disc, an American based company. The only problem was the band was going through a few difficulties with management and direction – with anything successful you always find this

happens, there's outside forces pushing and pulling the band.

Then Gary decided that, as we'd been going as a nine piece for so many years and covered so much ground, he wanted a fresh challenge and expanded it to a twenty odd piece and call it the All-Stars – and there are some great musicians in there.

Who are your main musical influences?

Art Blakey - he got my attention the most, then Philly Joe Jones, Elvin Jones, Buddy Rich, Gene Krupa, Max Roach – all the big drummers.

Then Harvey Mason, Steve Gadd, even the modern drummers – people I speak to a lot, Clark Tracey – Clark helped me a lot, he's not selfish. And I like the sound of Sebastian Rochford, Winston Clifford and Tom Skinner.

You teaching or coach jazz?

I used to run a little workshop over in Tottenham, North London in the mid-Eighties, and teaching drum basics to kids.

More recently I've been doing workshops either by myself or with Tim Richards and Kubryk. We'd go round schools as part of a deal in putting out *The Other Side* album. We visited ten London schools and taught the basics, how to improvise. We'd start with clapping exercises, then again on their instruments, round a chord sequence. They also had to copy a couple of tunes from the CD. I was surprised how much youngsters get into the tunes – my youngest daughter is eight, and so I have some understanding of children. You think that youngsters only listen to pop music, but if they get the chance, they're on to it!

My younger daughter has just taken up the recorder and she's really quick at getting the notation. The kids are the future for music. But for jazz, when I was getting into it, the influences were different, now they've got *so many* styles of music I think, and they're under pressure to get into the hip-hop style. A lot of drum-

mers who get to be good move into other things, start to wear their hair fancy, change their image. Then you see them on TV with a pop band - that's where they're making the money, you know?

You can't go round doing £30 gigs all your life. And the same thing happened to me – I ended up doing pop videos, and working with a band called Selector, which is a bit like ska with a rock element – sometimes you're on the bandstand, hating every minute of it. But it pays. And this naturally means you lose talented musicians from jazz but I can't blame them. I mean, I've got a mortgage, a family to support, and it means I do not listen to a lot of jazz now, though I still play it.

Your activities have moved on?

Yes, I tend to listen to a lot of current music nowadays and I'm getting more into production, producing dance music but I still like to think I'm making it tastefully, sometimes some jazz elements where they fit.

Also a guy from Japan suggested that Alan Weekes and I produce a ballad album mixing jazz and reggae, with a softer reggae edge. He picked the tunes, like Lullaby of Birdland. I ended up using brushes on the reggae tracks – a new concept where the high hat was creating the 2, 4, [beats] like the upbeat normally of the guitar, chic, boom-chic, chic, boom-chic, and we must have sold about 50,000 albums in Japan doing two albums! There was a singer called Sandra Cross on that album called *The Birth of Reggae Blue.*

They say drummers can make great producers. Sometimes people have [only] a rough idea of the piece and they are relying on you to give it what they can't explain to you. So your experience thinking about the overall sound can help as a producer and I have invested in some production tools – don't think I can be a drummer all my life!

I've got a mixing machine with sounds to create my own little things. This allows me to hear melodies and songs and the structure. Then I can set up the drum parts, play the bass lines, play the chords and any additional bits that I might hear, like a trumpet. Solo or collaborating, this is something I want to do more of. I've already co-produced some albums with people.

What about the health of jazz in the UK?

Well jazz, as we say, covers such a lot of things. As a kind of purist's style thing, if it stays like that, I think it's on the decline. Personally I might not be going out to look for the venues but I don't think there's that many places to play mainstream any more. When I look at the listings, it's not on the same scale.

Musicians marched down to parliament the other day [to protest against a new licensing threat] because jazz is probably the form that's played the most live in little bars, so there could be less opportunity.

Jazz is moving in all different directions. I haven't done that much research on jazz in the last few years because of Jazz Jamaica, but we played many jazz festivals - Montreux, Nice, New Orleans, Hungarian, St Lucia, Antigua – and you get *all* sorts of bands there now. You get Cuban, folk music from Eastern Europe, all under one umbrella. If you can look at jazz like that it's healthy, but if it's just mainstream, it probably is getting harder.

It's about drawing younger people in - my twenty-one year old daughter is into the most modern music but aware of Ella and Miles Davis because I was playing them while she was growing up. Robbie Williams's big band album has made some young people more aware of jazz - that's what it needs, pop stars reworking old jazz tunes. And some jazz segments are healthy.

But I and others intend to take the Jazz Ska thing to new dimensions - so watch this space!

Selected CDs		
Skaravan	Jazz Jamaica	[1996, Skazz]
Massive	Jazz Jamaica All Stars	[2001, Dune]
The Other Side	Tim Richards Trio	[1998, 33 Records]

Clark Tracey

Clark Tracey, born in 1961 in London's Middlesex Hospital (convenient for the Pizza Express) is a leading, vastly experienced drummer and bandleader who has worked with virtually all the major British players. Since starting commercial gigs in his early teens, he joined the groups of his father, Stan Tracey, when he was seventeen and has since regularly played with his groups including Continental Drift and Ellingtonia. Clark has also led a number of his own bands, with players including Iain Ballamy and Django Bates, followed by the long-standing (1984 – 1990) Quintet with Guy Barker, Jamie Talbot, Steve Melling and Alec Dankworth. He has also played or recorded with Gerard Presencer, Julian Arguelles, Dave O' Higgins, Nigel Hitchcock and numerous others.

Clark has worked with many visiting American bandleaders including Art Farmer, Buddy de Franco, James Moody and Red Rodney. He has also performed regularly with top vocalists including Tina May and Claire Martin.

Clark has written for and led a number of critically well-received CDs including *Full Speed Sideways* (1994) and *Stability* (2000). He has been awarded the British Jazz Award for 'Best Drums' three times, most recently in 2002. Like Art Blakey before him, he leads a quintet of rising players, the New Quintet, that came second in the Small Groups awards for 2002 and 2003.

What sort of music can you first remember listening to in the home?

The *very* earliest things – Blue Note things like Art Blakey and Hank Mobley albums.

Before jazz was there anything?

From day one, some music was always on. To find the first is really difficult – it could also have been Ravel, Bartok, Indian music and African classical music, anything that Stan was influenced by. Plus anything he'd just recorded. I was acquainted with his music too.

When you were quite young, you took an interest in piano and vibes.

It wasn't study; it was just because they were around! So from an early age, I was up on the piano stool working things out, and he showed me a few bits and pieces. The vibes thing started because Stan used to play the vibes and they were still in his music room, though he wasn't playing them anymore. Eventually they were set up and we used to improvise together, him sitting at the piano – it was always a waltz, I remember, always a waltz. He would play changes so that whatever black notes you played would fit the changes.

Some tuition from Stan then; besides the drums later, there were other instruments?

Yes, I started the drums aged thirteen. The other instruments - the recorder at school, and the clarinet. Also there was the violin at school – I was forced into taking violin lessons, because at my grammar school, in order to take music for O Level, you had to be taking an orchestral instrument; that's part of their syllabus. It wasn't like it is now, of course, there was no *percussion* teacher and they drafted in a violinist to teach us. After a few months, I said to them, 'Look I'm really not making this and I'm actually doing gigs now on drums and studying at home.' My headmaster, who happened to be a fan of Dad's – very useful – said 'All right, forget the violin, providing you really are doing the drums.'

When did the professional gigs start?

I left school at sixteen, and I'd already been doing paid gigs before that - I was in a duo with a pianist, Mark Ambler, who was having lessons with Stan – I would go down to Croydon and work with him. Eventually we did a couple of gigs here and there. That was jazz-rock-based music.

Then I was also involved with a very mainstream outfit called the Nonsuch Dance Orchestra or Dance Band – they lived around Nonsuch Park. These were all semi-pros out doing pubs. Plus I was in a punk band when I was just fifteen, just for a laugh!

When I was seventeen, just a year after I left school, Stan's chair became available. So that was that, I ended up doing it. That's *really* when I went professional, August 1978.

How did your music develop over the next few years?

In that early period I was really learning the ropes, how to behave on the road, how to interact with professional musicians and all their personalities.

At seventeen, I went on a Jazz Summer School in South Wales, a kind of *crash* course. In fact, that was the two weeks leading up to doing my first professional gig with Stan. I gained from the many hours playing *every* day, which was wonderful. The good things were that I met a few musicians such as Mike Mower and Martin Speake who were there too, so we've kept in touch as we used to jam and just have the occasional pub gig here and there for three pence. But ninety-eight percent of my work was

just with Stan until I was about twenty-one. It took a while to learn to operate with other people.

Playing in that band could have been a bit of a baptism of fire at that age.

Oh, I had *all kinds* of scathing comments; they all went on, which I can understand. I was absolutely raw, no formal training on the drums as such.

Difficult to get formal training then?

It was, yes. Trevor Tomkins was teaching at Barry Summer School – he still seems to be the number one teacher in this country and he's there at most of the jazz courses. Other than that it was a matter of go out and buy albums and immerse yourself in them.

The drummer Kenrick Rowe commented that when his friends took him to Ronnie Scott's he realised, listening to an American drummer, how much he had to learn. You probably had a similar experience?

Sure, the list of people I've learned from is endless. The earliest is Art Blakey whom I met when I was thirteen. You know, once after I had decided I was going to play drums, Art was giving a very rare workshop in London. My Mum took me along. And then a bit of behind the scenes, so we met him afterwards and hung out the remainder of the day. Then he was working at Ronnie's at night, so we went along there.

Once I was helping myself to Ronnie's, I'd listen there. In those days, people did two weeks and if you're not too busy as I wasn't, you could see them almost every night. Billy Higgins was there, coming there regularly with Cedar Walton - I used to clock just everything.

And Elvin Jones, a *huge* influence. The first time you see it or hear it, it doesn't make sense from the word go. It's almost an acquired taste, really.

Steve Melling commented that if you're

not doing what Elvin's doing, it's wrong.

Elvin has an *elasticity* with the time. It's fine by me and, I think, by the guys that work with him too. But I have heard some people *pooh-pooh* what he does and one player recently said – 'Do you think Elvin's any good?' Gasp. But we are talking about one of the demi-Gods of drumming for goodness sake.

Is Elvin making the drums the star function in the band?

He wouldn't see it that way at all. Working with Elvin, because he has this personalised *freedom* with the time, basically – I'd say he's pushed away all kinds of *boundaries* – you really do have to work *with* him. And you watch his bass player. He'll be watching Elvin most of the gig, because when Elvin does a fill, 'one' is not always going to be a *metronomic* one at the end of it. Can be a bit early, but mostly just a little bit after! Just a little breath, then a bang at the end of it! And the bass player's going – pause – then 'Ah, got it with you!'

And Art was the same – Art Blakey. Towards

the end of his playing career he was going more and more deaf unfortunately and if he ever crossed the beat or something, the other players aren't going to sit at the other end saying, 'Oh, he got it wrong' you know? You just go with Art every time.

Moving on to your playing career, you started a band in 1981 with Django Bates and Iain Ballamy.

Well that was my first venture into leading my own group and really, doing something different from what my Dad does. The way that group went really, Iain and Django bonded better than any Loctite I've ever seen and it was obvious they were going in one direction and I wasn't part of that. I was keen to know what it was, that was why I'd formed the band. So I backed off and basically fired everybody one night as nicely as I could, saying, 'Look, it's not working.'

Then in 1983, I put together a different band with people who were more like what *would* work - Guy Barker, Jamie Talbot, Steve Melling and eventually Alec Dankworth on bass. That was much more drummer-led, it was my ideas and direction. We had a modicum of success with it, pretty good considering and we released three CDs with that band. [*The Quintet, 1984 – 1990, was a very successful band.*]

Then I formed another group - the same time that the quintet was beginning its demise - with Gerard Presencer, when he was about sixteen or seventeen. We did quite a lot of work with that group.

Then Blakey died in 1990, and I and another drummer decided to form a tribute band for a gig and a recording. The way these things go, you can't let it end there, so we're still doing it. Well, *I'm* still doing it, the other drummer left for New York! The concept of two drummers doing Art Blakey solos is quite interesting! We split it up, most of it, but we combined for four tunes and one in particular, *New World*, written by Slide Hampton, was a Blakey solo that we know intimately – I still do it, for the Blakey solo – he used to refer to this kind of format of his solos all the time for years, uses the basic rhythm he used right from the Fifties.

What do you especially like about Art Blakey?

Art certainly stands out from the crowd. His range of sound is impressive but it's not all shouting, 'Hey, look at me!' It's not that, it's just his voice is *so* special.

There's one thing he told me a long time ago as well. In his era you *had* to stand out to be something. He told me about how a certain tap dancer moved, a certain lick that everybody knew was *his*, and Blakey said that's when he started his press rolls; you know, his enormous hurricanes out of nowhere – and that was Blakey. By the end, he had loads of these 'signatures'.

And back with the bands...

After the quartet and the quintet, I decided to put together a new band with Nigel Hitchcock, Dave O'Higgins, Mark Nightingale, Steve Melling and Arnie Somogyi. We did a fair number of gigs with that, we went abroad and we did a CD. And I found it really hard to get work for it after that! *Really* difficult.

Was the whole industry going through a bad patch?

It was the beginning of the Nineties, then and it still is really hard. Doesn't matter what you put together. I mean I even did the *Full Speed Sideways* CD in 1994 with that band which got great reviews.

You've been doing a variety of things since then, including working with Claire Martin.

Well, the Claire Martin relationship has been nearly fifteen years now. I'm on all except two of her CDs in the nineties. We had a gap when she wanted to go in a different direction musi-

cally, but now she wants to do more jazz stuff, so we're back and I love it!

Your album *Stability* in 2000 was highly rated: how did you select the pieces for that?

Well, it's a concoction really, it sums up all the things I hadn't been recording since *Full Speed Sideways*.

And five of them are with the Locrian String Quartet. Do you write for string quartet?

I wish I had that luxury. I got involved with that because when I was married to Tina May, she had some string quartet arrangements written for one of her CDs. Then I decided I'll have a go at that for her next CD and recorded a couple of things. Some of the material wasn't recorded , so we've used those pieces on *Stability*.

Are they a special quartet? There's lots of exciting pizzicato.

I did find it a bit daunting. I once asked one of the busiest writers for TV and film, 'How on earth do you write for strings?' – having grown up with Ravel quartets and the rest of it, didn't know where to begin really. He said, 'Basically, Clark, whatever you write, they'll play.' So if you've got the right guys, they'll play it!

One strength is that the writing has a

smooth integration between the jazz and classical playing.

I'm very glad that's happened, because that's the hardest thing - to fuse the two together. And you want to get the classical players involved a little bit too. And obviously the way you write for a classical musician is going to be slightly different. My way is to write four groups of triplets [in a bar] but miss out the middle one, 'da - da, da - da', and that's as near as dammit to a jazz feel. And that's what we did for a couple of them. But a lot of the tracks actually didn't require that, they're pretty straight eights anyway, like the pizzicato number. I'd love to do some more of it, it was a joy.

You still do some arranging for Claire Martin and Tina May?

I have done an arrangement for Claire when she wanted a string quartet and Geoff Gascoyne's contributed quite a few good arrangements. I was Tina's musical director and wrote everything for her while we were together.

Can we move to how, long ago, you learned jazz chords and harmonies?

Well, it's a bit silly having someone like Stan Tracey as your Dad and ignoring it, but that's what I did. It's your Dad talking to you so you mustn't listen to him! I found out the hard way basically. Anyway you can imagine, looking over a bass player's shoulder, playing a tune, 'Ah, C and a circle means diminished then!' And half diminished, that's written like that – a circle with a line through it.' So I was working it out, asking friends, everything.

Am I right that drummers have to know a piece as well as anyone else on the stand?

I see the drummer as an important ingredient in the band, remembering if there's an odd number of bars coming up and when and producing a *colour* behind at the same time as everybody else.

It's not just drummers who aren't always

aware of things; it *can be* that the musicians you're working *with* don't consider you need to know.

I mean, on a slightly different level, it still surprises me when a band is deciding what to play with its back to you and just turns round and gives you a count. You don't know if it's brushes, sticks, what is the tempo, just those four crochets – it could go in any direction! Maybe they'd like a loud Elviny thing, because of the type of tune it is or a little 'Girl from Ipanema' style - you've got no idea until the four beats. Even then, you may not have been told what the tune is.

That seems unprofessional?

It's unbelievable - still can happen, it happened last week to me!

Of course, the audience can be in the same position, suffering from lack of communication.

Oh, yeah. Some people are good communicators, some aren't.

Some are there just to be musicians, only musicians?

Yes, I mean Stan's like that. Makes me laugh sometimes. We did one in Liverpool last week and he announced the first tune before we played it, and then didn't say anything for the rest of the gig! That was it! He doesn't like talking - so it's just finish the tune, and 'Now, what shall we play?'

Sometimes, he won't tell us what he's playing either; he'll just keep improvising till he hits something he wants to play! That's fine because you're with him from the beginning, and you can pick it up almost even before he has. Sometimes you think, 'It's going into *Autumn Leaves*, isn't it? Yeah, got it.'

This is how you can all amuse each other on stage a bit?

Yeah, it's interesting how important humour is in what we do. We listened, Stan and I, to a jazz radio programme on the way to a recent gig and

didn't really enjoy anything we heard. About ten minutes after we'd heard it in almost stunned silence, wondering if we were in the same profession, he said, 'You know what it is, *none* of them made me smile! All deadly serious! No-one was having *fun* with it!' That has a lot to do with it, probably all tied up in the personalities involved, I suppose. I mean when you share a musical moment with somebody else and it can make you all smile.

You know, the audiences laugh sometimes because they can tell what's going on. I did a concert with Stan and Andy Cleyndert on bass and we have a pretty good rapport going now. In his solo, Andy started doing double stops and it sounded like, 'dum dum dum, dum dum do', like Red Indian school. I'd been quiet but then I just picked up my sticks and played, 'dum, duga, dum, duga, dum, duga', and Stan looked up and the whole audience looked up and laughed. It's just taking the mickey but it's not unmusical, just a personal thing between Andy and me. So if the audience pick up on that, great and I think that's important.

Incidentally, you do work with Dave Newton sometimes – the Bootleg album?

Not as much as I'd like to. That *Bootleg*, with the Octet, was a special project, in a year. We did probably about half a dozen gigs. I do also play with Dave when there's the occasional gig with the Alan Barnes Quartet.

So not often, unfortunately. We used to work *all* the time – I first met him with Martin Taylor in the early Eighties and we did three tours and a couple of albums, including in his title, *Making the Move*, just as he was moving down to London. Then he joined Tina's quartet, I suggested him on piano, so we were together for six or seven years, working with Tina who was very busy. Since he left that band we've hardly worked together. That's how it goes. He's put together his own trio and works with Alan Barnes and of course, Stacey Kent. Stacey doesn't have a drummer these days, so we rarely cross paths.

There's a few players, you have immediate

rapport on and off the stage, and then you hardly ever work with them, it's crazy. Someone like Alan Skidmore, we did a lot of travelling together, a number of high pressure gigs for a number of years but we never play together now.

I had a special kind of relationship because we're all the sons of fathers in the same business. We had a band with Alec Dankworth on bass, just the three of us, and called it How's your Father. We toured with that for about six months, we got a large number of gigs together with that!

Who do you reckon to be your main musical influences?

Roy Haynes was the first, after Bryan Spring, that is - Roy was and still is a huge influence. Definitely left his mark on my technique.

Bryan played me some of Roy's stuff the first time and I went overboard on him. I came to realise *everyone* has played with Roy Haynes because I started collecting every recording I could. So the earliest I found was 1947 with Lester Young, and I just heard his new CD on the radio. And if you want to build a wide collection of jazz CDs you can get his collection – who *hasn't* he recorded with – Bird, Coltrane, Chick Corea!

Roy has his own trademarks. There's this lovely line, 'Elvin did it, Max Roach did it, Roy Haynes did it 'n did-it 'nn did-it, n didit, 'n buggered it, 'n did it'. He's got this amazing technique – superb and so crisp and clean, big spaces, big *musical* spaces, you know, that's the first thing that rubbed off on me, he was really playing *melodically* the first time I heard him in an album with Roland Kirk called *Out in the Afternoon* which heavily features his playing. It was the first time I'd heard a drummer taking a solo over a walking bass line which I do infrequently with guys now. Marvellous. I think it also helps the listener maybe to follow the tune.

I'm amazed not only by some members of the audience who said this but even by some musicians I have respect for, who have come up to me and said, 'Were you following the se-quence?' Well, *of course*, it's what we all do. Others will say I could hear you referring to the tune there, or the middle eight bars there.

Some musicians comment that playing with others, you can sometimes learn to anticipate what others will play.

Yes, just like you can in a conversation, sometimes you can see it coming. Sometimes he'll then go off another way and smile at you 'musically.' The whole thing's marvellous in that respect. You get the spontaneous interaction.

Have you ever flirted with free jazz?

Yes, I did some of that in my 18-21 year old patch. I did some stuff with Mike Osborne and the bass player Paul Rogers, one of the most avant-garde players on the scene now, an excellent musician. We did a few gigs as a trio.

The way I feel about it is that it's better to play it than to listen to it. It is verging on self-indulgent a lot of the time and it's not always inviting an audience to be a part of it.

Stan Tracey went into free jazz for a while.

Yes, that was during the big movement in the Seventies, but you know, he never really *enjoyed* it. There was one recording he did, it actually went out on a broadcast. It was a large ensemble, not his, and, you know, the red light went on and it all just began, and half an hour later it ended. And at one point everyone was just in his or her own world, and Stan just looked around on this session and played 'God Save the Queen' – and nobody noticed! So what's the point?

Is there a Tracey sense of humour?

Oh yes, you might think its highly disrespectful but on the other hand, why didn't anybody notice that he'd done that? How disrespectful was that in itself? I don't suggest all of it's like that but I do enjoy playing it, especially if you get the right people - Mike Osborne and Paul Rogers were a joy to work with - big ears and playing off each other all the time – they would influence you and there's a real *conversation* happening.

Also Tony Oxley, he's right at the heart of that. Some players do it because that's them! There aren't that many around any more, but at the time it was a *very* new thing, very experimental. I always thought you had to learn how to do it within the constraints without getting rid of them first. You have to have gone through a certain amount of study, technical development and maybe even experience, before you can say, 'Well, I don't want to do that'. Because then you can hear the maturity of the musician and the person coming out - being able to converse with somebody else.

One of my favourite recordings - that I would happily take on a desert island - is my old man doing an improvised duet with Keith Tippett with two pianos and the interplay is *absolutely* marvellous. That to me is what avant-garde should be about. It's bouncing, really bouncing for a whole hour! A lot of it just sounds like classical composition. It's still out, Blue Note International reissued it.

Do you teach or coach in jazz?

I've recently started teaching in a secondary school, admittedly motivated in part by financial gain, I must hold up my hands on that. I always felt a bit uncomfortable teaching; maybe I wasn't a very good communicator about expressing my thoughts, translating my thoughts onto a drum kit.

But the more I've done it over the last seven or eight years, the more comfortable I feel. So I feel quite at ease teaching anybody now, at any level.

Is it right that with drummers, even more than other jazz instruments, there's an aural tradition, you learn through listening? So teaching it can never be easy.

Well, that's damn true. I think one of the benefits of the *melodic* instrumental school is there's

been so many books written and so many tunes written they can just go and open a page and practice that tune for an hour. But it's a different story for drummers. There are the drum *rudiments*, most of which are outmoded these days I think. But they're small exercises, often only a bar or two bars long, to develop certain things in your playing, originally for military drummers. So it's hard to see a relationship with what I do now. But I do make sure that any drummer I'm teaching knows of their existence, because the *majority* of them we *do* use all the time. So they're important at that level before moving on.

What do you think about the general health of jazz in the UK? Where and what are the new jazz people coming through going to play?

Well, that issue's always there, though there are more players of a higher quality these days – it's *always* been a problem where to play. One contribution I've made is my current quintet is made up of players that I consider to be at the top of their generation – I've had them for a couple of years, a couple in the band are twenty-two and a couple are thirty-two. So that's a platform for them to compose and learn how to interact, behave, you know, get all the protocols.

So now to your future; what directions do you think you will be developing in?

Well, I think what I *really* need is to be pushing myself harder because other people are pushing themselves hard. I mean the album *Stability* came about through two or three business lunches with record managers before that happened and getting the music together was an achievement for someone like me. Getting the musicians to play on it was the *easiest* bit.

I've got a few ideas for a new album and with *Stability* being two years old now, I know Linn Records would like to do something...

Those compositions of yours on Stability seem quite strong – I do like Lounge Blues, perhaps it could be used commercially in a number of ways?

I wish it was! Yeah, I could have done a whole album of my things on there, but there was stuff available from a previous project and I wanted to get those recorded properly. Also I'm aware that whenever us lot get a chance to make a CD, it's almost always full of originals. I don't think that all our best work comes out because we've had to write something for a CD. So a combination including standards seems good. But who knows?

We've just released our debut CD, and there are plans for further recording on dates in 2004 - which will be my twenty-fifth professional anniversary.

I think it's all about motivation and direction, seeing a goal and going for it. We have to be our own *managers* as well. And honestly, sitting at home waiting for the phone to ring - I've done that but, if you want more, you've got to find it, go and get it. Make things available to people!

I understand I have a reputation as

bandleader as well and we have another week at Ronnie's this year, plus various bits and pieces. So I will be pushing this quintet more - that's one of my goals to really get some work for that band! Lovely players!

Selected CDs	
Stability	Clark Tracey
	[2000, Linn]
Too Darn Hot	Claire Martin
	[2002 , Linn]
Seventy Something	Stan Tracey Trio
	[2004, Trio]
Website: www.clarktracey.com	

Index